EXTRAORDINARY HISTORY

Melbourne Regional Chamber of Commerce
on Florida's Space Coast, 1919 to 2025, and Beyond

William C. Potter

©2024 All rights reserved.

Independently published
William C. Potter
Melbourne, Florida, U.S.A.

ISBNs
979-8-9889048-7-8 - Hardcover
979-8-9889048-5-4 – Softcover
979-8-9889048-6-1– Epub

Table of Contents

FOREWORD 4
TIMELINE OF HISTORY 4
    1919 - 1925 5
    1957 – 1967 5
    1970 – 1991 6
    2010 – 2024 7
CHAPTER ONE A Concise History of South Brevard County from 1859 until 2023 8
CHAPTER TWO What is a Chamber of Commerce? 43
CHAPTER THREE Origins of Chambers in Melbourne and Eau Gallie: 1919 until the End of World War II 47
CHAPTER FOUR The Chambers of Commerce During The Early Years of the Space Age: 1946 To 1969 67
CHAPTER FIVE The Chamber Leads the Efforts To Create A New City 113
CHAPTER SIX The Consolidated Chamber Flexes its Muscles: 1969 To 1978 . 128
CHAPTER SEVEN The Strawbridge Years: 1978 until 1988 144
CHAPTER EIGHT The Chamber as an Incubator 161
CHAPTER NINE Accreditation 168
CHAPTER TEN Chamber-Airport Relations 171
CHAPTER ELEVEN The Malta Years: 1989 until 1995 178
CHAPTER TWELVE The Bohlmann Years: 1996 To 2005 188
CHAPTER THIRTEEN Meyer, Michaels, and Malesic: 2005 until 2017 195
CHAPTER FOURTEEN AYERS: 2017 until Present 206
EPILOGUE 215
AFTERWORD By: Michael Ayers 218
ACKNOWLEDGEMENTS 221
APPENDICES 224
    APPENDIX A: Population Growth in South Brevard County 225
    APPENDIX B: Chief Executives of the Melbourne Regional Chamber and its Predecessors 226
    APPENDIX C: Chairs of the Melbourne Regional Chamber and its Predecessors 230
    APPENDIX D: Chamber Financial Performance: 2004 To 2022 (USD) 235
BIBLIOGRAPHY 238
ABOUT THE AUTHORS 240
INDEX 242

FOREWORD

By William C. Potter

During the past few years, I have felt the need to write histories of some of the local institutions with which I have been engaged in substantive ways. I began with a history of the Melbourne Orlando International Airport and followed that effort by co-authoring, with Bill Jurgens, a history of intercollegiate athletics at Florida Institute of Technology. Although I do not think that my interest in writing these histories has risen quite to the intensity of a compulsion or an obsession, I suspect that this urge to preserve history is, at least subconsciously, a product of my advanced age and a recognition of my mortality. Hopefully, however, my motivation is also, at least partially, to create and preserve a record of institutions that have served our community well and will continue to do so in the future.

In any event, I hope that my penchant for local history will benefit the community. The Melbourne Regional Chamber of Commerce and the predecessor organizations that spawned it have had a significant impact on the community. That impact includes not only the economic development and job opportunities that have been created but also the development of the community infrastructure that supports the quality of life in Brevard County.

I do not pretend to have some extraordinary insight that demands the readers' attention. Nor do I claim unusual intellect that deserves deference. Without question, my version of local history may leave ample room for disagreement and critique. I will undoubtedly overstate the importance of some events while understating the significance of others in the view of the readers. Similarly, I will undoubtedly describe some individuals in a manner that is not completely objective as it is only human to have one's views shaped by incomplete knowledge. I hope that I will be fair in my treatment of my colleagues at the chamber, but I will apologize in advance to anyone who is offended by my observations.

As far as my involvement with the Chamber of Commerce is concerned, readers may well conclude that this is not an objective account of my role. They may say that I have overstated my positive contributions while understating my deficiencies. Without question, they will be correct in that critique. There is little doubt that I will succumb to the trait of human nature that makes one unable to objectively evaluate himself.

Despite all the foregoing caveats, it is worthwhile to record the history of the chambers of commerce in South Brevard County and their impact on the communities they serve. It is beyond debate that the chambers of commerce, in the various iterations they have taken, have impacted the community that, in many ways, exceeds the impact of other private, not-for-profit organizations. Even as the community has matured and other organizations have assumed important roles, the chamber continues to have the largest, most influential, and diverse constituency of any business group in the community. That means that the chamber will continue to have a significant voice in determining how the community evolves, including the nature and extent of its economic opportunities and the quality of the infrastructure that serves the community.

I hope that recording this history will provide a context that will help the chamber continue its vital role in shaping our community. Moreover, I hope that this will cause young leaders in Brevard County to recognize the chamber as a vehicle through which they can make a meaningful impact and experience the satisfaction of being part of an endeavor that transcends personal interests and serves the greater good.

"Chamber of Commerce" is not a proprietary phrase or title that may be restricted in terms of its use. Over the time covered by this history, many organizations have called themselves chambers of commerce, and many of these organizations have come, gone, and reappeared again during the more than 100 years that the Melbourne Regional Chamber has been in existence. Efforts have been made periodically to unify all the economic promotional efforts under one banner by mergers and consolidations of chambers of commerce. Groups of businesspeople may decide that they could have more representation if they create a new organization, and a new chamber of commerce would arise. It is a great tribute to the leadership of the Melbourne Regional Chamber that it has been able to maintain its identity amid this endless evolution of business groups.

As you will read, not only has the Melbourne Regional Chamber remained an anchor for business interests in Brevard County, but it has served as an incubator for many other organizations which have spun off from the chamber and assumed important roles in our community. From the Community Foundation for Brevard to Keep Brevard Beautiful to Junior Achievement, the Melbourne Regional Chamber has recognized community needs and spawned organizations to fill those needs.

This 1962 photo in the Brevard Sentinel-Star shows the Melbourne Chamber of Commerce office. The building now houses the offices of Brevard County.

TIMELINE OF HISTORY

This collage was compiled from photos taken during the chamber's annual "fly-in" to Tallahassee to meet with its local legislative delegation regarding legislative issues of interest to the chamber. These photos were taken during the 2023 visit.

1919 - 1925

September 10, 1919
Orlando Sentinel made the first mention of the Melbourne Chamber of Commerce in a newspaper.

March 6, 1923
Cocoa Tribune made the first mention of the Eau Gallie Chamber of Commerce in a newspaper.

August 8, 1925
The Melbourne Chamber of Commerce formally incorporated and hired a full-time executive director.

1957 – 1967

October 1957
The West Melbourne Chamber of Commerce was founded.

October 1958
The South Brevard Beaches Chamber of Commerce was founded.

July 1959
The first Palm Bay Chamber of Commerce was founded.

February 20, 1962
John Glenn blasted off from Cape Canaveral and became the first American to orbit the Earth.

September 1, 1967
The Eau Gallie Chamber of Commerce, the Melbourne Chamber of Commerce, the West Melbourne Chamber of Commerce, and the South Brevard Beaches Chamber of Commerce all dissolved and united to form the Metropolitan South Brevard Chamber of Commerce. The Palm Bay Chamber of Commerce declined to join.

1970 – 1991

February 6, 1970: Metropolitan South Brevard Chamber of Commerce changed its name to Melbourne Area Chamber of Commerce.

August 6, 1973: The Melbourne Area Chamber of Commerce joined with the South Brevard Board of Realtors to acquire a vacated A&P grocery store on Strawbridge Avenue and renovate it as the two organizations' headquarters. In May 1984, the Chamber purchased the Board's interest and then occupied the building as its headquarters until May 2024.

May 20, 1981: The Melbourne Area Chamber Foundation was founded; its name changed to The Community Foundation of South Brevard on February 11, 1983; its current name is Community Foundation for Brevard.

November 18, 1982: Melbourne Area Chamber of Commerce changed its name to The Chamber of Commerce of South Brevard.

December 15, 1984: The Chamber of Commerce of South Brevard was accredited by the United States Chamber of Commerce, a distinction that less than 2% of chambers achieve. January 1, 1987: Chamber of Commerce of South Brevard merged with the Palm Bay Area Chamber of Commerce to form the Greater South Brevard Area Chamber of Commerce.

June 22, 1987: Greater South Brevard Area Chamber of Commerce hosted President Ronald Reagan at a town hall meeting at the Melbourne Civic Auditorium.

August 12, 1991: Greater South Brevard Area Chamber of Commerce changed its name to Melbourne-Palm Bay Area Chamber of Commerce.

2010 – 2024

July 16, 2010: Melbourne-Palm Bay Area Chamber of Commerce changed its name to the Melbourne Regional Chamber of East Central Florida.

February 23, 2010: The Melbourne Regional Chamber of Commerce of East Central Florida achieved five-star rating from the United States Chamber of Commerce, a distinction which less than 1.5% of chambers achieve.

2018: The Viera Business Alliance was formed as a division of the chamber.

February 21, 2024: Melbourne Regional Chamber of East Central Florida changed its name to the Melbourne Regional Chamber of Florida's Space Coast.

May 20, 2024: Chamber sold its office building on Strawbridge Avenue, where it had operated for more than 50 years; leased a temporary office on NASA Boulevard at the airport.

July 31, 2024: Michael Ayers resigned as President of the Chamber in order to accept a position as senior executive of his family's manufacturing business.

August 14, 2024: Anne Conroy-Baiter selected as President and CEO of the Chamber.

CHAPTER ONE

A Concise History of South Brevard County from 1859 until 2023

To adequately evaluate the history of the Melbourne Regional Chamber and its forerunners, it is helpful to create a perspective through which to understand how the community served by the Chamber has evolved. This chapter will try to do so in a concise manner.

John Carol Houston IV was the earliest European-American settler in what is now known as South Brevard County. In 1859, the Army sent Houston to conduct a census of Seminole Indians in the Indian River Area. Houston was smitten with the area, which he named Arlington. He took a leave from the Army and traveled there with his wife and ten slaves to build a cabin. In 1869, William Henry Gleason, a former Lieutenant Governor of Florida, acquired almost thirty square miles of real estate extending from the Indian River Lagoon to Lake Washington. Gleason founded the town of Eau Gallie in 1869, and a United States Post Office was created in 1871. The precise source of the name Eau Gallie is not known. "Eau" means water in French. "Gallie" is not a French word. However, Eau Gallie is known to mean "rocky water." Eau Gallie was incorporated on May 22, 1893.

The first European-American and African American people to settle in what is now Melbourne arrived in 1877. The settlers included Richard W. Goode and his father, John Goode, as well as Cornthwaite John Hector, Captain Peter Wright, Balaam Allen, the Wright Brothers, and Thomas Mason. Captain Wright, Allen, and Brothers were African American formerly enslaved men. They settled around the narrow peninsula between Crane Creek and the Indian River and initially named the settlement "Crane Creek." By June 1880, Crane Creek consisted of six families, 21 people, and a post office. In July 1880, the name of the town was changed to Melbourne. Hector had formerly lived in Melbourne, Australia, and most historians assume that Hector promoted the name change.

The first European-American settler of what is now Palm Bay was John Tillman, who settled there in the late 1870s. Tillman constructed a wharf on the north side of Turkey Creek and, by the late 1880s, had created a steamboat stop as well as orange and banana groves. Later, in 1894, the Florida East Coast Railroad was extended to the town of Tillman, and a significant lumber operation was created. The town was renamed "Palm Bay" in the 1920s. It is presumed that the abundant sabal palm trees at the mouth of Turkey Creek inspired that name.

By 1910, Melbourne had grown to a population of 157 people. The economic drivers of the community were farming, ranching, and fishing. Transportation was provided primarily by the railroad since roads were mostly sandy wagon trails. East-west travel was particularly difficult due to the formidable barrier formed by the St. Johns River, although there was an old Indian trail leading west from Melbourne, which led to a primitive public ferry run by the Union Cypress Company crossing the St. Johns at North Indian Field.

George Washington Hopkins was an experienced lumberman from Michigan who, in 1902, began buying property in Osceola County, west of the St. Johns River. By 1907, he owned some 58,000 acres of virgin timber. His holdings included 225 million feet of cypress in the Jane Green Penna-Wah and Wolf Creek swamps. In 1911 he contracted with a Louisiana lumber firm owned by Charles and Milton Clark to build and run a lumber mill in an area south of Crane Creek and just outside the Melbourne city limits. That area became known as Hopkins. Hopkins was a company town, complete with a commissary owned by the lumber mill, company housing rented to the employees, and even its own currency.

The Union Cypress Company was incorporated in December 1911 to own and operate the lumber mill and to construct and support a railroad from the lumber mill to Hopkins' timberland in Osceola County. A contract between the Union Cypress and George Hopkins dated December 11, 1911, bound the Union Cypress to cut, finish, and market all cypress and pine on Hopkins's timberland, for which it would pay Hopkins $4 per 1,000 feet for cypress and $1 per 1,000 feet for pine. To accomplish this, the railroad needed to be built across the St. Johns River, a complex and expensive undertaking. The Union Cypress Company became a primary industry in south Brevard County and thrived for several years. By 1919, 50,506,362 pounds, consisting primarily of lumber, was shipped from Hopkins on the Florida East Coast Railroad. During World War I, lumber production had increased to 60,000 feet per day. The mill and the

Union Cypress Railroad ran until the death of George Hopkins in January 1925.

Settlement of the barrier island of South Brevard County by European Americans began a few years after the end of the Civil War. The first settlers were veterans of the Union Army. The first land sales were to Charles Latham in 1881 and Cyrus Graves in 1883 at a price of $1.25 per acre. Shortly thereafter, two brothers from Georgia, Robert and Charlie Smith, homesteaded Mullet Creek. Their descendants continue to live there today and run Honest John's Fish Camp. Pineapples were the first cash crop on the barrier island. In 1888, Alfred Wilcox founded the Melbourne Beach Investment Company. The first project of the company was to build a road from the Indian River to the Atlantic Ocean, naming the road Ocean Avenue. The project included a pier on the river with rails stretching eastward along Ocean Avenue to the ocean. Initially, the rail car was pushed by hand, transporting passengers from the ferry, which landed at the pier to the ocean. The rail car was later motorized. In 1923, the residents along Ocean Avenue incorporated the area as Melbourne Beach.

Ernest Kouwen-Hoven bought a one-square-mile tract of land on the barrier island east of Melbourne in 1915. His intent was to develop a resort on the property, giving it the name of Indialantic-by-the-Sea for its location between the Indian River and the Atlantic Ocean. In 1919, Kouwen-Hoven began to build a 16-foot-wide toll bridge spanning the river between Melbourne and Indialantic. The toll bridge was financed by bonds issued by Kouwen-Hoven and completed in 1921. The new bridge brought the first automobiles to the barrier island.

Developers in Melbourne Beach and Indialantic were part of the land "boom" that overwhelmed Florida in the mid-1920s. As was typical throughout Florida during that period, the land was promoted and marketed at prices that would not be realistic for another 30 years.

The Indialantic Casino opened in 1924 and became a center of entertainment for Brevard County. The Indialantic Hotel, featuring tennis courts and a 9-hole golf course, opened in 1926 and drew visitors from all over the globe until it closed during the Great Depression.

Great Drainage Project in Back Country Helps Melbourne Grow

THE development of agricultural lands surrounding a city always benefits that community and stimulates its growth. And this is another reason why Melbourne, the Midway City, is certain to expand rapidly.

Brevard County has a great extent of rich tillable lands whose fertility has already made the Indian River section well known for its fine fruits, vegetables and stock. Some of the back-country, however, as in other parts of Florida, must be reclaimed by drainage before it is fit for successful agriculture.

Sixty-six thousand acres of the back-country west of Melbourne is actually being reclaimed at the present time and prepared for cultivation. A huge network of drainage canals is now opening this vast area of rich lands for agricultural purposes. All this land will be tributary to Melbourne and will help Melbourne grow.

Melbourne possesses many advantages that are worthy of the consideration of homeseeker and investor—its location halfway down the East Coast on the Indian River and Atlantic Ocean, its splendid transportation facilities, its progressive community spirit, its modern improvements and its many recreational appeals.

There are opportunities and pleasures for everyone in Melbourne. We invite you to come and see for yourself what this likeable community has to offer you.

Chamber of Commerce
Melbourne
Brevard County .... Florida

This advertisement was sponsored by the Melbourne Chamber of Commerce and it ran in several newspapers in major cities in Florida on March 11, 1925.

Construction of a new concrete and steel bridge between Indialantic and Melbourne began in 1941 but was delayed during World War II and not completed until 1947. This bridge, with a center span that opened for boats, would remain in place until the current high-rise causeway was completed in 1985.

Indialantic was not a municipality until 1952 when it was incorporated as Indialantic-By-The Sea.

Between these early settlements in south Brevard County and World War II, the area stayed rural with an economy based primarily on agriculture and commercial fishing, along with some tourism and winter visitors. The area struggled through the economic challenges of the Great Depression, like most rural areas in the southern United States, until World War II changed the area forever. Both Melbourne and Eau Gallie defaulted on their outstanding bonds during the Great Depression. The book "A Tribute to Melbourne's Pioneers," published by the City of Melbourne Centennial Committee in 1976, traces the financial problems of the two cities to the boom years of the mid-1920s. According to that publication, the land boom caused the cities to issue bonds to build streets, sidewalks, sewers, and public utilities, which could be repaid only if the cities collected ad valorem taxes from landowners. When the land values plummeted, and owners were unable to pay taxes on the land, default on the bonds was unavoidable.

"A Tribute to Melbourne's Pioneers" also describes the squabble that took place from 1939 to 1940 between south Brevard County and the north and central portions of the county over the location of a proposed deepwater port. Eau Gallie argued that the port should be created by the excavation of an inlet at Canova Beach, arguing that a natural harbor already existed at Eau Gallie. Titusville residents, on the other hand, contended that the port should be close to Titusville, where the Haulover Canal already existed. As such, another inlet would be unnecessary. Central Brevard leaders advanced the argument that Canaveral Harbor was the logical location for a deepwater port. The argument was settled by the decision to launch missiles from Cape Canaveral and the Merritt Island Launch Area, and the result was the development of Port Canaveral, now the largest passenger cruise port in the world.

For much of its existence, Brevard County was a sleepy community marked by its citrus industry, excellent fishing, and pervasive mosquitos. Its population in 1940 was 16,142 with citrus and fishing as the backbone of its economy. The county experienced a notable evolution during World War II when the U.S. Navy set up three Naval Air Stations to train pilots for the war. However, by 1950, the population had only increased to 23,653.

Following the Naval Expansion Act of 1939, the Navy bought 1,900 acres of scrubland on the barrier island south of Cocoa Beach. In December 1939, the Navy began construction of the Banana River Naval Air Station on the land. The station was commissioned on 1 October 1940. During World War II, the Banana River Naval Air Station was used for seaplane patrol operations as well as a blimp squadron that conducted search and rescue operations along Florida's coast. In addition, A PBM seaplane pilot training program and an advanced navigation school were based at the squadron. At its height, 391 officers, 2492 service personnel, and 587 civilians were stationed at the Banana River Naval Air Station. The station was deactivated on 1 August 1947, and the area was transferred to the Air Force on 1 September 1948.

At a meeting on July 21, 1941, the Eau Gallie City Council enacted a resolution that acknowledged that the Melbourne-Eau Gallie Airport, as improved, now consisted of "four runways each 4000 feet long and 150 feet wide, is served by a full power radio beacon and broadcasting station and will shortly have proper lighting facilities and fueling facilities." The resolution noted that the airport could be "a valuable facility for the Government in carrying out the defense program." The resolution concluded by tendering the Melbourne-Eau Gallie Airport to the United States "for such use as shall deem desirable to said Government." On July 8, 1941, the Melbourne City Commission adopted a resolution tendering the airport to the federal government. An article in the *Melbourne Times* on February 6, 1942, two months after the Japanese attack on Pearl Harbor, reported that the Navy Department contemplated taking over the airport as a secondary base and that, if approved, $3 million to $5 million worth of improvements would be made to the airport.

Shortly thereafter, with the nation at war in both Europe and the Pacific, the 77th Congress enacted Public Law 438, which authorized the Navy to proceed with constructing the Melbourne Naval Air Station and its auxiliary fields. On April 23, 1942, Secretary of the Navy Knox made an announcement that the Melbourne-Eau Gallie Airport would become a major Naval Air Station, without specifying the details of the operations to be conducted there. On May 27, 1942, the U.S. Navy announced that it would set up eight new operational training facilities, seven of which were in Florida, including one at the Melbourne Municipal Airport, with auxiliary fields at Malabar and Valkaria. The announcement said that this was part of the Navy's plan to produce 30,000 new Naval aviators per year. The announcement further said that the projected cost was five million dollars for each facility and that it expected them to be operational by August 1, 1942.

The minutes of the May 25, 1943, meeting of the Eau Gallie City Council show that representatives of Melbourne and Eau Gallie met with federal officials to sign the agreement whereby the Navy became responsible for operations and maintenance of the Melbourne-Eau Gallie Airport as a Naval training base. Those minutes also refer to case number 136-ORL pending in the Federal District Court for the Southern District of Florida, whereby the United States government used its eminent domain powers to get 2378.5 acres of property by a Declaration of Taking for "runways and airport nucleus." This was a mere formality because, by that time, the Navy had been improving and running the base for almost one year.

By the end of 1943, 775 student pilots had undergone training at NAS Melbourne, 546 of whom had graduated. Only 35 had failed training, while another 20 had been killed during training. Overall, it was quite an impressive success. Training was initially conducted in the Grumman F4F Wildcat aircraft. Later, the Grumman 6F Hellcat became the aircraft of choice.

During the first 11 months of 1944, 1128 student pilots underwent training at NAS Melbourne. Of that number, 916 graduated, 62 washed out and 27 were killed. Again, an impressive rate of success, particularly when one considers that the instructors were training twice as many students per month as they had trained during 1943.

By March 1944 Melbourne NAS had reached its full personnel complement of 361 officers and 1184 enlisted personnel. That coincided with the transfer of all remaining Wildcats to other training bases, leaving Melbourne with 150 F6F Hellcats for training. In mid-1945 the number of planes was reduced to 75 for the rest of the war.

Melbourne NAS provided operational flight training, which meant that the students had previously completed primary flight training, intermediate flight training, instrument flight training and advanced flight training. Thus, the students had already earned their wings prior to arriving at Melbourne NAS. That explains why there were few deaths during training in Melbourne.

With the Japanese surrender and the end of World War II, thoughts at once turned to the postwar economy and, more specifically, how military assets might be converted to civilian use. An article in the Miami Herald on September 13, 1945, reported that the presence of naval air stations at Melbourne, Banana River and Titusville-Cocoa had awakened Brevard County officials to the potential for development in the county. The article further speculated that the Titusville-Cocoa field, having already stopped its naval operations, was a field for commercial operations. Since the Melbourne field was to be kept and operated by the Navy until June 1946, the article postulated that no private use could be considered for the Melbourne field at that time.

In October 1946, the Navy had created a revocable permit with the cities of Melbourne and Eau Gallie, allowing the cities to run the airport on an interim basis. That permit was approved by the Eau Gallie City Council on October 12, 1946. The permit was dated November 25, 1946, and allowed the two cities to assume responsibilities for the facility. The agreement called for costs to be shared equally by the cities.

Eau Gallie quickly grew weary of the obligations it had assumed in sharing the cost of running the airport. A meeting of the Eau Gallie

City Council on February 17, 1947, included a discussion of the costs being incurred in supporting the facility and the fact that Eau Gallie wanted to pay only those expenses related to the operation of the airfield.

On February 21, 1947, the city of Melbourne adopted a resolution to consider the federal government's offer to transfer the property of the naval air station to Melbourne. Attached to the minutes of that meeting was a letter from the city of Eau Gallie, waiving its claim to any part of the airport. The July 25, 1947, minutes of the Eau Gallie City Council reflect that Eau Gallie had executed a quitclaim deed waiving all rights to the airport.

On August 8, 1947, Naval Air Station Melbourne was conveyed by quitclaim deed to the city of Melbourne. Added property was conveyed to the city by quitclaim deeds dated April 20, 1948, and August 6, 1949. Altogether, 2370 acres were conveyed to the city. The auxiliary fields at Malabar and Valkaria were conveyed to other grantees. The Malabar field was conveyed to the Air Force, which used it for telemetry purposes, while the Valkaria field was conveyed to Brevard County, which maintains a general aviation facility there.

The deeds to Melbourne conveyed not only the real property, including the naval air station, but also the buildings, structures, improvements, and equipment on the property. The deeds contained the covenants, conditions, and restrictions required by the Surplus Property Act, as amended.

World War II had transformed the United States in an irreversible manner. The United States was forced to shed its self-isolation and was thrust into the role of leader of the free world, a burden with which it has struggled in the ensuing seventy-five years. Similarly, for Melbourne and south Brevard County, the presence of the Melbourne Naval Air Station and the Banana River Naval Air Station irreversibly transformed the community. As said in Karen Raley and Ann Raley Flotte's book, "Images of America, Melbourne, and Eau Gallie": "With the war, the fortunes and character of Eau Gallie and Melbourne became inextricably tied to the national economy, identity, and purpose."

In the late 1940s and early 1950s, the county underwent massive changes with the advent of the U.S. space program. On June 1, 1948, the Navy transferred the former Banana River Naval Air Station to the United States Air Force. In May 1949, President Truman signed the legislation that set up the Joint Long-Range Proving Ground (JLRPG). The Air Force renamed the facility for the JLRPG but shortly thereafter changed the name to Cape Canaveral Auxiliary Air Force Base. Work began in 1949 to build an access road and launch facility at Cape Canaveral. The first rocket launched at the Cape was a V-2 rocket named Bumper 8 on July 24, 1950. In 1951, the Air Force established the Air Force Missile Test Center at Patrick AFB.

Cape Canaveral was chosen as the site for rocket launches to take advantage of the Earth's rotation. The linear velocity of the Earth's surface is greatest toward the equator, and the southern location of Cape Canaveral allowed missile launches in the same direction as the Earth's rotation. The sparse settlement and missile launches over the ocean rather than populated areas were also helpful.

Between the establishment of JLRPG in 1949 and 1957, launch activities at Cape Canaveral were intermittent and were given a low priority by the United States Government. That changed when the Soviets launched Sputnik in October 1957. That event was a wake-up call to the United States and caused grave alarm in the country regarding not only the space and missile program but also the status of American technological education. Not only did the launch of Sputnik serve as an impetus to revamp and reinvigorate U.S. space programs, it also caused a reexamination of the American education system.

These activities of the U.S. space program dramatically changed the essential nature of Brevard County as tens of thousands of technicians, scientists, and engineers moved to East Central Florida to support the activities at Cape Canaveral.

TOURIST CENTER — William C. Fielder is pictured standing by the Eau Gallie Chamber of Commerce's Big Orange, a tourist registration and information center which opened this week for the 1954-55 season. [Sentinel Foto]

This 1954 photograph of the "Big Orange" shows the concrete structure that for many years was located on north U.S. 1 and served as the tourist information center for the Eau Gallie Chamber of Commerce.

The City of West Melbourne was created in 1959. As set forth on the city's website, West Melbourne was created specifically to avoid annexation by the City of Melbourne and to prevent the levying of ad valorem taxes.

The race for the moon and the development of the space industry in Brevard County set the stage for a series of momentous events that would shape the way south Brevard County would evolve during the ensuing 65 years.

The earliest of these events took place in 1950 when Radiation Inc. decided to set up its start-up enterprise at the airport in Melbourne. That decision had an enormous impact on Brevard County, particularly the southern part of the county. Homer Denius and George Shaw were engineers at Melpar, an engineering-manufacturing company in Virginia. Melpar had done a great deal of business with the U.S. Navy during World War II. When launch activities began at Cape Canaveral, Denius and Shaw saw the launch of a V-2 rocket from Cape Canaveral in 1950. The Navy asked Melpar to establish a branch in Florida to support the Navy's launch activities, specifically through the production of telemetry equipment. When the owner of Melpar declined, Denius and Shaw decided to form a venture of their own to exploit the business opportunity. Denius invested $20,000 for 80 percent of the company, and Shaw invested $5,000 for 20 percent. In looking for a place to locate their business near Cape Canaveral, they decided to lease one of the former Navy buildings at Melbourne's airport. That decision was to have an enormous and enduring positive impact on Brevard County and, indeed, Central Florida. The evolution of Radiation and its later permutations into Harris and now L3Harris, and the company's effects on the community would continue for years to come.

L3 Harris has had an enormously positive effect on the county, not only providing thousands of high-skilled jobs but also financially supporting dozens of community organizations while attracting other high-tech industries eager to tap the pool of skilled workers created by Radiation and L3 Harris. While those contributions are widely recognized, what is not known is that Radiation came close to leaving the community in the mid-fifties. Radiation had won a contract to digitally install instruments in some planes that were to fly through nuclear tests. However, the existing runways at Melbourne Airport were too short for the planes designated in the contract. Radiation offered to pay for lengthening the runway in exchange for the free use of some buildings at the airport, but the airport declined the offer. Since the program was highly classified, Radiation was limited in what it could present in its efforts to persuade the city to lengthen the runway. Radiation co-founder George Shaw later explained: "Fort Lauderdale, Orlando and Miami were willing to do almost anything to get us to move there." We wound up building our own facility for the project in Orlando where the runways were long enough, but we almost left the Melbourne area." Shaw further explained: "Neither Mr. Denius nor I wanted to move to Orlando." I suspect the fact that they were both avid sailors had something to do with their reluctance to move. It is difficult to imagine how different Brevard County would be had they moved the company at that time. Brevard would be a remarkably different community with a vastly different economic base.

Harris Intertype Corporation acquired Radiation in 1967. Although Harris was the surviving entity, it was Radiation that took over Harris. Harris Intertype was a producer of printing equipment, and its leaders were prescient enough to understand that digitization would soon make printing equipment obsolete. On the other side of the merger, Radiation officials were far-sighted enough to resist merging with a company in which Radiation would disappear. Instead, Radiation looked for and found a merger partner that would rely heavily on Radiation to provide the leadership, technology, strategic vision, and innovation for the future direction of the combined company. That is exactly what happened. As reported in *Florida Today* on October 28, 1976: "Melding of the South Brevard firm's electronics expertise with Harris' traditional printing equipment products has led to a virtual revolution in information-handling and communications techniques. Harris, as a result has become one of the leading companies in the fast-growing electronics industry." That same news article traced the founding of Radiation and its growth, including its move to the Palm Bay campus in 1959. In 1962, Dr. Joe Boyd, the Director of the University of Michigan's Institute of Science and Technology, joined Radiation as President and led the five-year growth plan which culminated in the merger with Harris. Although the merger in 1967 resulted in Dr. Boyd moving to the Cleveland headquarters of Harris as Executive Vice-President of the merged company, he would soon return to South Brevard, this time as Chief Executive Officer of Harris.

On October 28, 1969, *Florida Today* reported that Radiation had signed a lease with the Melbourne Airport Authority under which It leased sixty-five acres of airport property bounded by NASA Boulevard on the north, Woody Burke Road on the west, and Hibiscus Boulevard on the south. This lease also included an option for Radiation to buy the property. This site would become Harris's corporate headquarters.

By October 1976, Harris employed more than 5,500 workers in Florida, making it one of the state's five largest industrial employers.

On February 24, 1977, *Florida Today* reported that Harris projected it would create 3000 more jobs in South Brevard within five years. Later that year, on July 7, 1977, *Florida Today* reported that Harris was planning a $6 million expansion at Melbourne Airport, where it would construct facilities for its Satellite Communications Division. Harris predicted that the employment within that division would double its 650 employees in two to three years. The construction would bring Harris's total space in South Brevard to over 1.3 million square feet.

Florida Today reported even better news on August 25, 1977, when Harris announced that it was moving its headquarters from Cleveland to a site at the Melbourne Airport, near the terminal. The headquarters building would share the site with the Satellite Communications Division which had announced its expansion plans in July. The news article further noted that this site was near the place where Radiation had launched back in 1950. Richard Tullis, who was CEO of Harris at the time of the announcement, said the decision was a logical move to place the headquarters close to the core of the company. Tullis explained that 20 years before, Harris Intertype had annual sales of about $60 million, all from the sale of printing equipment. At the time of the move to Florida, its annual sales were about $650 million, seventy-five percent of which was from the sale of advanced electronics products. This move would make Harris the largest industrial firm headquartered in Florida. The decision by Harris was game-changing for south Brevard County, not only because of Harris' direct economic impact but because it gave the area credibility and a labor pool that attracted aerospace companies that would follow Harris to the region.

The next landmark event that forever changed the nature of Brevard County was the founding of the Florida Institute of Technology in 1958.

Among those drawn to the Cape and the U.S. space program in the 1950s was a young senior engineer in RCA's Systems Analysis section of the Missile Test Project. Jerome Keuper held a doctorate from the University of Virginia and a master's degree from Stanford University in addition to his undergraduate degree from Massachusetts Institute of Technology. Prior to joining RCA in 1958, Keuper had worked for Remington Arms Company in Bridgeport, Connecticut. While at Remington, Keuper had taught calculus at night at the Bridgeport Engineering Institute (BEI). BEI had been set up to provide education to people working in technical jobs looking to build their knowledge. BEI instructors were people employed in the subject matter that they taught at night.

Even before arriving in Florida with his wife and daughter in early 1958, Dr. Keuper had given thought to the possibility of creating something akin to BEI that would allow engineers and scientists at Cape Canaveral to continue their education. He had even explored the idea of establishing a branch of BEI near the Cape but was urged to begin an independent institution of his own. When he arrived at RCA, Keuper immediately embarked on this venture. Keuper began discussing his idea of starting a college modeled after BEI with three of his team members at RCA, George Peters, Donya Dixon, and Robert Kelly, all of whom enthusiastically embraced the idea. Soon Harold Dibble joined them, an RCA inertial guidance engineer who had taught in UCLA's evening engineering program.

This group, led by Keuper, soon put together a plan to form Brevard Engineering Institute. The plan contemplated that classes would be conducted three nights per week and would include classes in mechanical and electrical engineering, leading to an associate degree.

Graduate-level courses would be added later. The faculty and administration of the college would consist of people employed in local industry who would teach the subject area related to their employment. There would be no full-time professors or administrators. Keuper would serve as President, Dibble as Dean, Peters as head of the Mathematics Department, Kelly as Chief Financial Officer, and Dixon as the school's corporate Secretary.

In May 1958, Dr. Keuper officially announced that classes would begin in the fall of that year. Brevard County Public Schools agreed to rent the new college three classrooms in what was then Eau Gallie Junior High School (present-day West Shore Junior/Senior High School). In response to the opinions of prospective students, the name of the institution was changed from Brevard Engineering Institute to Brevard Engineering College (BEC) in June 1958. In July, BEC announced that it would offer nine classes: Advanced Calculus, Transients in Linear Systems, Statistics and Probability Theory I, Modern Algebra, Advanced Circuitry Analysis, Servomechanisms, Electromagnetic Fields, Transistor Theory I, and Numerical Analysis.

A meeting of prospective faculty members was held in September 1958. At the meeting, it was announced that 114 undergraduates and 40 graduate students had enrolled. Six of the students were women, and the average age of the students was thirty-three. Twenty-three faculty members were appointed, eight of whom held doctorates. Nearly all students and faculty members were employed by contractors at Cape Canaveral, including seventy-five students employed at RCA.

BEC faced a crisis in March 1959 when the Brevard County School Board threatened not to renew BEC's lease on the classrooms in Eau Gallie Junior High School. Woodrow Darden, the Superintendent of Brevard Public Schools, voiced several reasons for this action, including parking congestion and speculation that BEC would duplicate a junior college, which was contemplated by Brevard Public Schools but not yet developed. However, it is probable that Darden's opposition to BEC arose when he discovered that BEC's students included two African American students. Only when those two students voluntarily dropped out was Darden's objection placated.

By the fall of 1959, the issue of classrooms had been resolved with the aid of Homer Denius and George Shaw, the founders of Radiation, Inc. Shaw and Denius were avid supporters of BEC from the outset and remained supporters until their deaths. They came to the rescue in 1959 by persuading the First National Bank of Melbourne, a bank of which they had been among the founders, to allow BEC to occupy a building owned by the bank. The building on Waverly Place in Melbourne had previously been occupied by the Methodist Church. In the fall of 1959, BEC began its second year of classes in the old Methodist Church building. African American students returned to BEC. In September 1959, when BEC began its second year of classes, 247 students enrolled, including 149 graduate students and 98 undergraduates.

Following its year in the old church building, BEC relocated its classes to an old building at Melbourne Airport. That building was a former Navy barracks used during World War II when the airport was a training base for Naval aviators. The building had been leased to Radiation which sublet part of the building to BEC.

Another problem facing BEC at the outset was finances. Although RCA and other contractors at the space center had policies reimbursing their employees for college courses, those policies required that the courses be taken at an accredited institution. Although BEC had undertaken the process of becoming accredited, it was a lengthy endeavor that would not be completed for several years. Keuper wrote a letter to Dr. Robert Sarnoff, CEO of RCA, explaining the dilemma. Sarnoff delegated Irving Wolff, a vice president of RCA and Chair of its education committee, to visit BEC and make a recommendation on the issue of tuition reimbursement. Wolff visited Keuper and BEC in June 1959 and became fast friends with Keuper and a great advocate for BEC. Following Wolff's recommendation, RCA began to reimburse its employees for tuition paid to BEC, and most of the other contractors at the Cape followed suit.

In 1961, BEC's prospects brightened considerably when it was the fortunate beneficiary of the closure of the University of Melbourne. In 1951, a group of residents had a vision of setting up a liberal arts college, to be known as the University of Melbourne. The University received a gift of thirty-five acres of land on Country Club Drive in Melbourne from a local funeral homeowner, V.C. Brownlie. The University of Melbourne constructed a small classroom and library building on the site. However, by 1961 the leaders of the University of Melbourne recognized that they lacked the resources to continue their dream of a liberal arts college. They closed the university and donated the assets of the defunct college to BEC. On August 21, 1961, the Cocoa Tribune reported that BEC had moved its operations to the site. On July 31, 1962, the Cocoa Tribune said that BEC, with 457 students now enrolled, was undertaking the construction of two more classroom buildings on the site. By March 1963, The Evening Tribune reported that work had begun on a sixth building on the site. In January 1965. The Tribune reported the dedication of a library building that had been built on the campus (that building is not the current library but was converted to the Keuper Administration Building when the Evans Library was constructed).

The Cocoa Tribune reported on June 14, 1961, that BEC would conduct its first commencement on the following day. The ceremony was held at Melbourne High School, and Joseph Weil, Dean of the School of Engineering at the University of Florida, was the commencement speaker.

Keuper and other officials of BEC continued to press for the college's accreditation. In 1960, the Florida Association of Colleges and Universities (FACU) rejected BEC's application for membership. In 1962, FACU held its annual meeting in conjunction with the regional accrediting body, the Southern Association of Colleges and Schools (SACS). BEC was allowed to attend that meeting as an observer but continued to meet strong opposition from other Florida colleges. BEC continued its efforts for accreditation, and, on December 3, 1964, the Cocoa Tribune reported that BEC had succeeded and was now "an accredited resident senior college of engineering and science."

In 1961, BEC applied to the Florida Secretary of State for a new charter. In January 1962, Florida Secretary of State Tom Adams approved the request, including approval of the authority for the exclusive use of the name "Florida Institute of Space Technology." BEC demonstrated that it intended to become a more broad-based university when it announced its intention to expand its curriculum beyond science and engineering. The Cocoa Tribune reported on March 14, 1962, that it was creating an Institute of Management Studies. The stated goal of the institute was to "provide the broad base of management studies upon which the company training function can build and develop the specific company's philosophies, methods and procedures."

As a newly founded institution with no endowment, BEC was in a constant state of financial instability. An effort to address the financial needs of the college led Keuper to initiate discussions with the Disciples of Christ church which had founded Texas Christian University. Robert Bruce, former Executive Director of the St. Petersburg Chamber of Commerce, had been instrumental in the founding of Florida Presbyterian College (now Eckerd College) in St. Petersburg. Bruce convinced Keuper that they could set up a similar institution in Brevard County by entering into an agreement with the Disciples of Christ. Bruce also indicated to Keuper, either explicitly or implicitly, that the church would be able to invest several million dollars in the college. The proposal generated substantial enthusiasm from both BEC and the church. At the 71st annual meeting of the Disciples of Christ in May 1962, Keuper addressed the meeting and presented a preliminary agreement that had been negotiated by BEC and church representatives. The Disciples enthusiastically endorsed the plan, and it began to appear likely that Florida Christian University would be created. However, financial issues soon doomed the project. Bruce, while assuring Keuper that the church would invest millions, had assured the church that no financial investment would be needed. The negotiations quickly ended when it became clear that no funds would be forthcoming.

Another challenge that faced BEC during the early 1960s was the possibility of a state university being created at Cape Canaveral. In 1960, Florida Governor Farris Bryant had recognized the need for expanding the post-secondary education system in Florida. Bryant tasked the Education Committee of the Governor's Council of 100 to recommend a plan for Florida's post-secondary needs. BEC viewed the possibility of a state institution at the Cape as an existential threat. The creation of a new state institution in central Florida became a contentious political issue that attracted the attention of the most powerful political interests in the state, as well as business interests that could profit from such a venture. BEC used all its influence to discourage the establishment of a state institution, arguing that BEC was willing and able to meet educational needs in the region. The political debate on both sides was vigorous. In May 1962, the Education Committee of the Council of 100 recommended to Governor Bryant that the state should set up a space science university in central Florida. This resulted in the establishment in 1963 of Florida Technological University (FTU) east of Orlando, later renamed to University of Central Florida, which is now one of the largest undergraduate universities in the country. FTU opened in 1968 and, as Keuper predicted, has posed challenges to the Florida Institute of Technology (FIT), competing not only for students but for research funding and corporate partnerships.

In June 1962, BEC conducted its second commencement, awarding degrees to thirty-eight graduates, including one woman. Honorary degrees were awarded to Secretary of State Tom Adams and astronaut Gus Grissom. For the summer term of 1962, 448 students enrolled, including 313 undergraduates and 135 graduate students.

In 1962, Keuper recognized that the college could not progress with part-time leadership. Dr. Keuper retired from the RCA in October 1962 to devote all his energies to BEC. After BEC received full accreditation from SACS, the door was opened to receive research contracts. The Evening Tribune reported on December 4, 1964, that BEC had received its first industry-sponsored research contract. The contract with Dow Chemical obligated BEC to develop a mathematical model relating to the release of gases resulting from fuel releases.

The construction of dormitories signaled that BEC had evolved far beyond the idea of night classes for part-time students. On December 28, 1964, the Cocoa Tribune reported that a groundbreaking had been held for Brownlie Hall, the school's first dormitory.

In 1966, BEC amended its Articles of Incorporation to change its name to "Florida Institute of Technology, Inc." Since that time, the school has been informally referred to as "F.I.T." and, more recently, "Florida Tech."

Florida Tech has continued to be a pillar of the Brevard community, not only educationally but also culturally and economically. The university is one of the essential institutions which, collectively, have enabled the area to attract a high-tech economic base with a highly skilled workforce.

Another event that was the catalyst for dramatic change in south Brevard County occurred in 1959 when General Development Corporation (GDC) acquired 48,500 acres of land in Palm Bay, extending from U.S. 1 to the St. Johns River and extending 12 miles from north to south. GDC was a land development company created in 1958 by a merger between Florida Canada Corporation and the Mackle Brothers. Mackle Brothers, at one point, was the largest homebuilding company in Florida. The Orlando Sentinel reported on June 30, 1959, that GDC had paid more than $18 million for the property and intended to build a huge housing development named "Port Malabar". GDC told the newspaper that it intended to construct 30,000 homes and sell 105,000 homesites on the property. The June 30 article also showed that GDC had sold a 60-acre tract to Radiation, with a possibility for an adjoining 60-acre parcel. Radiation would expand its operations from Melbourne Airport and locate its primary manufacturing facilities on the Port Malabar site. The article described Radiation expansion as the "backbone" of the Port Malabar development. An article in the Orlando Sentinel on September 16, 1959, showed that GDC and Radiation were placing jointly sponsored advertisements in newspapers and technical journals publicizing the availability of homes and jobs in Port Malabar. George Shaw, senior vice president of Radiation, explained: "The tie-in of first-class homes and good jobs should enable our company to attract the kind of highly trained men we need in our technical work." Obviously, gender equity awareness had not yet reached the area.

The acquisition of Port Malabar by GDC had an enormous impact on the development of south Brevard County. That impact was not always positive. The Mackle brothers would end up leaving GDC due to a dispute with its chairperson, Gardner Cowles, and they would form the Deltona Corporation, which competed with GDC. By the late 1970s, GDC had sold thousands of lots but lacked the cash to complete the construction of the promised infrastructure. It continued to sell unimproved lots to generate cash to build infrastructure for lots sold a decade earlier. In the late 1980s, senior management of GDC was indicted for criminal fraud and two of the senior executives were convicted, although their convictions were overturned on appeal. GDC filed a Chapter 11 bankruptcy petition in April 1990. The Atlantic Gulf Communities would acquire the assets of GDC through the bankruptcy proceedings but would file a bankruptcy petition themselves in 2001.

Despite the checkered history of GDC and its successors, the development of Port Malabar has undisputedly had a dramatic and irrevocable effect on the area. The development created a huge inventory of affordable real estate, which has attracted people from all over the nation and internationally. It has brought not only retirees but also working-age residents who have filled the need for workers created by Brevard County's burgeoning economic base. Palm Bay is now the most populous city in the county.

The 1969 merger of the municipalities of Melbourne and Eau Gallie was another event that would have a transformational effect on South Brevard County and shape the community's nature for many decades. The critical role played by the recently combined Metropolitan South Brevard Chamber of Commerce is the subject of Chapter Five of this book and is certainly one of the most significant accomplishments in the chamber's history.

The early 1970s in Brevard County were defined by the general crash in the local economy that began as the Apollo Program for lunar exploration began to wind down at the Space Center. Thousands of people were laid off as employment declined. The New York Times reported on July 16, 1970, that NASA employment at Kennedy Space Center had declined by over 7,000 jobs during the previous year. By October 1975, the unemployment rate, as reported by

Florida Today on November 19, 1975, had reached a devastating level at 17.7 percent. Even by June 1976, unemployment remained at the painful level of 14.5 percent.

That made Collins Radio's decision in 1973 to find a new facility in Melbourne an extraordinarily important move for the community. That decision by Collins signified the first time since the onset of the economic decline caused by the end of the Apollo Program that a major aerospace firm or even a major employer of any sort had recognized that the U.S. space program had created a highly attractive labor force in central Florida. This trained workforce made the area an unusually desirable locale for high-tech industries.

In 1933, Arthur Collins founded Collins Radio Company in Cedar Rapids, Iowa. During World War II, Collins designed the Collins Autotune radio transmitter, 90,000 of which were used in British and American planes during the war. After the war, Collins expanded its markets into a variety of commercial and military communication goods, including products for the U.S. space program. In 1973, Collins was merged into North American Rockwell Corporation.

By the late 1960s, Collins had also become a leading supplier of avionics, marketed as Collins Pro Line avionics, in the general aviation heavy twin-engine turboprop and business jet markets. In 1972, Harry M. Passman, a highly innovative engineer and Vice President of General Aviation Avionics, recognized that there was an untapped avionics market for Collins in small single-engine and light twin-engine planes produced by companies like Beechcraft, Cessna, and Piper. Passman presented a business plan and received approval from top Collins management to cautiously go ahead with the development of a new, lightweight, panel-mounted, cost-competitive line of avionics for small general aviation aircraft.

While engineering work was quietly proceeding on the new avionics product line, Passman became concerned that the line would have difficulty meeting cost targets in the Cedar Rapids operating environment. He was particularly concerned that allocated overhead costs would be too much of a burden for the new line of products. He also believed that the Cedar Rapids environment would stifle manufacturing innovation and the ability to attack the status quo of the older, inflexible business systems serving the broad base of Collins government and commercial businesses. With Collins already employing 7,000 people in Cedar Rapids, Passman also concluded that the ability to expand there might be restricted by the limited size of the area's labor market.

In early 1973 Collins contracted with a firm specializing in site evaluation and selection services to provide a list of potential locations in which to set up a manufacturing operation for its new avionics product line. Together Collins and the site selection firm developed an extensive list of site requirements and desired attributes. At the top of the list were that the site has a large pool of available labor, that suitable land be available for industrial development, that the public education system is of high quality, and that the location is near an interstate highway and close to an airport with commercial air service. The firm developed a list of potential sites for the new Collins operation, and Melbourne, Florida, was one of the locations on the "shortlist."

In the spring of 1973, top Collins executives Clare I. Rice, Vice President and General Manager of Collins Avionics, and Harry M. Passman, Vice President of Collins General Aviation Avionics, visited Melbourne and met with John E. McCauley, Executive Director of the Brevard Economic Development Council. During their two-day visit, the Collins executives also met with Edward L. Foster, Director of Aviation for the Melbourne Regional Airport; the Superintendent of Brevard County Schools; and representatives of the South Brevard Chamber of Commerce.

Shortly after visiting Melbourne and other potential sites, Clare Rice and Harry Passman approved the selection of Melbourne, Florida, as the production site for the new avionics product line.

As previously noted, the decision to locate Collins in Melbourne could not have come at a better time for the community, which had been mired in the depths of the economic downturn following the end of the Apollo Program. Collins has continued to flourish and expand in Melbourne during the ensuing 50 years. It has morphed from Collins Radio to Rockwell Collins to Collins Aerospace and is now a subsidiary of Raytheon Technologies. Collins currently employs more than 1,500 people in Melbourne.

This 1973 advertisement sponsored by the chamber touted the membership benefits in anticipation of the chamber's upcoming membership drive.

In 1975, Suntree Country Club was created, and the housing development surrounding the golf course began. Suntree's development has had a substantial positive effect on south Brevard County. Currently, more than 4,500 homes have been built in Suntree. The country club now consists of two 18-hole championship golf courses, making Suntree a highly desirable residential area.

Another institution that has had a dramatic impact on South Brevard County is Health First, which is now the largest private employer in the county. Brevard Hospital Association was originally chartered on August 7, 1932, by a Circuit Court Judge in Brevard County. The hospital consisted of a single-story building on U.S. 1 in Melbourne on land donated by Mr. and Mrs. John Rodes. It was later reincorporated by the Florida Department of State on January 27, 1969. The hospital was financed by a $30,000 loan from the National Industry Recovery Act. Groundbreaking took place in the fall of 1936, and the formal opening took place on June 8, 1937. The City of Melbourne was originally responsible for the hospital's operation, but in 1945, the city transferred ownership to the Brevard Hospital Association.

In the early 1960s, a new hospital was built at its current location on Hickory Street in Melbourne, consisting of a modern facility with 322 beds. In 1979, the facility was expanded to 528 beds. On August 4, 1986, the hospital's name was changed from Brevard Hospital to Holmes Regional Medical Center (HRMC) in honor of James Holmes, a local insurance agent who had served as chair of the hospital board for many years. In 1992, HRMC built a 104,000-square-foot, 60-bed hospital on Malabar Road in Palm Bay known as Palm Bay Community Hospital (PBCH). PBCH has since been expanded to more than double its original size.

In 1995, HRMC, PBCH and Cape Canaveral Hospital joined together to create a single not-for-profit healthcare system named Health First, Inc. Health First then created Health First Health Plans to offer Medicare supplemental policies in 1996. In April 2011, Health First opened Viera Hospital, a 100-bed hospital on Wickham Road in Viera.

Today, Health First employs more than 9,500 associates with a payroll of more than $664 million. Its financial impact in 2022 was estimated to be $869 million.

The largest employer in Brevard County is Brevard Public Schools with more than 9,500 employees. Brevard is always at or near the top of school districts in Florida in terms of student achievement, dropout rates, and other metrics. This is not surprising given the number of well-educated engineers and scientists employed in the aerospace industry in the county. Those parents demand quality education for their children. The prominence of Melbourne High School during the 1950s and 60's, as described hereinafter in Chapter Four was at least partially a result of the influx of aerospace workers.

The dramatic fluctuations in employment in the aerospace industry posed great challenges for the Brevard Public Schools. During the 1950s and 1960s, as space workers poured into the county to work on the Mercury, Gemini, and Apollo Programs to put a man on the moon, that growth spurt posed enormous problems in providing classrooms and teachers to meet the demand. The Miami Herald reported on June 7, 1953, that the demand for new classrooms was causing Brevard Public Schools to defer teacher pay raises, thereby impacting the district's ability to hire teachers. An article in the Orlando Sentinel on June 12, 1960, noted that between 1950 and 1960, classrooms in the county had increased from 117 to 802 while pupil enrollment had rocketed from 3,659 to 21,757. Salaries for starting teachers during that time had increased from $2,250 to $3,800. By June 23, 1974, Florida Today reported that there were 60,767 students enrolled in Brevard Public Schools and that the cost of educating a student had increased by 239% over the past 10 years. As the Apollo Program came to an end and employment at the space center plummeted, the problem was a surplus of classrooms. As the Shuttle Program expanded, enrollment in public schools began to expand again. In 2015, it was estimated that 74,000 students were enrolled in Brevard Public Schools.

Another seismic shift in south Brevard County occurred in 1985 when Grumman Corporation selected the Melbourne Airport as the site for one of its largest programs. In 1974, George Skurla became the President of Grumman Corporation, which was headquartered in Bethpage, Long Island, in New York. Grumman had been the contractor for the lunar excursion module (LEM), designed to transport the Apollo astronauts from the spacecraft to the moon's surface and back. Skurla had led the program and lived in Satellite Beach. When the program ended and Skurka was reassigned to Bethpage, he kept his house in Satellite Beach. His wife would spend much of each year at their Florida home, and George would often travel to spend weekends in Satellite Beach. When George, an unusually gregarious person, traveled through Melbourne Airport, he often stopped to visit Ed Foster, the Director of Aviation. I suspect they shared many stories that improved with age since Ed was a former Naval aviator who had flown a variety of Grumman-built aircraft.

When Grumman began to pursue the U.S. Army and Air Force surveillance and target attack radar system (J-STARS) contract in 1984, George assembled a team to survey airports around the country to find a suitable site to fulfill the contract. As George related it to me, the team initially returned with a list of potential sites that did not include Melbourne. One of the requirements for a site was that Grumman needed to have assurances that it would have a clear line of sight for 1,000 feet to test its signals. The team was concerned that Melbourne could not ensure such an uninterrupted line of sight. Skurla instructed the team to take another look and not return with a list that omitted Melbourne.

Grumman's pursuit of the J-STARS program and the decision to locate the program in Melbourne are discussed in Skurla's book "Inside the Iron Works: How Grumman's Glory Days Faded." As related in the book, Grumman had been almost exclusively a contractor for the Navy. Skurla described Grumman's winning bid for J-STARS—as causing "astonishment in the electronics community." Grumman had executed an earlier contract for a program named the "Pave Mover Radar Program," which consisted of putting a 12-foot radar on an F-111 aircraft. That technology proved to be the enabling technology for J-STARS. Initially, there was a dispute as to whether to install the J-STARS system on a U-2 rather than a commercial 707 plane. The Army even pushed for a helicopter-borne system. Grumman was able to persuade the government that the 707 was the best platform, as it was able to accommodate 18 display consoles along with all the data processing and cooling systems.

After it was announced that the contract would be awarded to Grumman, the question remained whether it would be performed in Melbourne. Lt. Gen. Melvin F. "Nick" Chubb, commander of the electronics center at Hanscom Air Force Base in Massachusetts, contacted Skurla to voice his concern about Grumman's plans to perform the contract in Florida. Chubb opined that it would be difficult to convince the needed workers, particularly software developers, to move to Melbourne. Skurla observed: "This was a shock because Grumman has already cut some good deals with Melbourne for the facility we were to build at the Melbourne airport, which was an F6F operational training base in World War Two." Although Chubb's call caused Grumman to take another look at its decision to locate in Melbourne, that second look only solidified its confidence in its first decision. Chubb acknowledged that Grumman had made the correct decision. Marty Dandridge, General Manager of the Grumman operation in Melbourne (and later a member of the Melbourne Airport Authority) said that Chubb "loved us after a while."

On October 2, 1985, Florida Today welcomed Grumman Corporation to the Melbourne Airport and noted that Grumman had won a $657 million contract for J-STARS and had leased a site at the airport where it intended to construct a 188,000-square-foot facility that would employ 400 workers with a $35 million annual payroll.

Today Northrop Grumman's Melbourne operation encompasses 17 buildings on its 109-acre campus. As described on the Melbourne, Florida, page of the company's website, the "Melbourne site features a premier facility for the development and rapid prototyping of advanced surveillance and battle management systems." It continues: "Here, we design, develop, and test advanced manned aircraft and battle management command and control systems."

An article in Florida Today on June 13, 2022, reported that Northrop Grumman's employment in Melbourne at the end of 2020 was 4,714. The article further revealed the company's plans to immediately hire several hundred more employees with skills in electronics, logistics, software engineering, cyber-security, and other technical fields.

The development of Viera began in 1989 and has had an enormous impact on Brevard County. A. Duda and Sons, doing business as the Cocoa Ranch, had been a large agricultural/cattle operation in Brevard County for many years. In 1990, the company renamed one of its subsidiaries, The Viera Company, to begin the development of a portion of its property for a variety of uses. The original Development of Regional Impact (DRI) filed by the Viera Company in 1990 contemplated the development of 3,000 acres with mixed uses. In 1992, the DRI was expanded to encompass 6,000 acres, and a 2006 amendment expanded the development to 11,567 acres. The ensuing development has been impressive. Not only has Viera become the government center of Brevard County with the main courthouse, primary county administrative offices, and school district offices, but the development includes up-scale shopping venues, extensive recreational facilities, and even a baseball complex that has housed major league baseball spring training. The variety of housing is nothing short of astounding, ranging from multi-million-dollar mansions to affordable middle-class homes. The 2020 census revealed that 11,687 people lived in Viera East (that portion of Viera lying east of Interstate 95), while Viera West had a population of 16,688.

CHAPTER NOTES

- All citations related to the meetings of the governing bodies of the cities of Melbourne and Eau Gallie are derived from either a review of the official minutes of those bodies or from a summary of those minutes prepared by Cathleen Wysor, who was the city clerk of Melbourne from 1994 to 2020. Both the minutes and Wysor's summary were provided to the authors by Kevin McKeown, the current city clerk of Melbourne.
- The settling of the towns in south Brevard County is discussed in the following publications:

- "Crossroad Towns Remembered: A Look Back at Brevard and Indian River Pioneer Communities," by Weona Cleveland, published by Florida Today in 1994.
- "Melbourne and Eau Gallie (Images of America)," by Karen Raley and Ann Raley Flotte, published in 2002 by Arcadia Publishing.
- "A Tribute to Melbourne's Pioneers," published by the City of Melbourne Centennial Committee in 1989.
- "Brevard County: From Cape of the Canes to Space Coast," by Elaine Murray Stone, published by Windsor Publications in 1988.
- "Melbourne Beach and Indialantic (Images of America) by Frank J. Thomas, published by Acadia Publishing in 1999.
- "Melbourne: A Century of Memories," published by the Melbourne Area Chamber of Commerce Centennial Committee in 1980.
- "The Melbourne Bicentennial Book," published by the Melbourne Bicentennial Committee in 1976.
- For a comprehensive history of the logging era in south Brevard County, see "Melbourne's Logging Era, 1912 to 1932, (Images of America)" by Ed Vosatka, published by Arcadia Publishing in 2012.
- Information about the establishment of the JLRPG and the first launches at Cape Canaveral is taken from "Evolution of the 45th Space Wing"
- (https[://www.patrick.af.mil/library/factsheet.asp?id=4514).
- For more about the early launches at Cape Canaveral, see "70 Years Ago: First Launch from Cape Canaveral," by Uri, John, published on July 24, 2020, on the NASA website at nasa.gov/feature/70-years-ago-first-launch-from-cape-canaveral.
- The discussion of the early activities of Radiation, Inc. is partially based upon *Radiation, Inc.: An Anthology of Defining Stories* by A.B. Amis and John G. Johnson, published by George P. Burdell Publishing in 2019. These subjects are also extensively described in *High Tech Among the Palmettos: The Story of Radiation, Inc., and How It Changed the Face of South Brevard County* by Frank Perkins, published by Oak Publishing in 2014. See pages V, 13, 25 to 43. The discussion is further based upon conversations between the author and his friends Homer Denius and George Shaw, both of whom are now deceased.

- The quotations from George Shaw about the effort to extend the runway at the Melbourne Airport and the possibility of moving Radiation from Melbourne are taken from FYI: The Harris Magazine of Technology at Work, Fall 1995 edition, published by Harris Corporation. The author was provided a copy of this publication by Harry Deffebach, a former senior executive of Harris Corporation.
- Harris officials proclaimed that company officers looked to acquire Radiation because they "became fully convinced of a natural confluence between print and electronic communication methods." See "The Harris Story," an internal publication compiled by Harris Corporation written by William D. Ellis of Editorial Services, Inc. and published on June 30, 1972. The author was provided with a copy of this publication by Harry Deffebach.
- For more information about Radiation, L3 Harris, Collins Radio, and Grumman Corporation see "Melbourne Orlando International Airport: A History from 1928 to 2022," by William C. Potter, independently published in 2022.
- Information regarding Keuper's arrival at RCA, his desire to set up an educational institution and the challenges during the first two years of the college is taken from Patterson, Gordon "Countdown to College: Launching Florida Institute of Technology," Florida Historical Quarterly, Volume 77, Number 2, Fall 1998.
- The article by Patterson, Gordon, "Space University: Lift-Off of Florida Institute of Technology," Florida Historical Quarterly, Volume 79, Number 1, Summer 2000, describes the challenges faced by BEC during the early 1960s, including its efforts to gain accreditation, its negotiations with the Disciples of Christ, and its efforts to forestall a state university in the area.
- An article in Florida Today newspaper on May 25, 1969, describes the University of Melbourne and its gift to BEC.
- Other sources describing the founding of the college and its early challenges include:
- Cleveland, Weona. "Crossroad Towns Remembered: A Look Back at Brevard and Indian River Pioneer Communities." Florida Today, 1994. See page 87. Patterson, Gordon. "Florida Institute of Technology." Arcadia Publishing, 2000.

- For information about the merger of Melbourne and Eau Gallie, see Potter, William "Melbourne Orlando International Airport: A History from 1928 to 2022," self-published in 2022.

- For the fraud case against the executives of General Development Corporation, see US v. Brown, 79 F. 3rd 1550 (1996).
- For the history of Collins Radio, see "The First Fifty Years"—A history of Collins Radio Company and the Collins Divisions of Rockwell International" by Ken C. Braband, published by Rockwell International in 1983.
- Much of the information about the location of Collins Radio in Melbourne was taken from the information written by Ted Fuhrer in "Melbourne Orlando International Airport: A History from 1928 to 2022, "ibid. See pages 64 to 70.
- The information about Health First's economic impact is taken largely from https://hf.org/news/health-firsts-economic-impact-brevard-county-approaches-900-million-recent-report. As to the historical development of HRMC, PBCH and Health First, see Florida Today issues of June 25, 1979, May 14, 1989, and August 6, 1992. Information regarding the original charter of Brevard Hospital Association, Incorporated, and its subsequent reincorporation can be viewed on the website of the Florida Department of State at dos.fl.gov/sunbiz/search/.
- The information about the Brevard Schools Foundation comes from a Florida Today article of December 30, 1989, and from the website of the Foundation at https://brevardschoolsfoundation.org/who-we-are/history.
- The information regarding the school desegregation lawsuit is based upon an article in the Orlando Sentinel dated September 19, 1976.
- Grumman's success in being awarded the J-STARS program, the decision to locate in Melbourne, the quotes from Skurla and Dandridge and Lt. Gen. Chubb's misgivings about Melbourne are all discussed in "Inside the Iron Works: How Grumman's Glory Days Ended" by George M. Skurla and William H. Gregory, published in 2004 by the Naval Institute Press. See pages 209-219. Ironically, the pejorative title of the book refers to the merger of Northrop and Grumman, an event that has substantially benefited south Brevard County, resulting in the relocation of even more jobs to the Melbourne facility.

- The information about Grumman is also partially based on the author's discussions with George Skurla, Martin Dandridge, Al Verderosa, and other Grumman officials.

- Northrop Grumman's information about their Melbourne facility appears on their website at: www.northropgrumman.com/careers/northrop-grumman-in-melbourne-florida.
- Information about the development of Suntree is taken from the webpage of the Suntree Master Homeowners Association at suntreeflorida.com and the webpage of the Suntree Country Club at suntree.com/default.aspx.
- The information about the development of Viera is taken from the webpage of A. Duda and Sons at "History" (http://www.duda.com).
- Appendix A is a chart illustrating the population expansion of the areas served by the Melbourne Regional Chamber and is intended to prove the extraordinary growth during the Chamber's existence.

CHAPTER TWO

What is a Chamber of Commerce?

Businesses have long banded together to promote their common interests. The first European chamber of commerce was founded in France in 1599.

There is conflicting information about the first Chamber of Commerce in the United States. Some sources say it started in New York in 1768, while others show that it was created in Charleston, South Carolina, in 1773.

In 1773, a chamber of commerce was formed in Boston. That chamber organized and implemented the Boston Tea Party. Despite numerous efforts, only a few chambers have been able to launch such a momentous inaugural project in the ensuing 250 years.

By 1912, the U.S. Department of Commerce estimated that there were 1,968 business groups in the U.S. with a combined membership of more than 348,000. In the early 1900s, there were also three large regional business groups: the American Association of Commercial Executives, the Southern Commercial Secretaries Association, and the Central Association of Commercial Secretaries. In 1912, President William Howard Taft called a meeting in Washington of commercial and trade associations and included those three regional groups. The Bureau of Manufacturers of the Department of Commerce organized the meeting. The result of the meeting on April 22, 1912, was the formation of the United States Chamber of Commerce, creating a unified voice to speak to governments on behalf of business.

The Association of Chamber of Commerce Executives (ACCE) defines a chamber of commerce as "an organization of businesses seeking to further their collective interests while advancing their community, region, state or nation." ACCE asserts that chambers have existed in the U.S. for over two centuries, predating the Charleston, Boston, and New York chambers. ACCE acknowledges that the missions of chambers vary substantially but asserts that they all tend to focus on five primary goals: 1. Building communities to which residents, visitors, and investors are attracted; 2. Promoting those communities; 3. Creating a pro-business climate within the communities; 4. Providing a unified voice to represent employers in the communities; and 5. Creating networks that facilitate efficient transactions.

ACCE reports that there are more than 7,500 chambers of commerce in the United States, some of which may be called by other names, such as boards of trade or business councils. ACCE recognizes that the service territory of a chamber is rarely defined by a political district but more likely represents the catchment area of the membership of the chamber. There are no rules governing the number of chambers that may exist in or serve a specific geographic area. ACCE recognizes that chambers dissolve and merge from time to time, based upon economic or political conditions.

ACCE recognizes that there are endless varieties of chambers, although most are run as not-for-profit entities under section 501(C)(6) of the Internal Revenue Code. Unlike 501 (C) (3) entities, chambers are allowed to lobby and take positions on proposed legislation, although they may be subject to local, state, and federal laws on lobbying activities and political contributions.

The relationship between local chambers of commerce and state and national organizations also varies considerably. Some local chambers cultivate close relationships with the state and/or national chambers, while others have no formal relationship with their state and national counterparts. The state and national organizations have no authority to regulate or monitor the activities or positions of the local chambers.

The U.S. Chamber of Commerce does have an accreditation program that allows the national organization to review the structure and programs of local, regional, and state chambers when they seek accreditation. Of the more than 7,500 chambers in the U.S., only 194 chambers were accredited by the national chamber as of 2023. The Melbourne Regional Chamber is one of this number. According to the U.S. Chamber of Commerce, accreditation is "a prestigious honor that distinguishes the high quality, expertise and strong leadership displayed by accredited state and local chambers of commerce." It further asserts that the accreditation process is "the only program of its kind that defines excellence in chamber planning and recognizes chambers for outstanding contributions toward positive change in their communities."

CHAPTER NOTES

- The information about the U.S. Chamber of Commerce was taken from the United States Chamber of Commerce. "U.S. Chamber of Commerce: The Early Years" (https://www.uschamber.com/sites/default/files/uscc_HistoryBook.pdf).
- The information about the Association of Chamber of Commerce Executives was gleaned from "What is a Chamber?" (https://web.archive.org/web/20131023062940/http://www.acce.org/whtisachamber/).
- The information about the accreditation process is taken from uschamber.com/chamber-accreditation-program.

CHAPTER THREE

Origins of Chambers in Melbourne and Eau Gallie: 1919 until the End of World War II

I was unable to find documents that conclusively validate the founding dates of the Melbourne and Eau Gallie chambers. The current administration of the Melbourne Regional Chamber has been relying on documentation that states that it was founded in 1925. They have begun initial planning for 2025 events celebrating the 100th anniversary of the chamber. However, my research makes it quite clear that both Melbourne and Eau Gallie had chambers prior to 1925. It was 1925 that marked the first time that the Melbourne Chamber of Commerce was formally incorporated as a corporate entity with a full-time executive manager. An article in The Miami Herald on August 8, 1925, noted that: "A reorganization of the Melbourne Chamber of Commerce to provide it with the foundation and stabilizing qualities of a corporation is being arranged by the officers of the chamber. The change will involve the employment of an executive secretary to devote his entire time to the affairs handled by the chamber." Thus, 1925 was a significant date in the history of the Melbourne Chamber. It was the year that the organization formally became a corporation. However, the earliest reference to the Melbourne Chamber of Commerce, which I found, was a September 10, 1919, article in the Orlando Sentinel. The article said that six members from the Melbourne Chamber of Commerce had appeared as guests at a meeting of the Orlando Board of Trade. The purpose of the visit was to inform the Orlando leaders that bonds had been issued to build a new bridge and road from Orlando to the ocean via Melbourne. Stanley S. Lichty was the spokesperson for the Melbourne delegation. An article in the Orlando Sentinel three days later indicated that the delegation from Melbourne included Lichty as well as J. O. Campbell, Charles H. Stewart, Reverend H. Cary-Elwes, Ernest Kouwen-Hoven, and C.P. Singleton. The delegation had traveled from Melbourne by automobile, stopping in St. Cloud and Kissimmee along the way. The article in the Sentinel reflected that the Orlando people present at the meeting were "really and truly interested in the Orlando-to-the-Sea road and especially the Melbourne-Indialantic bridge."

The road between Melbourne and Orlando was the subject of a resolution of the chamber presented to the Brevard County Board of Commissioners, reported by The Cocoa Tribune on April 22, 1920. The resolution, signed by Elton Hall, Secretary of the Melbourne Chamber, said in part: "Whereas. 'The Cross State Road' from Melbourne to Kissimmee, the completion of which means much to this section and will open territory that we are desirous of benefiting. "The resolution went on to ask the commission to request that the State Road Department begin to make the necessary surveys and cost estimates to plan the construction of the road. The County Commission adopted the resolution on a motion by John B. Rodes and sent it to the State Road Department.

On June 27, 1920, The Palm Beach Post published a letter from Elton Hall informing readers of a meeting to be held in Melbourne on June 30 to discuss the merits of the Melbourne-Kissimmee Road as a cross-state artery. According to Hall's letter, only a 17-mile section between Melbourne and Kissimmee remained to be improved to create a road that would span Florida from the Atlantic to the Gulf. The meeting was also touted as a forum at which to discuss a "constitutional amendment to permit the Legislature to bond for a statewide system of good roads."

A report of that June 30 meeting in the Tampa Tribune on July 2, 1920, described it as "What may be considered as one of the most important good roads conferences ever held in Florida." An editorial in The Tampa Tribune on July 21, 1920, said: "The Times and the Melbourne Chamber of Commerce call upon the people of that section to lend every assistance to put through this important project this summer and fall so as to have it ready for the tourist season this winter." The editorial continued: "Melbourne will be brought into prominence by the completion of this cross-state highway as it will be a junction point of interest to the thousands of motorists in the winter season coming up from the lower east coast and crossing to the west coast and coming from the west coast to visit the lower east coast."

It is striking that the first news articles that I found had to do with the bridge between Melbourne and Indialantic and the highway from Melbourne to Kissimmee, because several decades later, during the 1960s, 1970s, and 1980s, those issues would continue to be among the most urgent issues faced by the chamber's transportation committee. Although the bridge between Melbourne and Indialantic was opened as a 16-foot-wide toll bridge in 1921, it was a flat bridge with a span in the middle which opened on demand for boats of all kinds. The colossal traffic jams that result from bridge openings were a significant hindrance to local commerce and residents. For many years, convincing transportation planners to replace that bridge with a four-lane, high-rise bridge was at the top of the chamber's road priorities.

The road between Melbourne and Kissimmee had been built but was a two-lane road that resembled a roller coaster more than a road. As a result, the creation of a four-lane road for U.S. Highway 192 between Melbourne and Kissimmee joined the bridge at the top of the road priority list of the chamber for many years until the 1980s.

Demonstrating that its transportation interests extended beyond the Melbourne-Kissimmee Road, the Melbourne Chamber of Commerce presented another road resolution, this one signed by Leroy W. Cooper, secretary of the chamber, to the County Commission. On September 22, 1921, the Cocoa Tribune published the resolution that addressed the "deplorable condition" of the Dixie Highway (now U.S. Highway One) through Brevard County.
An article in The Miami Herald on October 14, 1921, showed that the Melbourne Chamber's transportation interests were not only not confined to a single road but extended to other forms of transportation. The article showed that the chamber had been presented with a proposal from S.D. Noel to form the Melbourne Railway and Navigation Company. The plan presented by Noel contemplated the construction of an inlet that would give seagoing vessels access to the Indian River.

The Melbourne Chamber's interest in railway transportation was further demonstrated by a resolution reported in The Tampa Tribune on October 22, 1921. That resolution addressed a threatened railway strike and called upon the federal government to take prompt action to prevent or settle such a strike.

The first mention which I found about the Eau Gallie Chamber of Commerce also related to transportation issues. The Cocoa Tribune reported on March 6, 1923, that representatives of the Eau Gallie Chamber had attended a meeting with Harry Green, the Division Engineer of the State Road Department, discussing what was needed to make the "main highway through the county at least safe and passable." I assume that the "main highway' refers to the Dixie Highway (now U.S. Highway One).

The first mention of the chamber in the minutes of the Melbourne City Council appeared in the minutes of January 8, 1925. The council proved that no matter was too mundane to escape the council's oversight when it granted permission to the Melbourne Chamber of Commerce to have benches, tables, and a dancing platform erected at Campbell Point. Shortly thereafter, the council acknowledged receipt of a letter from Joseph Masch, secretary of the chamber, recommending that the city buy 808 feet of real property on Front Street south of the Indialantic bridge for park purposes and as a "suitable place for entertainment of winter visitors." Although not reflected in the minutes, the city must have followed up on the recommendation since Front Street Park still is an important recreational facility today.

The road known as the Dixie Highway continued to be a topic of significant discussion, as reported by the Pensacola News Journal on July 15, 1924. The article described a meeting between Governor Cary Hardee and a group described as the Association of Chambers of Commerce, which included Albert Vorkeller, chairperson of the "good roads committee of the Melbourne Chamber of Commerce," as well as representatives from Daytona and St. Augustine. The group told the Governor that progress on the road was "discouraging," in response to which Hardee promised to take the matter up with Chair Phillips and Chief Engineer Cresap of the road department.

Further discussion of the cross-state road through Kissimmee was reported by The Miami Herald on August 10, 1924. The article indicated that C. E. Melton, vice-president and general manager of the Union Cypress Company, operator of the ferry across the St. Johns River on the route between Melbourne and Kissimmee, had told the Melbourne Chamber of Commerce that its ferry operation was a significant source of income for the company. The chamber responded by finding it "irksome" that construction of the highway had been delayed and reacted by appointing a committee to learn the source of the delays. The Melbourne Chamber criticized the idea of the railway company running a ferry and attributed delays in progress on the cross-state road to the existence of the ferry. A letter from Melton published in The Miami Herald on August 14 responding to that earlier article in the Herald related that he had demonstrated the fiscal impact of the ferry operation to the Melbourne Chamber and had proven that the ferry operation was proper and reasonable.

The Melbourne Times reported on January 22, 1925, that the Melbourne Chamber of Commerce had held its annual banquet a few days earlier and that "upward of 150 members, wives and friends came together for a feast of good things." The newspaper reported that David Peel functioned as toastmaster and that the remarks of the speakers "were designed to lift thought above personal affairs into the larger world of community betterment for which the chamber of commerce stands." The article continued: "That the program of speeches and music was appreciated and attested by rounds of applause." Aside from its failure to recognize gender equity, the article was noteworthy when one considers an attendance of 150 people in a town of a few hundred citizens.

Representatives of the Eau Gallie Chamber of Commerce, led by W. Lansing Gleason, appeared before the Melbourne City Council at the council meeting of January 29, 1925. Speaking on behalf of the Eau Gallie Chamber, Gleason objected to Melbourne's proposed annexation of property north of Melbourne, arguing that Eau Gallie would more appropriately annex the property. The Eau Gallie representatives reappeared at the council meeting of February 17, 1925, to renew their objection.

An extensive article in The Miami Herald on March 10, 1925, described a $10,000 advertising campaign recently undertaken by the Melbourne Chamber. The article noted: "From a civic point of view, Melbourne is viewed upon by her neighboring cities and an admiring public as being exceptionally fortunate and is credited with having one of the most active and effective chambers of commerce on the Florida East Coast." The article showed that Melbourne Mayor Albert Vorkeller was serving as president of the chamber while the "pleasant and accommodating" Joseph Masch was secretary. The campaign entailed the placement of advertisements in various newspapers around the state and was reported to have generated so much interest that the chamber had increased its staff to respond to inquiries generated by the campaign. The ads touted Melbourne as the "Midway City" due to its location between Miami and Jacksonville and promoted the area as an agricultural and citrus center.

An advertisement by the Melbourne Chamber in the Tampa Bay Times on March 8, 1925, headlined: "What a Wonderful Location for a Home." Another chamber ad in the Palm Beach Post on March 18 proclaimed: "The Logical Location for a Large City."

This advertisement was sponsored by the Melbourne Chamber of Commerce. During the first quarter of 1925, it appeared multiple times in the Miami Herald, Palm Beach Post, Tampa Tribune, Tampa Bay Times, Miami News, and Orlando Sentinel.

Brevard County was not immune to the schisms that have often plagued the county. On October 20, 1925, the Melbourne Times reported that the Eau Gallie Chamber of Commerce had hosted a meeting with officials from Cocoa to discuss Cocoa's plan to divide the county into three parts. Representatives from the two towns agreed that it was not a propitious time to consider such a proposal.

On December 24, 1925, the Eau Gallie Record showed that the Inlet Committee of the Eau Gallie Chamber of Commerce had traveled to Cocoa to meet with representatives of the Cocoa Chamber and the Titusville Chamber regarding an inlet. The Eau Gallie representatives were C.C. Canova, John O. Shares, and Dr. William J. Creel. Mr. Canova made a presentation of the proposal complete with drawings and engineering studies. Although the news article does not make clear the proposed location of the inlet, it was somewhere near the present east end of the Eau Gallie Causeway Boulevard in the area known as Canova Beach. All representatives at the meeting expressed interest in the project and agreed to appoint members to a joint committee to pursue the proposal.

The Miami Herald reported on April 8, 1926, that the meeting of the Eau Gallie Chamber of Commerce held the previous day had entailed discussions regarding "industrial and agricultural matters." The industrial committee of the chamber showed that it had been advertising for industrial prospects to locate in Eau Gallie and had succeeded in attracting several prospects. The agricultural interests present at the meeting had noted that there was no county agent in Brevard County, and it was decided that the chamber should ask the county to employ an agent who could provide advice to farmers. Attendees at the meeting further reported that chamber delegates had appeared before the county commission to complain that tolls on the Eau Gallie Bridge were higher than tolls on the Melbourne-Indialantic Bridge and had been assured that tolls on the two bridges would be equalized. Another topic of discussion at the meeting was steps that could be taken to entertain winter visitors. One proposal was that an excursion steamer be bought to provide free pleasure trips on the Indian River. A special committee was appointed to probe that possibility. The last action at the meeting was the appointment of a special committee to urge voter turnout on April

16, when a bond issue for constructing a municipal golf course would be considered.

The idea of an inlet near Eau Gallie was even more ambitious than the plans presented by Canova at Cocoa in December 1925. The Orlando Sentinel reported on June 25, 1926, that Judge John O. Shares, standing for the Eau Gallie Chamber of Commerce and the Associated Chambers of Commerce of Brevard County, had visited Orlando the previous day to meet with former Orlando mayor James Giles. Shares presented the idea of opening a water route from Orlando to the ocean at Eau Gallie. Share supported that: "A waterway connecting Orlando with the sea is not only possible but could be constructed with such comparative ease that it only remains for the people of the city and section to realize the wonderful opportunities to get them behind the project and put it through."

The idea of a navigational channel connecting Eau Gallie and points west did not die easily. On September 20, 1926, the Fort Myers News-Press reported that a delegation of the Eau Gallie Chamber of Commerce had visited Fort Myers to present the idea of a boat line from Eau Gallie to Fort Myers via the Caloosahatchee River. R. E. L. Niel, executive secretary of the Eau Gallie Chamber, acknowledged that the project seemed to be "up in the air" at present and agreed to postpone further investigations until a later date.

The Eau Gallie Chamber engaged in charitable activities and business advocacy initiatives. The minutes of the Eau Gallie City Council of November 20, 1926, reflect that the city donated $441.24 to the chamber to aid "hurricane sufferers of South Florida." The city council meeting of April 4, 1927, reflects another donation from the city to the chamber for $50.00, but the purpose of the gift was not disclosed.

The interests of the Melbourne Chamber were not limited to commercial activities and transportation matters. The Fort Myers News-Press reported on May 13, 1927, that C.P. Singleton had found the remains of a Jefferson Mammoth elephant near Melbourne. The remains, reported to be at least 25,000 years old, were kept at the Melbourne Chamber of Commerce for "some time" before being shipped to the Department of Geology at Amherst College in Massachusetts.

A notice in The Cocoa Tribune on July 22, 1927, announced a meeting of the Associated Chambers of Commerce of Brevard County. That association was described as including the officers and directors of the chambers of commerce in Titusville, Cocoa, Rockledge, and Melbourne. The association was an early effort to ensure that the various chambers in Brevard County harmonized and coordinated their goals and efforts. This meeting was to have as its guest of honor Colonel Gilbert A. Youngberg, a retired officer of the Corps of Engineers. The title of Colonel Youngberg's speech was to be "waterways of Brevard County." The speech would include discussions of the "East Coast Canal, the Upper St. Johns-Indian River Canal, and the Brevard Ship Canal or inlet connecting the waters of the Atlantic Ocean with the waters of the Indian River." It is informative that the chambers in 1927 were fixated on the potential commercial benefits of waterways even as motor vehicles and airplanes were proliferating.

The Tallahassee Democrat showed in its issue of August 23, 1927, that officials of the Eau Gallie Chamber of Commerce were in Tallahassee that week to voice concerns to Governor Martin about road issues. One of the chamber officials was Dr. W. J. Creel, who was not only president of the chamber but also a member of the state legislature. Judge John O. Shares, president of the Associated Chambers of Commerce of Brevard County and an appointee to the Florida Inland Navigation Commission, attended the meeting as did the chamber executive Robert E.I. Niel. The delegation protested the proposed location of an extension of the Dixie Highway, which, they argued, would impede access to Eau Gallie's harbor by constructing a draw bridge across the harbor. They urged, instead, that the highway extension use the existing bridge lying west of the harbor. Their arguments were persuasive since the current path of U.S. 1 lies west of the harbor.

The South Florida Developer, a newspaper in Stuart, Florida, reported on October 21, 1927, that the Melbourne Chamber of Commerce was amid a ten-day "patronize home industry campaign." The campaign also looked to convey the message that Melbourne could prosper only if there was "a united effort among the citizens, all working for a common good, and to the end that Melbourne may be made to take on new life and grow as never before." This campaign obviously presaged the "buy local" campaigns which are not uncommon today.

Even in those early days, the Melbourne Chamber kept a relationship with the U.S. Chamber of Commerce. An article in the Vero Beach Press Journal on March 27, 1928, reported that Colvin Brown, Manager of the Organization Service of the Chamber of Commerce of the United States, would address the Melbourne Chamber of Commerce on April 24. The newspaper noted: "This will be an opportunity for Sebastian people to hear a man of note."

The Cocoa Tribune of May 18, 1928, reported that County Agricultural Agent W. R. Briggs spoke to the Melbourne Chamber membership. The news article observed: "Subjects of agriculture, horticulture and the growing of fruits and vegetables were discussed with much enthusiasm by the membership present." That was a sign of progress in that the county now had an agricultural agent, only a couple of years after the Eau Gallie Chamber had complained about the lack of such an agent.

The existence of the Associated Chambers of Commerce of Brevard County was insufficient to satisfy the urge to have a new united effort of chambers of commerce. The Vero Beach Press Journal of November 9, 1928, disclosed that, on the following day, Melbourne would host the fall meeting of the Association of Chambers of Commerce of the East Coast of Florida. That organization, with our old acquaintances J. J. Shares as president and Robert E. L. Niels as secretary, was described as including the chambers of commerce from Jacksonville to Key West.

Although the relationship between Orlando International Airport and Melbourne Orlando International Airport has sometimes been strained in recent years, it was not always that way. The Orlando Sentinel of March 29, 1929, reported that officials of the Orlando Chamber of Commerce had visited the Melbourne Chamber for a joint meeting of the Melbourne Chamber, Rotary and Kiwanis clubs. The purpose of the visit was to offer advice about the airport being constructed in Melbourne. Orlando officials had flown to

Melbourne for the meeting and their flight was 40 minutes going east and 35 minutes for the return flight.

The Miami News of December 8, 1929, hinted about the effect of the 1929 stock market crash on the Melbourne Chamber. The article said that the chamber had been "not very active since financial difficulties came." However, the article showed that the chamber "will be resumed and a paid secretary will be employed" and a new board of 12 directors would be elected for 1930.

Indeed, the Melbourne Chamber was back at work in 1930. The Fort Lauderdale News reported on December 1, 1920, that the Melbourne Chamber had published a "beautiful little pamphlet" that proclaimed Melbourne to be "A City Ideally Located." The pamphlet touted Melbourne as being "on the banks of the famous Indian River, midway between Jacksonville and Miami, and halfway between Daytona and Palm Beach." The publication continued: "Imagine an ideal location for both work and play. Picture the blue-green Indian River flowing idly by. Visualize the waves of the broad Atlantic breaking against a wide sandy beach." One must tolerate a bit of literary license during a depression.

The Tallahassee Democrat of October 14, 1931, reported a significant event for the Melbourne Chamber. On October 17, the chamber will host the dedication of the new bridge over Crane Creek. The bridge would be the latest link in the highway system on Florida's East Coast and a significant part of the Dixie Highway.

The Fort Pierce News-Tribune of December 20, 1932, revealed that the Melbourne Chamber was taking the lead in another issue of great concern to businesspeople and citizens in east central Florida. The Melbourne Chamber had called a meeting of municipal and civic representatives between New Smyrna and Stuart to devise a plan to address gas prices in the region which were said to be much higher than elsewhere in Florida.

At the June 14, 1932, meeting of the Melbourne City Council, the Melbourne Chamber presented an interesting proposal. The chamber asked that the city negotiate a monthly fee to be paid by the city to the Indialantic Corporation to end the toll on the Indialantic bridge. That proposal was quickly rejected by the city.

No matter was too mundane to avoid council attention. On July 12, 1934, the Melbourne City Council agreed to share the cost of a loudspeaker with the Melbourne Chamber. The cost for each party was $75.

On July 9, 1934, the Eau Gallie Chamber of Commerce notified the City of Eau Gallie at its council meeting that the Florida East Coast Railroad had applied to the State Railroad Commission for permission to close its Eau Gallie station. It is unclear whether that permission was granted.

Another challenge for the Melbourne Chamber was described in The Miami Herald on March 31, 1935, under the headline: "Group Protests Illegal Fishing: Melbourne Chamber of Commerce has Indignation Meeting." The described meeting hosted a group of sports fishermen, led by Al Mathers, who complained that commercial fishermen were illegally netting fish in Sebastian Inlet. As a result of the meeting, telegrams were sent to Governor Sholtz and the conservation commissioner, and letters sent to State Representatives Noah B. Butt and J. J. Parrish. The Bradenton Herald reported on April 25, 1935, that, at the request of the Melbourne Chamber of Commerce, the U.S. Coast Guard had dispatched a 75-foot patrol boat from Fort Lauderdale to investigate reported disturbances among rival fishermen.

The Florida Cross State Canal became the target of several chambers of commerce in 1935. The Miami News reported on September 28, 1935 that six southeast Florida chambers of commerce had met in Dania the previous day, at a meeting presided over by W. E. Fitch, secretary of the Melbourne Chamber of Commerce. The purpose of the meeting was to resurrect the Florida East Coast Association of Chambers of Commerce to fight the proposed canal.

Secretary Fitch appears to have been an energetic advocate with a strong feeling that local chambers should band together to pursue common goals. A few days after presiding over the Dania meeting, Fitch addressed the Cocoa Chamber at its monthly luncheon. As reported in The Cocoa Tribune on October 10, 1935, Fitch proposed that the chambers within the "Indian River district," which he defined as the area between Daytona Beach and West Palm Beach, should band together in joint advertising for the district.

The Cocoa Tribune issue of July 30, 1936, said that the Melbourne Chamber bought a cabana which it would erect on the corner of the Dixie Highway and New Haven Avenue for use as its headquarters. There are a couple of things that are noteworthy about that disclosure. The first is that the headquarters were to be located at a site only a few hundred yards from the site of the Chamber headquarters at the time of this writing, some 88 years later. The second notable thing was that, for the first time, the Chamber was referred to as "The Greater Melbourne Chamber of Commerce." It is unclear what changes had been made to cause the name change.

Only a few months later, an article in The Cocoa Tribune made the name issue even more puzzling. The article dated January 12, 1937, described a meeting in Hollywood, Florida, of the East Coast Association, Inc. which urged the members of the organization to unite to demand that the State Road Department make needed improvements to the Dixie Highway. Present at that meeting were representatives of the chambers of commerce in Miami, Miami Beach, Vero Beach, Hollywood, and Fort Lauderdale, as well F. M. Sawyer, now described as secretary of the Melbourne-Cocoa Chamber of Commerce. This is the only occasion in which a chamber was described as "Melbourne-Cocoa" and it is unclear whether that was a typographical error, a temporary merging of two entities or simply a change of name by the Melbourne Chamber. In any event, the change did not continue long.

The bridge between Indialantic and Melbourne stayed a topic of interest in 1938. A decision had been made to replace the bridge with a causeway. On February 17, 1938, The Cocoa Tribune reported that State Senator J. J. Parrish had promised the Melbourne Chamber of Commerce that the State Road Department Dredge "Oriente" would be moved to Melbourne within a few days to begin dredging fill material for the new causeway.

The inlet at Sebastian remained another issue for the Melbourne Chamber in 1938. An article in the Vero Beach Press Journal on July 29, 1938, revealed that at a recent membership meeting of the Melbourne Chamber of Commerce, the chamber had endorsed federal improvement of the inlet and had appointed a committee to address the matter with federal officials. A group of residents in northern Indian River County had protested improvement of the inlet, arguing that high water during storms would flood and damage citrus groves in the area.

The Melbourne Chamber of Commerce remained engaged in the issue of the proposed deepwater port at Cape Canaveral. The Cocoa Tribune issue of May 4, 1939, related that a local bill had been filed in the legislature to create the Canaveral Harbor District, looking to extend the district to south Brevard County. Elton Hall, the secretary of the Melbourne Chamber of Commerce, appeared before the county commission to protest the inclusion of Melbourne and Eau Gallie in the district. The chamber acknowledged that the development of the harbor was a positive act but argued that south Brevard residents were already heavily taxed. The idea of extending the tax district for Port Canaveral to the entire county was periodically revived as late as the 1970s and 1980s. However, when Port Canaveral began running profitably without the need to levy local ad valorem taxes, the idea became moot.

Disputes between sections of the county have a long history in Brevard. From its early history to the present day, there have been issues that created conflict among the north, central and south areas of Brevard County, worsened by the fact that the county is 72 miles long. As described above, there were proponents in 1925 to dividing the county into three separate, smaller counties. On the other hand, there have always been and there remain today civic leaders who strive to find common interests of the sections of the county and to promote those common interests. A Cocoa Tribune editorial of October 5, 1939, harshly criticized the Melbourne Chamber of Commerce for a resolution which the chamber had adopted about roads in the county. The editorial even argued that the chamber "had a case of bad manners which will only cause grief to Melbourne in the future, and which has already certainly engendered bad feelings between the two communities and in Central Florida." These disagreements over roads in the county appear to have been generated by the impending development of the Banana River Naval Air Station which had been authorized by the Naval Expansion Act of 1938. The intra-county dispute was over which roads would be built to access the base. The newspaper was supporting the idea of a road from Cocoa to Merritt Island to the ocean and south to the new air base. The editorial also criticized the City of Melbourne for its resolution the previous week opposing the creation of Port Canaveral. While conflicts between the sections of the county persist to this day, such comments are less common than in the past.

In 1942, W. W. Kerr was named president of the Melbourne Chamber of Commerce. The Miami Herald reported on November 13, 1942, that H. B. Fielding had been reappointed as executive secretary and that Lieutenant C. H. McNulty had been appointed finance officer. It was unclear how Lieutenant McNulty would manage both his chamber responsibilities and his military duties. McNulty would later buy several banks throughout small towns in central Florida and would become well-known in the state not only for his business dealings but for his amorous activities.

Road and port disputes aside, one thing upon which the different sections of the county could agree was the need to control mosquitos. The Cocoa Tribune indicated in its issue of July 29, 1943, that both the Melbourne Chamber and the Eau Gallie Chamber had appointed delegates to join an effort spearheaded by the Greater Cocoa Chamber of Commerce Mosquito Control Committee to work out an orderly plan for mosquito control. During the 1940s and 1950s, stories about mosquitos in Brevard County were legendary and all historical accounts included tales of these pests. The county had been part of Mosquito County until 1844.

On November 2, 1943, The Miami Herald noted that Howard G. Blake, who was then serving as head of the Eau Gallie Chamber of Commerce and as Mayor of the City of Eau Gallie, was seeking reelection as mayor. The article noted that Blake had been a leader in obtaining federal approval to construct a canal from the upper St. Johns River to the ocean and, thereby, create a port in Eau Gallie. The story claimed that originally It had been planned to make Sebastian the port terminal, but that Blake had been able to get a bill amended to provide that the terminal would be in Eau Gallie. It requires a lot of imagination to picture Eau Gallie as a deepwater port like Port Canaveral's current scope.

With the end of the war in sight, the efforts of the chambers turned to the post-war economy. On December 17, 1944, The Miami News reported that the Melbourne Chamber of Commerce had devised a plan for a series of advertisements in national magazines aimed at attracting "postwar industries and pay rolls." A major part of the program, it was said, would not begin until the end of the war in Europe. On February 18, 1945, The Miami News reported that those ads had begun in ten northern newspapers. An added enticement was that they offered a free trip to Melbourne to those who wrote the "most logical letter of why they would locate an industry in Melbourne." The ads sparked some interest. A total of 125 responses were received in a single day.

> **73 Business Opportunities**
>
> **To Men Now Thinking of the Future—Melbourne**
>
> Florida's fastest growing industrial city offers three prizes, including round trip transportation to executives who write stating why they contemplate bringing or starting new industry in Melbourne. For more complete details, address President, CHAMBER OF COMMERCE, Melbourne, Fla.

Ad placed in numerous newspapers in January 1945.

CHAPTER NOTES

- References to the minutes of the Eau Gallie City Council and Melbourne City Council are taken from a summary of those minutes prepared by Cathleen Wysor, who was City Clerk of Melbourne from 1994 to 2020, as well as the minutes of these bodies provided to me by Kevin McKeown, the current City Clerk of Melbourne.
- The Dixie Highway was a network of connected paved roads constructed and expanded from 1915 to 1929. There were several routes on the highway, including a western route, an eastern route, a central route, and a Carolina route. In Florida, the route ran down the east coast from Jacksonville to Miami. It was funded and promoted by a group of businesses under the name of the Dixie Highway Association, led by Miami developer Carl G. Fisher. The federal government played only a minor role in developing the highway network but did provide increasing funding between the early 1920s and 1927. In 1927, the Dixie Highway was taken over by the federal government as part of the U.S. Route system, and the part of the Dixie Highway in Florida became U.S. Highway One. See Ingram, Tammy: *Dixie Highway: Road Building and the Making of the Modern South, 1900-1930.* Chapel Hill, The University of North Carolina Press (2014).
- The plan presented by Noel in 1921 to cut an inlet connecting the Indian River to the ocean was different from the decades-long effort that resulted in the construction of the Sebastian Inlet. The proposed inlet discussed by Canova in 1925 was at the east end of the present Eau Gallie Causeway, which would have led to the creation of a port in Eau Gallie harbor.
- The first Sebastian Inlet was dug at its current location in 1905 by private individuals, but it quickly filled in since there were no funds to support it. Roy O. Couch was the head of a group that lobbied for years for the construction of the inlet at Sebastian. In 1918, Couch led an effort that formed the Sebastian Inlet Association. The association was able to convince the War Department to issue a permit to allow dredging of the inlet but left it up to the association to maintain it. On May 23, 1919, the Sebastian Inlet District was created by the Florida Legislature, creating a tax district to construct and support the inlet to "maintain a navigational channel connecting the Indian River and the Atlantic Ocean." Following

construction of the inlet, it was periodically closed due to maintenance issues. During World War II, it remained closed during most of the war. It was re-opened in 1948 and has remained open since that time. The Miami Herald issue of September 15, 1948, reported that the last barrier reef blocking the inlet had been "blasted away." In the 1950s and early 1960s citizens of Brevard County lobbied vigorously for construction of a bridge over Sebastian Inlet. To entice Indian River County to support the bridge and to pave Highway A1A north to the bridge, Brevard County ceded almost three miles of land south of the bridge to Indian River County. With this act and the unceasing efforts of State Representative James Pruitt of Melbourne, the bridge over the inlet was opened on February 27, 1965. For the history of the inlet and the bridge see the website of the Sebastian Inlet Tax District at sitd.us/history-of-sebastian-inlet.

- The formation of the organizations known as the Associated Chambers of Commerce of Brevard County and the Association of Chambers of Commerce of the East Coast of Florida suggest later efforts to assure that the chambers of commerce of Brevard County were working for common goals whenever possible rather than engaging in destructive competition. The creation of the Council of Chambers in the 1990s was a similar attempt. The creation of the Brevard Economic Development Council by the Brevard County Commission during the 1960s was an attempt to ensure that industrial development efforts in the county were coordinated and consistent and that communities were not competing against one another in a destructive manner. The formation of the Economic Development Council of Florida's Space Coast in the early 1990s continued that quest for a coordinated effort.
- The repeated efforts to increase navigational channels for maritime transportation were not confined to Brevard County. The most prominent effort was the Cross Florida Barge Canal. The vision of cutting a canal from one coast of Florida to the other and creating a direct path for commercial boat traffic had been first proposed during the early 19th Century. In 1935, the Army Corps of Engineers made plans for the Gulf Atlantic Ship Canal which was envisioned to be a 30-foot-deep waterway which would cross the state through Ocala. The canal would entail a series of locks and dams that would take the waterway west to Yankeetown on the Gulf Coast. Construction began in 1935 but was interrupted for decades by environmental concerns. Construction began again in 1964 but was

stopped when a group of environmentalists led by Marjorie Harris Carr argued that the Oklawaha River would be destroyed by the canal. President Richard Nixon permanently halted construction in 1971 after $75 million had been spent on the project. Today, the remnants of the Cross Florida Barge Canal are part of the Marjorie Harris Carr Cross Florida Greenway which provides pristine hiking and bike trails. For more on the Cross Florida Barge Canal see *Ditch of Dreams*: *The Cross Florida Barge Canal and the Struggle for Florida's Future,* by Steven Noll and David Tegeder, University Press of Florida; Reprint Edition (2015).

CHAPTER FOUR

The Chambers of Commerce During The Early Years of the Space Age: 1946 To 1969

This ad was sponsored by the Melbourne Chamber of Commerce and the City of Melbourne and was published in the Orlando Evening Star on July 22, 1947.

Following World War II, the advent of the U.S. space program transformed Brevard County. On June 1, 1948, the Navy transferred the former Banana River Naval Air Station to the United States Air Force. In May 1949, President Truman signed the legislation that set up the Joint Long-Range Proving Ground (JLRPG). The Air Force renamed the base the Joint Long-Range Proving Ground but shortly thereafter changed the name to Patrick Air Force Base.

Launch facilities at Cape Canaveral were built in 1950, and the first rocket launched was a V-2 rocket named Bumper 8 on July 24, 1950. In 1951, the Air Force established the Air Force Missile Test Center at Patrick AFB.

During the time between the establishment of JLRPG in 1949 and 1957, launch activities at Cape Canaveral were intermittent and were given a low priority by the U.S. Government. That changed dramatically when the Soviets launched Sputnik in October 1957. That event was a wake-up call to the United States and caused alarm in the country as to not only the space and missile program but also American technological education. Not only did the launch of Sputnik serve as an impetus to revamp and reinvigorate U.S. space programs, but it caused a reexamination of the American education system.

These activities of the U.S. space program dramatically and instantly changed the essential nature of Brevard County as tens of thousands of technicians, scientists, and engineers moved to east central Florida to support the activities at Cape Canaveral.

The Melbourne Regional Chamber and its predecessors would play an indispensable role in the transition of south Brevard County from a small community with an economy based primarily on fishing, agriculture, and tourism to an economy employing tens of thousands of scientists and engineers at some of the best-known aerospace and defense contractors in the world.

The Miami Herald reported on October 20, 1946, that the Melbourne Chamber's membership drive had thus far collected $1,750 in membership fees from new members "from as far south as Grant."

Following the end of the war, the Melbourne Chamber focused on drawing visitors to the ocean beaches. The Miami News reported on January 23, 1947, that the Melbourne Chamber was sponsoring the construction of a boardwalk 350 feet long and 16 feet wide on the ocean beach. Construction would also include a parking area and freshwater showers with a bandstand at one end of the boardwalk.

The interests of the chamber were not limited to beaches. On February 27, 1947, the Miami Herald reported that the Melbourne Chamber of Commerce had gone on record favoring a Brevard County ordinance that required fencing to keep cattle off the highways, an action which would make travel to the area safer for visitors. In another demonstration of its diverse interests, the Melbourne Chamber endorsed, according to a Miami Herald article of March 6, 1947, a proposal by Dale Jacobus for a community-owned radio station. According to Jacobus, the station would be used to promote Melbourne and its industries and could be incorporated for $50,000. Notably, Dale Jacobus was the father of retired Judge Bruce Jacobus and grandfather of current Judge Curt Jacobus.

Memorial Day, 1947 was marked by a big event for south Brevard County, with a fish fry sponsored by the Melbourne Chamber of Commerce. As reported by the Cocoa Tribune on June 6, 1947, the event celebrated the completion of the $1 million causeway from Melbourne to the ocean beaches. The chamber reported that it had served more than 2,500 pounds of fried fish to more than 3,000 attendees at the celebration. The main speaker at the event was the president of Florida Power and Light Company, who announced plans to spend $85 million in expansion throughout its service area, which was projected to grow from 820,000 to 1,150,000 people.

An article in The Miami Herald on December 9, 1947, described another attempt by the chamber to draw visitors to the area. The article showed that the Florida Flying Alligator Club would hold its annual meeting at the Melbourne Municipal Airport in January 1948. Vic Robbins, manager of Robbins Skyways and President of the Melbourne Chamber, was the general chairman of the meeting. Robbins expected about 2,000 pilots and 500 to 1,000 aircraft at the meeting.

Air Show!

Melbourne Airport

former
Naval Air Station

Sun., Feb. 15 - One o'clock

- **BETTY SKELTON**
  Acrobatics

- **WOODY EDMUNDSON**
  Acrobatics

- **JOHNNY BOYD**
  Bat Wing Jump

- **CARL DUNN**
  Farmers Act

and many other attractions to thrill you
at this 3 hour performance

Sponsored by
The Melbourne
Chamber of Commerce

Adults $1.00 plus tax

Children 50c plus tax

The Melbourne Chamber of Commerce sponsored this ad promoting an air show at the Melbourne Airport on February 15, 1948.

The Miami Herald reported on January 24, 1948, that the Melbourne Chamber was undertaking "an intensive beautification program." The plans included planting new landscaping all along the three highway approaches to the city.

An advertisement in The Cocoa Tribune on February 1, 1948, publicized an air show sponsored by the Melbourne Chamber to be held at the Melbourne Airport on Sunday, February 15. Admission to the three-hour-long show was $1 for adults and 50 cents for children. The headline acts were aerobatic experts Betty Skelton and Woody Edmundson and "bat wing jumper" Johnny Boyd.

To focus on promoting the ocean beaches, chamber members formed another organization known as the "Sea Island Association." One of the first recorded efforts of the association, in coordination with the chamber, was reported by Walter Edge in The Miami Herald on May 26, 1948, wherein he said that the chamber and the Sea Island Association were discussing advertising and promotion of Melbourne's beaches. Among their decisions was the idea to offer an all-expense paid, one-week trip to "Melbourne's Beaches of the Sea Island" to the winners of the annual Leesburg Watermelon Festival beauty contest. They also decided that Melbourne would send a representative to the contest and that the representative would be chaperoned by someone from the chamber.

On June 2, 1948, The Miami Herald announced that the chamber and the Sea Island Association had selected Pat Callahan as their representative to the Leesburg beauty contest. At that same meeting, the chamber had authorized an order for 10,000 folders promoting Melbourne's beaches as "a summer resort as well as a winter playground." These folders were to be distributed throughout central and north Florida.

That same news article of June 2, 1948, reported that the chamber board had directed the chamber executive, Sarah W. Knight, to write to state officials to inquire if the state intended to make improvements to Highway U.S. 192, noting that it had been under water for several weeks during the previous summer. This was notable because the deplorable condition of U.S. Highway 192 continued to be at the top of the chamber's goals for at least the next

40 years until the 1990s when reconstruction of the road and expansion to four-lanes began. The road's construction to four lanes was not finished until 2008. The Melbourne Chamber's efforts on U.S. 192 during those 40 years included dozens of resolutions, letters, and visits to Tallahassee, as well as securing support from every political candidate who ventured close to Melbourne during that time.

The Melbourne Chamber has long recognized that an adequate infrastructure was necessary to support economic growth in south Brevard County. Throughout its history, the chamber has been at the forefront of efforts to develop that infrastructure. The Miami Herald reported on July 8, 1948 that the Melbourne Chamber would hold two open meetings to inform the public of the urgent need to expand the sewer system, noting that the population had tripled since the system was built and the existing system was inadequate and a potential threat to public health. In a sign of the times, it was announced that the second meeting would be held in the "colored section."

A puzzling report appeared in the Miami News on July 25, 1948. The article said that the Melbourne Business and Professional Association would hold its annual meeting next week. The article showed that one of those proposed as an officer was Frank H. Little, former manager of the Melbourne Chamber of Commerce. It is unclear whether the organization was an offshoot of the chamber or a rival to the chamber.

The Melbourne Chamber and the Sea Island Association shared a significant accomplishment in the fall of 1948 when Walter Edge wrote in The Miami Herald on September 15, 1948, that the final barrier across the Sebastian Inlet had been cleared and two organizations were planning a celebration of the opening of the inlet. Roy Couch, who had been the primary catalyst for the inlet for many years, noted the jetties that extended into the ocean from the east end of the cut should be sufficient to "withstand any further efforts of mother nature to close the mouth of the inlet through storms that cause a great shifting of ocean sands." Couch further noted that a conservative estimate of the economic impact of the inlet would be at least $5,000 per day. That estimate was quite conservative as tens of thousands of people have come to the area in the ensuing 75 years to enjoy the fishing and other recreational activities at Sebastian Inlet. Sebastian Inlet became a state park in 1971. In 2011, the park hosted 722,683 visitors, making it the second-most visited of Florida's 152 state parks. The Florida Department of Environmental Protection determined that the park's economic impact on the area in 2011 exceeded $31 million.

By the end of 1948, business leaders were acutely aware of the significance of what was happening at Cape Canaveral and what would soon be Patrick Air Force Base and were eager to reap the economic benefits of the burgeoning activities. Walter Edge reported in The Miami Herald on November 3, 1948, that the Melbourne Chamber had enthusiastically endorsed the application of a bus line to provide service from Melbourne to the Banana River base that would become Patrick. The chamber announced its intention to put together a large delegation to appear before the Florida Railroad and Public Utilities Commission in support of the application. Edge's article noted that while no definite plans had been announced for the Naval Air Station that had recently been transferred from the Navy to the Air Force, such plans were "considered imminent."

The Miami News issue of November 19, 1948, showed that the Florida Flying Alligators would be returning to Melbourne again for their annual flight supported by the Melbourne Chamber. The organization noted that 300 planes and around 1,000 members had taken part the previous year, and they expected those numbers to double at the next event.

The Miami Herald reported on February 2, 1949, that Ernest L. Blackburn had been elected president of the Melbourne Chamber. More significantly, that same meeting voted to change the name of the organization to the Greater Melbourne Chamber of Commerce. The meeting discussion noted that the service area of the organization would go from Eau Gallie on the north to the Sebastian River on the south and would include the towns of Eau Gallie, Melbourne Beach, Indialantic Beach, Palm Bay, Malabar, Valkaria and Micco. It was noted that the constitution and bylaws of the chamber would be changed to ensure that all these areas had representation on the board of directors. Another article in the Miami Herald on February 22, 1949, explained that the service area, which Eau Gallie bounded on the north, the Sebastian River on the south, the St. Johns River on the west and the "Sea Island Beaches" on the east, would be divided into four districts, each of which would receive representation on the board of directors. Ernest L. Blackburn, president of the chamber, was quoted as saying that the primary objective of the chamber would be "selling the Greater Melbourne area to tourists as a year-round vacation resort, with specific emphasis on summer advantages, selling this area to prospective business firms, and to those interested in cattle, poultry, citrus, and other agriculture development."

An article by Milt Sosin in The Miami News on May 5, 1949, showed that plans for development of the space center were solidifying. The article said that the process of turning the air station into "a proving ground for guided missiles and other highly secret developments" was already underway. The article related that before the arrival of the "first experts in guided missiles," there would be hundreds of construction workers, engineers, and planners to make the base habitable again. The article further stated that the Greater Melbourne Chamber of Commerce and the Greater Cocoa Chamber of Commerce were "intense rivals in a race to develop their respective communities industrially, culturally and as tourist resorts." The article noted that both chambers were sparing no effort to provide for the influx of military and civilian personnel who were expected to "bring vast improvements in the economy of the area, which severely felt the loss of business when the air station closed down." The article explained that the Greater Melbourne Chamber of Commerce included Eau Gallie and several other communities. It also noted that the chamber had "profited by its wartime experience and was ready for Uncle Sam this time."

The rivalry between the Melbourne and Cocoa chambers in their efforts to tie themselves to the development of the missile range was illustrated by a photograph in The Cocoa Tribune on June 9, 1949, showing representatives of the two chambers of commerce posing with the commanding officer at the Banana River base at a dinner at the Bahama Beach Club in Indialantic honoring a large group of officers visiting the Banana River Joint Long-Range Proving Ground.

This ad was sponsored by the Greater Melbourne Chamber of Commerce in the Orlando Evening Star on January 14, 1949.

An article in the Orlando Evening Star on June 14, 1949, touted the Melbourne area as a great destination for a weekend getaway or a vacation. The article exclaimed: "And here is the biggest news yet. Central Florida's newest vacation land and playground is the Greater Melbourne Chamber of Commerce area, Melbourne, and Melbourne Beach, which have all the recreational and relaxational facilities which anyone could wish for between Jacksonville and Miami along Florida's East Coast."

The Miami Herald showed on July 12, 1949, that the Melbourne Chamber would be sponsoring a Labor Day celebration. It would include a three-day fishing tournament, boat races, a rodeo, a ball game, a beauty contest, several boxing matches, a square dance and even a calling contest. Congressman Sidney S. Herlong, Jr. would squeeze a speech into the agenda at some time. The celebration was described as an annual event of the chamber which drew thousands to the area. The Cocoa Tribune followed up on September 1, 1949, with a further description of the planned Labor Day event. The Tribune touted the beauty contest, with close to 70 contestants, as perhaps the most significant activity of the celebration, noting that the winner would be crowned "Miss Indian River" and would be eligible to compete in the Miss Florida pageant.

On September 10, 1949, The Miami Herald reported that the Greater Melbourne Chamber of Commerce was publishing a document designed to tell winter tourists the "better places in the Greater Melbourne area to stop," including hotels, tourist courts and cottages. H. E. Harris, executive secretary of the chamber, told the Herald that he expected a record influx of winter visitors.

An article in The Cocoa Tribune on October 13, 1949, noted that there were nine organizations in Brevard County which included "Chamber of Commerce" in their names, four of which were in north Brevard, four were in central Brevard, and only one, the Greater Melbourne Chamber of Commerce, was in south Brevard. The Tribune article praised the formation of an organization called the "Coordination Council of Brevard County," which consisted of representatives of each of the chambers. The Tribune noted: "We are hoping that such an organization will result in a much better understanding among the sections represented and that out of the formation will come better relations for the betterment of the county." This effort was only one of many attempts over several decades to foster good relations between the geographic areas of the county, efforts which have met varying degrees of success, but which have never ended the concerns.

The minutes of the Melbourne City Council on December 27, 1949, reflected that the Greater Melbourne Chamber of Commerce continued to advance the road construction agenda in south Brevard County. At that meeting, Chamber representatives Sidney Platt, John Jorgensen, and H. E. Harris presented a resolution urging the opening of Babcock Street to provide a connecting link between New Haven Avenue and the Indian River Bluff area of the city.

The Greater Melbourne Chamber of Commerce worked for several years to bring "Tin Can Tourists" to Melbourne. This was an organization of travelers who toured the country with their mobile homes and periodically gathered for reunions. The Melbourne City Council minutes of March 8, 1950, reflect that H. E. Harris of the chamber informed the council that the Tin Can Tourists wanted to set up its headquarters in Melbourne. The council directed the city manager to figure out whether the Naval Air Station property could be used for that purpose. At its following meeting of March 14, the council informed the chamber that the Civil Aeronautics Administration had approved the use of the airport by the Tin Can Tourists. The April 19, 1950, edition of The Miami Herald announced that they had determined to hold their Thanksgiving reunion in Melbourne on November 25, 1950, at Melbourne Airport. This would eventually result in the establishment of the mobile home development at the airport originally known as Trailer Haven and, later, as Tropical Haven. A letter from the chamber to the Melbourne City Council was read at the council meeting of November 28, 1950, praising the city for its efficiency in constructing the mobile home site at the airport.

On May 16, 1950, the Greater Melbourne Chamber of Commerce announced that it had endorsed the publication of a new city directory which would list all residents with their addresses, telephone numbers and occupations. In a sign of the times, the announcement in The Miami Herald disclosed that the "Negro census" would be conducted by the Melbourne Vocational School.

An article in The Cocoa Tribune on April 22, 1952, mentioned that the Greater Melbourne Chamber of Commerce was taking the lead in seeking improvement of U.S. 1 through Brevard County. The Melbourne Chamber had succeeded in obtaining supporting resolutions from the chambers and city councils of Melbourne, Cocoa, and Titusville.

The Orlando Sentinel edition of June 24, 1952, revealed that the Eau Gallie Chamber of Commerce had recently been formed and had undertaken a membership drive. The new organization decided to create a temporary office at the Oleanders Hotel at the west end of the Eau Gallie Causeway. By July 20, 1952, the Sentinel would report that the new organization was off to a strong start with 36 new members.

The Miami Herald reported on July 3, 1952, that the Greater Melbourne Chamber of Commerce had decided that its current facilities were inadequate and was in the process of constructing a new office building. The chamber had secured a 25-year lease of a county-owned parcel in Riverview Park, west of the Indian River Causeway. When completed, it was expected that the new office would have a value of around $15,000. To raise funds for the construction, the chamber undertook to sell bonds for $5,000. The Miami Herald stated on April 17, 1952, that the bonds had been over-subscribed. The Cocoa Tribune reported on October 14, 1952, that the new building had been dedicated during a ceremony and barbeque held the previous day.

The newly formed Eau Gallie Chamber of Commerce wasted no time in going to work for its community. The Miami Herald reported on August 9, 1952, that the chamber had succeeded in persuading the State Road Department to straighten out two dangerous curves in U.S. 1 through the city. The news article also reported that the chamber was pressing for completion of the Eau Gallie Causeway. A few days later, on August 10, The Miami News verified that work on straightening the curves would begin soon and verified that Eau

Gallie businessperson Carrie Rossetter had donated land to facilitate rerouting the road.

The Eau Gallie chamber proved that it was concerned with more than roads when it was reported in The Miami Herald on September 25, 1952, that the chamber would sponsor its first annual Eau Gallie Fishing Rodeo. Monthly and grand prizes would be awarded to anglers reporting the largest fish. Eligible fish had to be caught in an area bounded by Pineda on the north, Sebastian Inlet on the south and Lake Washington on the west.

The attempts to promote coordination among the various business groups in Brevard County was further illustrated by a report in The Cocoa Tribune on November 25, 1952, which described the efforts of the Brevard County U.S. Highway No. 1 Improvement Committee. This group, chaired by Melbourne Chamber President Walter A, Fordyce, included representatives from throughout the county and sought to promote the county-wide expansion to four lanes of U.S. 1.

A notable accomplishment for south Brevard County was announced in The Miami Herald on December 21, 1952, by Walter Fordyce, who was not only chamber president but also the city aviation director. Fordyce announced that Eastern Air Lines would begin service to Melbourne on January 31, 1953, and that the inauguration of service would be celebrated by an event sponsored by the Greater Melbourne Chamber of Commerce. A later announcement in The Cocoa Tribune on January 27. 1953, invited all the directors of all chambers of commerce in the county to attend the celebration. The invitation promised each a ride on one of Eastern's Silver Falcons.

An article in The Miami Herald on August 5, 1953, revealed that the Eau Gallie Chamber of Commerce, which had been formed in June 1952, had set up several ambitious goals. President Van G. Werley announced that the completion of the Eau Gallie Causeway was a key goal of the organization, as well as the production and distribution of a city map, mail delivery for rural Eau Gallie and a "shop at home" campaign.

Another sign of the diverse goals of the Greater Melbourne Chamber of Commerce was presented in an article in the Orlando Evening Star on February 6, 1954, which related that the chamber had enticed the University of Tampa to offer secretarial, general business, speedwriting and typing classes in Melbourne.

A few days later, the Evening Star showed that the Melbourne Chamber had even bigger ideas about attracting educational institutions to Melbourne. An article published on February 9, 1954, revealed that city aviation director Walter Fordyce had formed a committee to help him in his effort to have the proposed United States Air Force Academy located in Melbourne. Two chamber of commerce representatives were part of the seven-member committee. The article promised that plans would be made "for making Melbourne's official bid in Washington." There is little further information about Melbourne's bid, but it is known that the Air Force surveyed some 400 sites around the country before deciding to build the academy in Colorado Springs.

The Orlando Evening Star edition of February 10, 1954, outlined the Melbourne Chamber's continuing efforts to lure the Tin Can Tourists to the area. The chamber's executive director, Charles Herring, attended the group's annual meeting to extend an invitation for the group to hold its annual meeting at Trailer Haven at Melbourne Airport as it had for the past several years.

The Miami News reported on February 16, 1954, that the Greater Melbourne Chamber of Commerce had established two committees, a committee for highways, streets, traffic, and safety and a second committee for hotels and motels. Jack Fogg was appointed chair of the first committee while Sidney Platt was appointed to chair the hotels and motels committee. A few days later, on February 19, the Orlando Evening Star reported that the chamber had appointed a committee on Armed Forces to function as liaison with Patrick Air Force Base and formed a committee on industry. In all, the Evening Star reported the chamber had appointed 19 committees to execute its agenda for 1954.

A substantial effort for the Melbourne and Eau Gallie Chambers in 1954 entailed the support of a proposed $4 million bond issue which was the subject of a referendum in May 1954. The bonds were proposed to finance the expansion of U.S. 1 through Brevard County. The Orlando Evening Star reported on April 15, 1954, that the Melbourne Chamber had approved a resolution urging voters to support the proposal, noting that the bonds would be paid by an added gasoline tax and not by ad valorem taxes. On May 3, the Orlando Evening Star said that the Eau Gallie Chamber had also endorsed the proposal. The Cocoa Tribune indicated on May 7, 1954, that the bond issue had been approved when Brevard County freeholders voted better than 3 to 1 in favor of the proposal.

The issue of competition between the geographic sectors of the county remained a challenge. On June 15, 1954, The Cocoa Tribune reported that Charles Herring, executive director of the Melbourne Chamber, had made a plea for unity in the county. Herring noted: "As things are now, we are all running our own little show and divided we don't amount to a great deal."

The Eau Gallie Chamber of Commerce presented an interesting proposal in 1954. As reported in the Orlando Evening Star on August 4, 1954, the chamber directors recommended that the name of the city be changed to Eau Gallie Beach. Such a change would require approval by the state legislature, followed by a referendum of Eau Gallie voters. I could find no records of the outcome of this effort and the minutes of the Eau Gallie City Council do not reflect that the council ever considered the issue.

On July 22, 1954, the Orlando Evening Star reported that the Melbourne Chamber had presented a bold idea and that the chamber had appointed Lock Davidson as chair of a committee to study the feasibility of an "outside harbor" in the Indian River, south of the Melbourne Causeway. The concept was that sand would be dredged from the Indian River and used as fill to create a "sand spit" or breakwater, thereby creating a landlocked harbor. Environmental sensitivity, it seems, had not yet become a chamber priority. In any event, the concept quickly died an ignominious death.

The Orlando Evening Star reported on August 5, 1954, that the Melbourne Chamber was hard at work with a variety of projects. The chamber appointed a special committee to pursue a project to improve the harbor. It also reported that the chamber had lobbied state and county officials for provision of court facilities in South Brevard. This effort was a result of the fact that Titusville was the county seat and the site of most county services, such as court proceedings, tax assessor, sheriff's office, marriage licenses, clerk of the circuit court and other services. For residents of South Brevard, a trip to Titusville to access these services was a major undertaking. At the chamber's request, State Representative O. L. Burton introduced and passed legislation authorizing branch facilities for these "courthouse extension facilities."

A notable event for the Eau Gallie Chamber of Commerce was reported in the Orlando Evening Star on November 20, 1954, when the chamber's "Big Orange" tourist registration and information center was opened. The Big Orange was a concrete ball about 15 feet in diameter, painted orange with a service window to greet tourists, even serving them free orange juice. The Big Orange was a noted landmark that survived into the early 2000s. An article in Florida Today on October 9, 2005, purported to relate the history of the Big Orange but incorrectly said that it had been first built in 1966 while the photo in the Orlando Evening Star showed that it existed in 1954. However, the orange ran afoul of the building inspector and as reported in the Orlando Evening Star on October 18, 1966, "the faded yellow testimonial of what can happen to a tourist attraction if it isn't kept in good condition" was destroyed. However, as reported in The Sentinel on August 28, 1966, Eau Gallie Mayor Adger Smith convinced the Eau Gallie Chamber to undertake a project to build an improved big orange. Notably, construction of the new orange took place in the yard of the mayor's home with much of the work performed by the mayor himself. Anyone who knew Adger would not be surprised by his ability for physical work.

Another notable event for the Eau Gallie Chamber and the community occurred on February 22, 1955, when the chamber sponsored the dedication ceremonies of the W. J. Creel Bridge. The announcement of the ceremony published in The Orlando Sentinel on February 20 described the bridge as the "gateway to the Central East Coast beaches and Patrick Air Force Base."

Late that year, the Eau Gallie Chamber voted to cooperate with the other chambers in the county and the East Coast Highways Association of Florida in supporting a publicity program to educate the public about the upcoming establishment of four lanes on U.S. 1. That same meeting, reported by the Orlando Evening Star on August 5, 1955, discussed the request by the chamber to the City of Eau Gallie for $1,200 for operating expenses and a request for office space in the new Civic Center Building.

A report in The Orlando Sentinel on September 17, 1955, showed that issues about the county seat remained alive. The article reported that both the Eau Gallie Chamber and the Eau Gallie City Council had gone on record asking the county commission to move county facilities from Titusville. In this case, the chamber and city council recommended that the facilities be in Pineda, described as "a small settlement north of Eau Gallie," which was said to be the center of the 72-mile-long county as well as the population center of the county. That issue would remain contentious for many years until the Moore Justice Center and county administrative offices were constructed in Viera in the mid-1990s.

Activities at the Greater Melbourne Chamber of Commerce during 1956 were varied and impactful. The Miami Herald reported on January 26, 1956, that the proposed University of Melbourne had made a presentation to the chamber outlining its plans for construction of its campus on land in Melbourne which had been donated to it. Although the University of Melbourne proved to be financially unsustainable, it was significant in that when it became clear that the University of Melbourne was unfeasible it donated its land and building to Brevard Engineering College which was the precursor to Florida Institute of Technology. That land and building continues to be part of the main campus of Florida Tech.

In March 1956, the Greater Melbourne Chamber published its first brochure in six years in cooperation with the Town of Indialantic and City of Melbourne. An article in The Orlando Sentinel on March 24, 1956, described the color brochure as having 29 photographs and related that 30,000 copies had been printed. Chamber officials projected that the brochures would be placed in racks throughout the country.

The Orlando Sentinel reported on April 11, 1956, that the directors of the Melbourne Chamber had toured Melbourne High School the previous day to see its new facilities. Melbourne High School had moved to its present site on Babcock Street in September 1955 from its original home at the present Henegar Center on New Haven Avenue. The chamber delegation presented a certificate of appreciation to Principal B. Frank Brown, who was creating the first ungraded high school in the United States and developing a curriculum that would bring national recognition to Melbourne High School.

The Greater Melbourne Chamber also sustained its long-standing efforts regarding U.S. Highway One during 1956. The Orlando Evening Star reported on May 4, 1956, that the chamber board of directors had passed a resolution asking that steps be taken to speed up the establishment of four lanes on the highway through Melbourne and Eau Gallie. The resolution stressed that traffic on the road through Melbourne and Eau Gallie had increased so rapidly that it had reached a critical point and claimed that section of the highway had become the most congested area in Brevard County and perhaps "the entire East Coast."

The most significant action of the Greater Melbourne Chamber in 1956 was the publication and distribution of a fact sheet which outlined the impact on the Greater Melbourne Area of the launch activities at Cape Canaveral. The fact sheet, authored by Charles L. Herring, executive vice-president of the chamber, noted that the area's population had grown from 10,000 in 1950 to 35,000 in 1956 and would reach 75,000 by 1960. Within a six-mile radius of the chamber building, population had increased from 8,000 in 1946 to 30,000 in 1956, Herring noted that retail sales in the county had increased 96.7% during the last year alone. He estimated that new construction in the Greater Melbourne Area in 1957 would exceed $30 million, including more than $6 million for a new Melbourne water system.

With growth as dramatic as that outlined by Herring in his fact sheet, it became plain that water was a critical issue. As reported in The Orlando Sentinel on January 18, 1957, the Greater Melbourne Chamber enacted a resolution praising the city commissioners of

Melbourne for their vision in going ahead with the water distribution system, a project that had increased to $6.75 million. Water would remain a key future concern for the chamber and remained high on the list of chamber priorities for several decades. Even today, it is still true that the availability of reliable and safe potable water is one of the most critical needs to accommodate the growing population of the region.

While the Greater Melbourne Chamber of Commerce continued to carry out its action plans during 1955 and 1956, the Eau Gallie Chamber of Commerce foundered during these years. The Orlando Sentinel reported on March 15, 1957, that a group of Eau Gallie business owners had met to try to put new life into the Eau Gallie Chamber. A letter observed:" It seems obvious to them that the city needs an active and representative chamber to help keep it in step with the development of the rest of Brevard County."

The West Melbourne Chamber of Commerce was founded in October 1957. The organization began with a vigorous membership drive that netted 107 members by that date, according to The Orlando Sentinel issue of November 24, 1967. The chamber announced a 10-point program which included improvement of U.S. Highway 192, merchandizing the area through advertising, improving drainage, promoting development of business and industry, improving telephone service, and obtaining better financing for construction of homes and commercial buildings. On November 27, the Sentinel reported that the newly formed chamber had sent a telegram to Governor LeRoy Collins urging him to make an "automobile inspection tour of U.S. Highway 192 from Melbourne city limits to Brevard-Osceola County line" during his planned upcoming visit to Melbourne.

A statistical report compiled by the Greater Melbourne Chamber of Commerce was the subject of an article in The Orlando Sentinel on April 24, 1958. The report showed that the population of Brevard County now exceeded 90,000 people. The population of the Melbourne area, which is defined as those within a 6-mile radius of the chamber office, exceeded 35,500, contrasted with 8,000 in 1950. Melbourne's population was estimated to be 17,600 while Eau Gallie was estimated to be 7,500 people. The chamber concluded the report by boasting: "The Greater Melbourne Chamber of Commerce takes great pride in the terrific growth, development and prosperity of our several communities, because we feel that this organization has played an important part in the development of a comparatively unimportant section of Florida in 1950 to its present status of the fastest growing and most prosperous in the state." Modesty was not a high priority for the chamber.

The West Melbourne Chamber of Commerce continued its efforts to improve roads when it took the initiative to form a county-wide highway planning movement. The Cocoa Tribune reported on February 19, 1958, that the county group had set its priorities as 4-laning the Cocoa, Melbourne and Eau Gallie causeways, construction of a new causeway at City Point, and 4-laning of A1A from Indialantic to Cape Canaveral and north from Cape Canaveral to Titusville. The West Melbourne Chamber pursued this program and, on April 9, 1958, The Cocoa Tribune reported that Norman Lund, president of the West Melbourne Chamber, said that the U.S. Bureau of Public Roads had recommended that the Department of Defense pay half of the cost of 4-laning A1A from Indialantic to Cape Canaveral and the 4-laning of the causeway between Cocoa and Cocoa Beach.

According to The Orlando Sentinel issue of August 17, 1958, the West Melbourne Chamber of Commerce, then only 10 months old, had carried out its first goal, the resurfacing of U.S. 192 from the Melbourne city limits to John Rodes Boulevard. The article also noted that Brevard County had recently set up a zoning commission and that the West Melbourne Chamber would be working closely with the commission.

On September 14, 1958, The Orlando Sentinel reported the formation of the South Brevard Beaches Chamber of Commerce. It was reported that this new chamber would "represent the entire beach area from Sebastian Inlet to Patrick Air Force Base, a distance of about 25 miles." The new group announced an ambitious agenda, topped by construction of a bridge over Sebastian Inlet. Another report in the Sentinel on October 24 disclosed that the "longest" chamber had successfully organized, had set up 10 committees, and would become active after the first of the year.

Meanwhile, the newly reinvigorated Eau Gallie Chamber continued its renaissance when, as reported in The Orlando Sentinel on October 28, 1958, it got an office in the Eau Gallie Civic Center and employed a full-time secretary. The chamber reported that it had received more than 10,000 telephone calls and 6,000 visitors since setting up the office.

The Greater Melbourne Chamber suffered a setback when Charles L. Herring, who had been executive vice-president of the chamber for ten years, announced that he would retire on July 1, 1960. The Miami Herald reported on February 28, 1959, that Herring was leaving to enter private business. Herring's ten-year term was highlighted by effective actions. The same report in the Herald noted that the chamber was studying the idea of creating a Better Business Bureau and an industrial committee, two ideas which the chamber would pursue successfully.

The Orlando Sentinel reported on May 20, 1959, that the Eau Gallie Chamber had authorized its president to "investigate the feasibility of an area-wide Chamber of Commerce for industrial development." Throughout the history of chambers of commerce in Brevard County, the chambers have struggled to find methods for all the chambers to work together for common goals. There is no evidence that the effort led to such an organization. Similar efforts for a county-wide industrial development organization were reflected in a special act of the legislature creating a public industrial development agency, the Brevard Economic Development Agency, in 1967, which evolved into the present public-private Economic Development Commission of Florida's Space Coast in 1989.

On May 28, 1959, the Greater Melbourne Chamber announced a membership drive with a goal of reaching 500 members. An article in The Orlando Sentinel showed that the current membership was 200, so the membership drive had an extremely ambitious goal.

The Orlando Sentinel issue of July 7, 1959, reported that the newly formed Palm Bay Chamber of Commerce would install its officers on July 17. The chairman of the installation was the general manager of Port Malabar. He described the project as a "big residential and industrial community to be developed in Palm Bay." An article in the Sentinel the previous week, on June 30, had said that Radiation had become the first industry to locate in the industrial park. That article forecast that 30,000 homes would be constructed in Port Malabar while 105,000 homesites were planned. The Miami Herald reported on August 25 that State Representative L. B. Vocelle will address the charter meeting of the Palm Bay Chamber on September 10. Vocelle had said that he would discuss the upcoming referendum to change the boundary lines of Brevard and Indian River counties to the middle of the Sebastian Inlet.

The issue of the boundary line between the counties had arisen when the possibility of building a bridge over the Sebastian Inlet came to the fore. At that time, Sebastian Inlet was within Brevard County and the county line was about two and ½ miles south of the inlet. Indian River County agreed that it would pay for construction of the bridge over the inlet in exchange for moving the county line to the middle of the inlet. A referendum was needed to approve the move of the county boundary. As reported in The Cocoa Tribune on October 27, 1959, the South Brevard Beaches Chamber of Commerce was a primary advocate of approving the change. On October 30, 1959, the chamber sponsored an advertisement in The Cocoa Tribune urging voters to approve the proposal and "close the gap." The ad argued that approval of the change and construction of the bridge would "open new vistas of growth along our beautiful Atlantic coastline, affecting the future prosperity of both counties." Another advertisement by the chamber in the Tribune on November 2 added that passage of the referendum would "pave the way for development of the entire east coast."

The Miami Herald reported on November 4, 1959, that the referendum to change the county boundary was approved by more than a two-to-one margin. Readers will decide whether the result lived up to the hyperbole of the South Brevard Beaches Chamber ads.

The Brevard Edition of The Orlando Sentinel reported on January 20, 1960, that the Eau Gallie Chamber had "stepped up its activities during the past year in order to keep up with the county's fastest-growing city." The chamber reported that it had distributed more than 15,000 city maps.

The Miami Herald related in its issue of February 19, 1960, that the Melbourne Chamber had created a four-prong plan of action to make Melbourne "a better city in which to live and play." An industrial committee would "work with northern plants" interested in coming to Florida. The housing committee would "handle all housing problems," while the recreation committee would work on providing new recreation facilities. The final prong of the plan would work with city, county, and state governments "on matters pertaining to the betterment of Melbourne."

The Palm Bay Chamber as well was going strong in 1960. The Miami Herald reported on February 27, 1960, that the Palm Bay Chamber had sent a resolution to the State Road Board opposing the commencement of the Fort Pierce-Orlando extension of the Florida Turnpike until U.S. 1 had been four-laned through Brevard County.

The West Melbourne Chamber in 1960 was continuing its efforts to be a positive force in south Brevard County following Melbourne's failed effort in 1959 to annex areas in West Melbourne and the subsequent incorporation of the City of West Melbourne (which will be discussed in greater detail in Chapter Five below). Lonnie Coker, executive director of the West Melbourne Chamber was quoted in The Orlando Sentinel on March 3, 1960, as arguing that area consolidation is imperative to provide all the needed facilities of south Brevard. The Sentinel further reported on April 1, 1960, that the West Melbourne Chamber was spearheading an effort to form an Industrial Committee of 100 made up of leaders from throughout the county.

The South Brevard Beaches Chamber of Commerce sponsored this ad on October 30, 1959, urging Brevard County voters to vote in favor of an agreement with Indian River County ceding land south of Sebastian Inlet to Indian River County in exchange for construction of a bridge over the inlet.

The Palm Bay Chamber in 1960 was upset by what it believed to be the undercount of the Palm Bay population in the 1960 census. The Miami Herald related on June 17, 1960, that the Palm Bay census was reported as being 810 but city records showed 700 electric connections and more than 600 registered voters. The chamber called upon Congressman Syd Herlong to ask that the Census Bureau take another count.

It was not only Palm Bay which was disappointed in the census. The Miami Herald reported on June 16 that the Melbourne Chamber was supporting the city's attempt to increase the count for Melbourne. The census reported 11,911 residents for Melbourne while local officials thought the population was as many as 17,000.

The Orlando Sentinel showed on July 12, 1960, that the Palm Bay Chamber now had more than 100 members. The same article showed that there was now an organization known as the "South Brevard Chambers of Commerce Council." This organization was another attempt to ensure that the chambers in the area were coordinating their efforts and trying to avoid destructive competition. These efforts would eventually lead to the consolidation of the 5 chambers of south Brevard in 1967.

One of the first projects of the new council was to promote the creation of a fishing reef. The Orlando Sentinel related on July 15, 1960, that Richard Muldrew of the Greater Melbourne Chamber had taken the proposal to the Chambers of Commerce Council. The proposal was to create a "fishing haven" 2 to 3 miles offshore by sinking old automobiles weighed down with rocks. Although the proposal went nowhere, Dick Muldrew went on to serve as a County Commissioner and, later, a Circuit Judge. As an aside, Muldrew was the first county official elected as a Republican in an era when it was difficult to persuade the Supervisor of Elections to allow a person to register as a Republican.

The August 4, 1960, edition of The Miami Herald reported that the U.S. Census Bureau had made it official by announcing that Brevard County was the fastest-growing county in the United States. The report related the county's population had grown 370% during the

1950s, growing from 23,563 to 111,176. The newspaper related: "Brevard-which can trace its growth to the fast-rising rockets of the free world's most important space port- outstripped all competitors by twenty-four percent, the Bureau said." County Commissioner Lee Wenner noted that the official acknowledgement by the Census Bureau might help convince state and national agencies that Brevard had growth problems and needed help with roads, schools, hospitals, and other public services. Ralph L. Bickford, president of the Greater Melbourne Chamber, related that the designation was no surprise to him. The Census Bureau report included the information that only 13.5% was "natural growth" while the rest of the growth came from "immigration."

On August 11, 1960, The Miami Herald reported that the Greater Melbourne Chamber was exploring the possibility of setting up a Better Business Bureau. The chamber noted that such a bureau could be a means of "checking out suspected shysters." This was the start of what would become an important and effective function of the chamber for many decades.

Another issue which arose in 1960 and would garner the attention of the community for many years related to a proposed jai alai fronton. Not surprisingly, the issue of para-mutual gambling in the area would arouse the passions of citizens on both sides of the issue. The Miami Herald issue of November 18, 1960, related that the officers of the Greater Melbourne Chamber had declined to take a position, declaring it "too controversial." On the other hand, the South Brevard Beaches Chamber was described as a leading backer of the fronton. The West Melbourne Chamber had not been called upon to take a position. The chambers of commerce in south Brevard County would sit out that issue through all the referenda held in 1960, 1963, 1967 and 1969. Para-mutual gambling was narrowly approved in the 1969 referendum after suffering defeat in each of the three earlier elections.

The Eau Gallie Chamber was optimistic for 1961. On January 24, newly installed president Bert Pooley told The Orlando Sentinel that the chamber was undertaking a membership drive which he believed would result in the Eau Gallie Chamber being the largest chamber in the county. Pooley saw that such a result would be "only fitting for the county's largest city."

Annexation and municipal consolidation continue to be a hot topic in 1961. The Orlando Sentinel reported on February 17 that the South Brevard Beaches Chamber had released a strongly worded statement condemning any efforts by mainland cities to annex beach communities, declaring the chamber "against annexation of any beach city, town or area."

Events in Palm Bay in 1961 were also dynamic. J.J. Finnegan was not only president of the Palm Bay Chamber but was also, fittingly, executive director of General Development Corporation. The Orlando Evening Star reported on July 14, 1961, that Finnegan had told the Eau Gallie Rotary Club that his company would be building 3,000 homes per year in Port Malabar and that the total buildout in Port Malabar would be 60,000 homes.

Jackie Reid wrote in The Orlando Sentinel on September 20, 1961, that the South Brevard Beaches Chamber had reached a milestone in its progress when it opened its new office in Indialantic. The office, it was said, would be open 8 hours per day and would "inform tourists and newcomers of the potential of the area."

Not to be outdone, the Melbourne Chamber set ambitious goals for 1962. On January 23, 1962, the chamber announced told The Orlando Sentinel that it was undertaking a membership drive with the goal of increasing membership from 262 to 400 members.

The South Brevard Beaches Chamber tooted its own horn in an article in the Orlando Evening Star on January 31, 1962, when it listed its accomplishments since its organization in October 1958. It boasted of its role in spearheading the Sebastian Inlet bridge, as well as its establishment of a better business bureau, its lobbying for beachside post offices, its support for the establishment of the volunteer fire department, its role in developing Spessard Holland Park and its leadership in the Sidewalk Art Festival.

The Orlando Sentinel reported on February 6, 1962, that the Melbourne Chamber had outlined a wide range of activities for the year. The article noted that the chamber had a better business division to inform area businesses and prospective merchants. Additionally, the article described the efforts of the chamber's industrial committee which looked to lure new commerce and industry to the area. To assure readers that the chamber was employing modern technology, the article added that the chamber used "a mimeograph to keep a running reproduction of the ever-changing statistics."

The Orlando Evening Star showed on February 14, 1962, that the Eau Gallie Chamber had a current membership of 136. The chamber announced that it was kicking off a membership drive with a goal of increasing its membership to 250. On March 2, The Miami Herald reported that the Eau Gallie Chamber had received two citations from the Governor's Chamber of Commerce Merit Award program, thus becoming the only chamber in the state to receive more than one such award. Governor Farris Bryant announced that the Eau Gallie Chamber had won awards in the tourist promotion and community development categories.

The Melbourne Chamber informed The Orlando Sentinel on March 6, 1962, that it had formed a study committee to gather facts about the proposed jetport at Melbourne Airport. The chamber promised that it would gather facts from other cities facing the problems of jetports as well as data from manufacturers related to jet aircraft.

The project to four-lane U.S. 1 through Melbourne and Eau Gallie continued to occupy much of the efforts of the Melbourne and Eau Gallie chambers during 1962. Securing the right of way for this expansion proved problematic. The Miami Herald disclosed on March 31, 1962, that 36 landowners had declined to accept the money offered by the State Road Department for the right of way. As a result, the State Road Department was considering re-routing part of the highway to reduce the cost of right of way acquisition. In response to this possibility and to avoid re-routing, the Melbourne Chamber formed a mediation committee to serve between the department and landowners. The chamber announced that it had begun contacting the recalcitrant landowners and was making progress.

The Melbourne Chamber was also intimately involved in 1962 with the fledgling Brevard Engineering College and its efforts to stabilize itself. The college had been formed in 1957, providing courses for engineers and technicians employed in the space program. To achieve a more substantial financial foundation, the college began discussions with the Florida Christian Churches about merging that organization with the college to form a university in Melbourne. The model that the school and churches looked to emulate was Texas Christian University. The Melbourne Chamber joined with Brevard Engineering College to make the merger proposal to the Florida Christian Churches. The Miami Herald reported on May 18, 1962, that the churches had eagerly accepted the proposal. The Herald said that the churches were "ready to invest $300,000 immediately to get the college going and Brevard Engineering College and a new liberal arts college are expected to open on a full-time basis in September." The paper showed that the decision made college president Jerome Keuper "jubilant." The Tampa Bay Times issue of May 26 confirmed that the churches had appointed a committee to work with the Melbourne Chamber of Commerce to effectuate the merger. Unfortunately, it soon became clear that the churches had no money for this project and the proposed merger quickly unraveled.

A promising display of cooperation between the chambers of commerce in south Brevard County was shown by an article in The Orlando Sentinel on July 1, 1962. An article by Jackie Reid showed that, for the first time, the July 4 celebration in the area would be a joint effort by several organizations, including the chambers of commerce in Melbourne, West Melbourne, and the South Brevard Beaches. The article also included the information that the Melbourne Chamber had a women's division. I will leave it to the reader to decide whether the existence of a women's division was proper in those days or, as many others may argue, an example of prevailing misogyny.

Another milestone for the Melbourne Chamber in 1962 was the establishment of its headquarters on the Melbourne Causeway. A photograph in The Orlando Sentinel on August 19, 1962, described the office as "located on the banks of the Indian River" and "the scene of much activity aimed at promoting the area." That building would later become the office for several Brevard County commissioners and still is in use by the county today.

Improvement of U.S. 192 continued to be the top priority for the West Melbourne Chamber during 1963. The Orlando Evening Star reported on April 3 that the West Melbourne group was looking to create a joint effort with the Melbourne Chamber to exert pressure on the State Road Board to speed up improvements.

A top priority for the Palm Bay Chamber in 1963 was an effort to persuade the state to build a "space age university" in Palm Bay. The Orlando Evening Star edition of June 14 disclosed that this issue was the top goal for the Palm Bay group for 1963, followed by construction of a new building for the chamber office and support for a proposed Brevard Museum of Natural History. The idea of a space university referred to the effort undertaken by the state to develop a public university in central Florida that would provide education and research in support of the activities at Cape Canaveral and the Space Center. That project became highly controversial due to the many communities competing to be the site of the university. In addition, supporters of Brevard Engineering College ("BEC," now Florida Institute of Technology) were lobbying against the establishment of such a state university, arguing that BEC could satisfactorily serve the needs of the space industry. The South Brevard Chamber of Commerce council, a coordinating group with representatives of all five chambers in south Brevard, spearheaded a meeting of all chambers in the county where it was agreed to promote the choice of a site anywhere in the county. An article in The Miami Herald on July 20 noted that the only site suggested thus far in Brevard County was a 1000-acre site in Palm Bay offered by General Development Corporation. In any event, the efforts of Palm Bay and the council to lure the university were fruitless when the state made the decision to locate the new university near Alafaya Trail in eastern Orange County. The college was founded as Florida Technological University and later renamed as the University of Central Florida.

Further evidence of the efforts of the chambers of commerce in Brevard to avoid destructive competition among the organizations was described in The Cocoa Tribune on August 16, 1963. The newspaper reported that the Brevard County Chambers of Commerce Council, consisting of the presidents of all chambers in the county, had held its first meeting the previous evening. The stated purpose of the council was to "voluntarily associate to discuss matters of mutual interest and promote programs of common concern." Similar efforts among the chambers in the county to name and promote common goals have continued to the present time.

A significant effort of the Melbourne Chamber was reported in The Orlando Sentinel on October 30, 1963, when the chamber hosted the opening of Barnes Engineering Company near Melbourne Airport. The news article noted that the chamber hoped to make Barnes, a firm from Connecticut doing research and development work in infrared and electro-optics, the showpiece that would lure other electronics and instrumentation manufacturers to the area. The chamber added: "Our industrial climate, already excellent, is improving by leaps and bounds." The building constructed by Barnes would serve several companies in the area over many years. Florida Tech currently occupies the building and has used it as the home of its Applied Research Center.

All the chambers of Brevard were preoccupied with the World's Fair to be held in New York in 1964. The chambers organized a county-wide Brevard World Fair Authority to create a display on behalf of the county to be exhibited at the fair. The Cocoa Tribune reported on February 7, 1964, that the display was in jeopardy due to lack of funding. However, the good news was that all the chambers in the county, including the five in south Brevard, were working together to raise funds for the project. The Orlando Sentinel reported on March 27 that the Melbourne Chamber and the South Brevard Beaches Chamber had joined together to sell "discount" books, with the proceeds going to the fair exhibit.

The Miami News reported on February 16, 1964, that the Greater Melbourne Chamber of Commerce had established two groups: The first group was the Highways, Streets, Traffic and Safety Committee to be chaired by Jack Fogg. The second was the Hotel and Motel Committee to be chaired by Sidney Platt. Beyond these committees, The Orlando Evening Star reported on March 5 that the Melbourne Chamber's Industrial Committee was aggressively lobbying the

County Commission to establish a county industrial board that would encourage new industries to locate in the county. The chamber committee said: "It is hard to argue with success and Brevard has certainly succeeded in growing beyond the wildest predictions made a few years ago. Still, our economy would be more soundly based if we had more diversified industry and that is what the new plan is looking toward." This effort would result in a Special Act of the legislature that would authorize the establishment by the County Commission of the Brevard Economic Development Commission (BEDC). The BEDC would serve as the industrial development arm of the county for more than 20 years before it morphed into the public-private partnership Economic Development Council of Florida's Space Coast which exists today.

The efforts of the five chambers in south Brevard to work together were causing community activists to think beyond mere cooperation. The Orlando Sentinel showed on April 10, 1964, that E.H. Haupt, Jr., executive director of the South Brevard Beaches Chamber, had proposed consolidation of all chambers in south Brevard County. A meeting of directors of the Melbourne, Palm Bay, West Melbourne, Eau Gallie, and South Breaches chambers to discuss this possibility had been scheduled for April 22. Although it would take several years to bring this about, Haupt's idea would prevail. One immediate reaction to Haupt's proposal came from the Palm Bay Chamber. The Orlando Sentinel reported on April 12 that A. O. Eckwall, Palm Bay Chamber president, said that he would support the merger of all chambers in Brevard County but would not support the merger of chambers in south Brevard. These discussions about consolidation in April 1964 did not lead to immediate agreement among chamber officials but neither did they end the discussion. On October 23, 1964, The Miami Herald noted that the South Brevard Automobile Dealers Association asked that the chambers "unite into one South Brevard Chamber of Commerce in order to better serve the overall community."

The Melbourne Chamber conducted a nationwide search for a new executive director during 1964. The Miami Herald showed on May 21 that the Melbourne Chamber had hired William Moore. Moore's prior job had been as "top promoter" of the Kentucky Derby Festival. Moore's salary would be $12,000 per year. Moore promised that he would at once strive to increase cooperation among the chambers of south Brevard County.

The South Brevard Beaches Chamber of Commerce endorsed the idea of a toll causeway from Grant to the beaches. This idea has periodically been advanced but never gained practical traction. The Orlando Evening Star reported on June 2, 1964, that several bonding companies had expressed interest in exploring the financial feasibility of such a project. These investment bankers, eager for an opportunity to earn underwriting fees, seemed oblivious to the environmental outcry that such a project would arouse.

The Melbourne Chamber adopted a resolution that was published in The Orlando Sentinel on June 28, 1964, endorsing a water storage plan developed by the Central and Southern Flood Control District. The Melbourne Chamber had long known that adequate water was among the foremost issues that could limit growth in south Brevard County. The resolution said that "the municipalities within the County of Brevard are on the verge of a critical situation in the diminishing of the water supply to serve the ever-increasing populous (sic)." The chamber's sensitivity to this issue would cause it to be a leader in addressing water management issues for decades to come.

The South Brevard Chambers of Commerce Council, the group coordinating efforts of the five local chambers, noted that it was beginning its fifth year of operation in 1964. The Orlando Sentinel reported on July 31 that the council activities for the previous year had ranged from the effort to locate the space university in Brevard to the effort to set up a fishing reef off Sebastian Inlet.

The chambers also backed the proposal to create a state park at Sebastian Inlet. The Miami Herald reported on September 2, 1964, that the Melbourne Chamber "strongly urges" the development of such a park. Although this proposal would not come to fruition until 1971 with the establishment of Sebastian Inlet State Park, it would be a significant step in that direction. The 1,000-acre park has become the second most-visited state park in Florida with more than 700,000 visitors per year.

Another significant project for the Melbourne Chamber in 1964 was the first annual Space Bowl Game sponsored by the chamber at Melbourne High School Stadium. As described in The Orlando Sentinel on October 18, the high school football team from south Brevard with the best regular-season record would face off against another team from central or north Brevard, Orange, or Indian River County. The idea was promoted by Jonathan Dwight of Florida Air Academy, whose son Jamie would later become chair of the chamber. The idea resulted in an initial game between Satellite High and Orlando Boone High and a later game between Satellite and Vero Beach. However, after those first two games, the chamber decided that the game was not within its primary goals and turned it over to the City of Satellite Beach to administer.

An article by Jack Snyder in The Orlando Sentinel on December 20, 1964, described an issue that would occupy the attention of the local chambers for many years before being resolved. The report showed that U.S. 192 west of Melbourne had been proclaimed the worst road in Florida by an article in an American Automobile Association magazine. The article, appearing in The Florida Explorer described the road as "a roller coaster' that "appears to be slipping into the marsh on the right side." Following publication of the AAA article, the Melbourne Chamber passed a resolution asking that the road be rebuilt at once. As someone who first arrived in Melbourne in 1964, I can attest that for a newcomer, arriving in Melbourne via 192 caused one to wonder whether one was travelling to the end of the earth. To call the road "a roller coaster" was to insult most carnival rides and to omit the thrill one received when the wooden planks of the bridge over the St. Johns River flew up as cars crossed the bridge.

Another major transportation issue that would occupy all the local chambers of commerce first arose in 1984. The Miami Herald reported on May 8, 1984, that consulting engineers for the State Road Department had proposed a $41 million project which became known as the Banana River Expressway. This audacious proposal included a $36 million bond issue to finance the tollway which would include construction of a bridge from Pineda across the Banana and Indian rivers to the south boundary of Patrick Air Force Base. The proposed project then envisioned construction of a north-south tollway constructed in the Banana River that would connect the

Pineda Causeway with the Bennett Causeway (State Road 528) north of Cocoa. The second part of the proposed project envisioned widening the Bennett Causeway from two to four lanes and extending it to the St. Johns River, where it would connect to the Beeline Highway to Orlando, which was then under study by the East Central Florida Regional Planning Council. Not surprisingly, a project of such ambition immediately drew vocal supporters and detractors that would engage all the chambers in Brevard County during 1965.

The Orlando Evening Star issue of February 3, 1965, related that the Melbourne Chamber of Commerce planned to endorse both the Pineda Causeway and the Banana River Expressway. Chamber president E. Davison Potter also floated the idea of a professional baseball stadium for the City of Melbourne.

The South Brevard Beaches Chamber realized one of its biggest aims on February 12, 1965, when the new bridge over Sebastian Inlet was opened for traffic. The Orlando Sentinel reported on February 13 that: "Completion of the project is expected to spawn a development boom in both the South Brevard and North Indian River beach area."

The Miami Herald noted on March 19, 1965, that all members of the South Brevard Chambers of Commerce Council had endorsed the Banana River Expressway, except the Eau Gallie Chamber. Milton McGrath, president of the Eau Gallie Chamber, questioned the reliability of the feasibility and engineering studies which had been conducted about the proposal. The council did, however, unanimously approve resolutions urging the completion of improvements to U.S. 192 and State Road A1A.

The effort to promote the Banana River Expressway "met with disaster" according to The Orlando Evening Star issue of July 2, 1965. The news article showed that property owners in the Cocoa Beach area had organized to successfully oppose the project and that the State Road Department had withdrawn its application to the Army Corps of Engineers for permits to construct the road. The news article also showed that the Eau Gallie Chamber had proclaimed its support for the Pineda Causeway project now that the expressway had been abandoned.

Another issue that captured the attention of the chambers of commerce in south Brevard County in 1965 was the newly created Fourth District Court of Appeals. The Orlando Sentinel reported on September 8 that the Melbourne Chamber had enacted a resolution asking that the court be in Melbourne. The City of Melbourne had offered temporary quarters at the airport and promised to offer free land for a permanent site. Alas, the court was established in Vero Beach in 1965 and moved to West Palm Beach in 1967.

All was not well with the South Brevard Chambers of Commerce Council in 1965. The Orlando Sentinel reported on October 13 that Cliff Heiner had resigned as president of the West Melbourne Chamber and as president of the council. The newspaper speculated that his resignation was due to "the state of affairs in the council of area chambers" and concluded that "squabbles and dissention inside the council doesn't (sic) help the area."

The deplorable condition of U.S. 192 continued to be spotlighted by local chambers. The Miami Herald reported on November 13, 1965, that the Melbourne Chamber had urged state road officials to prioritize improvement of 192 in view of the "predicted Disney boom." The chamber resolution pronounced that the proposed Beeline Highway was "unneeded" and would further separate south Brevard from central Florida. The Beeline had been strongly recommended by the East Central Florida Regional Planning Council which described it as "a key economic lifeline for Brevard, Orange and Osceola counties." Even leaders in central Brevard were cautious about the Beeline, which many of these leaders regarded as being primarily promoted by Orange County leaders who wanted to "funnel off" business from Brevard to Orange. Although one might regard such concerns as paranoid, time has shown that competition between Orange and Brevard County economic interests is real and continuing. The lawsuit between the airports arising from Orlando's objection to the use of "Orlando" in the name of the Melbourne airport which took place between 2016 and 2022 is the most recent evidence of the competition.

Even amid consolidation discussions, the Eau Gallie Chamber did not lose sight of its priority projects. On January 16 ,1967, the Orlando Evening Star related that chamber president Joe Wickham was exhorting chamber members to write letters to the Army Corps of Engineers and the State Road Department expressing support for construction of the Pineda Causeway. Wickham also hoped to have 100 or more members in attendance at a public meeting conducted by the Army Corps on January 26.

One issue which bound all the chambers in the county in 1966 was that of the Manned Orbital Laboratory. When NASA announced that it was considering locating the MOL in California, all the chambers, as well as all public officials, raised an outcry in opposition to such a move. The Orlando Sentinel reported on February 13 that the Eau Gallie Chamber had passed a resolution which "launched a blistering attack upon the USAF and the Department of Defense."

The South Beaches Chamber declared a big victory when the Orlando Evening Star revealed on March 14 that reconstruction had begun on Highway A1A. Chamber president Art Proulx predicted that: "The next six months will change the character of the South Brevard motel business tremendously."

The Melbourne Chamber suffered a setback in 1966 when William A. Moore, who had been executive director of the group since 1964, died unexpectedly. Chamber president Cliff Higgins described Moore's passing as "a great loss to the city and its chamber."

The issue of consolidation of the chambers in south Brevard monopolized the time and energy of all five chambers during 1966. On May 14, the Orlando Evening Star reported that the Melbourne and West Melbourne chambers had agreed to merge into a single organization. Melbourne president Cliff Higgins and West Melbourne president Bud Huggins jointly made the announcement. Within a few weeks, The Orlando Sentinel showed on June 7 that the Melbourne and Eau Gallie chambers were trying to create a "greater South Brevard Chamber of Commerce" by merging all existing chambers. Unidentified officials of the two chambers acknowledged that some "old-timers" opposed the

This ad, sponsored by the Melbourne Chamber of Commerce, was published in the Orlando Sentinel and the Orlando Evening Star on March 10, 1966.

merger due to their fear that their community would lose its identity. However, those officials added: "We would be listened to more readily than would five small chambers of commerce, each with five different viewpoints." A couple of weeks later, on June 22, an official of the South Brevard Beaches Chamber told The Orlando Sentinel on June 22 that the chamber was ready to join the merger plan. On June 27, the Orlando Evening Starr quoted the South Brevard Beaches' executive director Elmer Haupt as saying that the merger would "prevent duplication of efforts to promote our fine South Brevard assets as a place to live and enjoy life." On June 30, Art Proulx, president of the beaches chamber, told the Orlando Evening Star that its members had approved the merger, and the chamber would be meeting with the Melbourne Chamber to work out the mechanics. In that same article, Eau Gallie Chamber president Ken Sanders said that a meeting of the South Brevard Council of Chambers would take place the following week to have further discussions about a merger.

It was not certain that the Eau Gallie Chamber would embrace the idea of merger. The Orlando Evening Star issue of July 15, 1966, related that there was a dispute within the Eau Gallie Chamber between its president Ken Sanders, who supported the idea of a merger, and Milton McGrath, a director and former president of the chamber and former mayor of the city, who opposed the idea. The Miami Herald reported on July 21 that the directors of the Eau Gallie Chamber had postponed any decision about a merger until some questions were answered. Specifically, the Eau Gallie group wanted to know where the chamber would be located, how it would be financed, what it would be named and the nature of the merged chamber's charter.

A factor that caused the Eau Gallie Chamber to be cautious about going ahead with consolidation was that the group had successfully undertaken a substantial expansion of its office building, nearly tripling its size. The Orlando Evening Star reported on August 4, 1966, that the expanded building, consisting of 1,312 square feet, would be dedicated the following Sunday with a speech by Patrick Air Force Base commander Colonel Joseph B. Williams.

By November 10, 1966, the Orlando Sentinel reported that Melbourne Chamber president Cliff Higgins, Eau Gallie Chamber president Ken Sanders, and Palm Bay Chamber president Warren Foster all urged a unified chamber for south Brevard. A few days later, on November 13, The Sentinel showed that the South Brevard Beaches Chamber was expected to give final approval of the merger the following week. The Orlando Evening Star reported on November 29 that Milton McGrath had changed his mind and now advocated for the merger.

The merger effort suffered a setback when the Palm Bay Chamber voted against it on December 11. As reported in The Orlando Sentinel on December 15, the chamber president Warren Foster was out of town when the vote occurred. Foster at once resigned as president in protest because the decision had been made a week before a meeting scheduled for December 19. Foster's resignation letter noted: "You failed to even honor the request that a decision be reached after the 19th of December meeting when all of you would have had an opportunity to hear all the pros and cons on the issue." An editorial in The Orlando Sentinel on December 20 took the Palm Bay Chamber to task in noting: "With chambers of commerce planning toward consolidation in both South and Central Brevard, it quickly becomes obvious that a single body like that of Palm Bay cannot hope to effectively serve its community by struggling along alone."

Following the meeting of December 19, the chambers of Eau Gallie and the South Brevard Beaches voted to join the previously merged chambers of Melbourne and West Melbourne. The Orlando Sentinel reported on December 24, 1966, that each of the chambers had appointed representatives to a chamber of commerce merger charter revision committee to create a proposed charter for a new chamber made up of what had formerly been four chambers. Tom Moldenhauer and Art Proulx would represent the South Beaches Chamber while Joe Wickham, Marshall Boykin, Abbott Herring, and Bert Pooley would represent the Eau Gallie Chamber. The Melbourne Chamber representatives were Bill Kercher, John Wilson, Beville Outlaw and W. D. Webb.

Although the issue of combining the chambers consumed much of their time and attention in 1966, that was far from the only heated issue facing the group. Another issue that accelerated the emotions of the business community in south Brevard had to do with the location of the proposed south campus of Brevard Junior College (later Brevard Community College, later Eastern Florida State College). The Orlando Sentinel reported on the controversy on August13 and August 17, 1966. The Eau Gallie Chamber made a bid when it conveyed an offer to donate an 80-acre site at the northwest corner of Wickham Park. Melbourne reacted by suggesting a site south of Crane Creek which would be part of a proposed urban renewal project. When it was pointed out that an urban renewal project would require years of bureaucratic approvals, Mayor Nate Friedland suggested a site at Melbourne Airport. When airport director Ken Allen pointed out that the airport must receive fair market value payment for its land, that idea died a rapid death. The Palm Bay Chamber was particularly outspoken in its opposition to the Wickham Park site. An article in The Orlando Sentinel on March 23, 1967, following the recommendation of the Wickham site by a state survey board, described the Palm Bay Chamber as "still one small voice of dissent in regard to selection of the new BJC facility." Although the controversy over the college site divided the community in 1966, the wisdom of the decision to build near Wickham Park seems obvious when one sees the bustling and impressive campus of Eastern Florida State College as it exists today.

Consolidation of the four chambers went ahead enthusiastically. The Orlando Evening Star reported on January 19, 1967, that the charter and by-laws of the new, combined organization had been drafted by the committee that had been appointed the previous month. The news article showed that the proposed charter had been approved by the Eau Gallie Chamber, subject only to an acceptable audit of each of the chambers. Following the audit, the proposed charter and by-laws would be given to the members of each chamber for a vote. Under the governing documents, the new chamber would be split into three districts for voting purposes and each district would elect nine directors. One district would be made up of the beach area between Patrick Air Force Base and Sebastian Inlet while the mainland would be divided into two areas with newly constructed NASA Boulevard as the dividing line. The Miami Herald reported on February 23 that the audits had been completed and the consolidation had been approved by the general membership of each organization. George Tomlinson wrote for The Orlando Sentinel on March 16 that on March 20 the chambers would begin to implement the merger. Tomlinson continued: "Could there be any greater cause for celebration? This is the biggest and most magnificent step forward South Brevard has made in years. It is a sign of things to come." The Orlando Evening Star followed up with a report on February 23 disclosing that the current boards of the chambers would meet jointly for the ensuing six months, after which a board of the new organization would be elected and seated. That report concluded: "The successful merging of all South Brevard's chambers is regarded by many civic officials as the first step towards the unification of all of South Brevard's communities." The Orlando Sentinel issue of March 16 noted: "The merger of all chambers of commerce in South Brevard marks a real milestone in the banishment of provincialism in this county." The op-ed continued: "Because of its unprecedented growth and the difficulty of identifying areawide leadership, Brevard has suffered from an unusually large dose of over-weaning local pride within its municipalities."

The enthusiasm for consolidation expressed by the news media was not sufficient to sway the Palm Bay Chamber. The Orlando Sentinel showed on April 26, 1967, that the directors of the Palm Bay Chamber had called a special meeting and had, for the second time in a year, overwhelmingly rejected the proposed merger.

As one of its first actions as a combined organization, the Metropolitan South Brevard Chamber of Commerce endorsed a proposal which would amend the Florida Constitution to allow the State of Florida and its political subdivisions to issue industrial revenue bonds. This action of the new chamber was reported in the Orlando Evening Star on April 27, 1967. This was a significant step that has enabled Brevard County and municipalities within Brevard to finance construction of dozens of industrial and manufacturing facilities employing tens of thousands of Brevardians.

The Orlando Sentinel reported on June 6, 1967, that the new chamber had hired Alfred Webster as the executive director of the merged organization. Webster, a retired Army Lieutenant Colonel, had been the deputy chief of the community relations division of the office of information at the Air Force Eastern Test Range. Prior to that, he had been on the staff and faculty of the Army Information School. Webster would prove to be a solid choice to lead the new organization.

The Miami Herald reported on August 4, 1967, that Joe Wickham, first president of the merged organization, had named four major improvement areas which the chamber would undertake, including organization improvement, business and economic development, community development and public affairs. Wickham said that subcommittees would be formed in each of the four areas. The Orlando Sentinel opined on October 22 that the four chambers had united into "one active, hard-working organization."

One effort of the newly merged organization resulted in the establishment of the Junior Achievement program in Brevard County, a program which has been an extraordinary success during the ensuing 55 years. The Orlando Sentinel reported on June 14, 1968, that the Metropolitan South Brevard Chamber of Commerce had formed a steering committee with a goal of setting up the program in Brevard County schools. The news article described the program as: "A nationally franchised program" whose participants "learn the free enterprise system by setting up and operation their own miniature corporations." A later article in The Sentinel on July 18, 1969, showed that Junior Achievement clubs would be introduced into four south Brevard County high schools in the fall of 1969, sponsored by the Metropolitan South Brevard Chamber of Commerce. Chamber Executive Director Al Webster revealed that 12 local businesses had shown support for the program.

Another significant activity of the recently consolidated chamber was described in an article in The Orlando Sentinel on January 16, 1968, when Executive Director Webster noted that with a completely merged chamber representing the entire area, the chamber was able to activate "what is very close to a bureau-oriented division" to fill a role like a Better Business Bureau. As Webster noted: This means we will cooperate with state, county, and federal agencies to investigate business activities and keep out unscrupulous and fraudulent business operations here." An article in Florida Today on November 6, 1968, reported that this new division had managed more than 5,500 complaints and requests for information since its start. This division of the chamber would remain an active and effective asset for the community for many years.

While some may argue the merits of the consolidation of the four chambers, most would agree that it has been a remarkable success. In an editorial on June 16, 1968, Florida Today urged the two chambers in central Brevard County to consider merging, noting: "For proof of the value of such a merger, these members have only to look less than 20 miles to the south where merger in its most solid form has worked - and worked well. The Metropolitan South Brevard Chamber of Commerce is now well into its second year standing for its 11 communities and has much more accomplishments to its credit that all the chambers which were absorbed." An editorial in The Orlando Sentinel on June 16, 1968, noted that the merger had brought "Business seminars, home shows, tourist committees, airport committees, public relations committees, boat shows, and a myriad of other projects which now represent the entire area, not just Melbourne, nor Indialantic, nor Eau Gallie." The editorial continued: "The best talent from all areas was pooled." Florida Today newspaper published an op-ed on September 29, 1968, which described the combined chamber as a "Model for Growth" and further noted: "The Metropolitan South Brevard Chamber of Commerce has a list of accomplishments to which it can point with pride, and which can be envied by medium-sized chambers anywhere." An editorial in Florida Today on December 21, 1969, further noted: "The Metropolitan South Brevard Chamber of Commerce has been the most unifying influence in the area for the past couple of years. Its efforts resulted in bringing Melbourne and Eau Gallie together. And it has been eminently successful in creating an atmosphere that encourages new business and industry and the expansion of existing firms." High praise indeed.

CHAPTER NOTES

- For more on the history of construction of U.S. Highway 192 see aaroads.com/guides/us-192-fl/,
- For more on the impact of the Sebastian Inlet on attracting visitors and its economic impact see Waymer, Jim, "Park is 2nd Most Visited in State Despite 10% Drop in Attendance," Florida Today, January 31, 2011.
- The information about the University of Melbourne and its gift to BEC is described in an article in Florida Today newspaper on May 25, 1969.
- For more on Melbourne High School and its national renown as the first ungraded high school in the United States, see Mary Anne Walker's article in The Cocoa Tribune on July 23, 1963. Walker described the school's philosophy as "not to bridal students academically, but to make each student inquiry oriented." Additionally, the October 8, 1962, issue of Newsweek Magazine ran a lengthy article on Melbourne High School in which it described the school as "probably the most unusual, complex and exciting public school in America." The article discussed the abolition of grades and the establishment of phases as well as the unusually extensive and diverse curriculum.

CHAPTER FIVE

The Chamber Leads the Efforts To Create A New City

Few political subjects raise emotions as quickly as the consolidation of municipalities or municipal services. Such discussions attract the immediate attention of not only those citizens who value their small towns and traditions but also politicians whose positions might be threatened by reorganization. Municipal employees often fear that their jobs might be eliminated or reduced by consolidation. Citizens often value their ability to influence government action in their small town and fear that their influence will be less in a larger city. All these concerns were voiced during the efforts to combine communities in south Brevard County during the 1960s.

The book, A *Tribute to Melbourne's Pioneers* maintains that there were many attempts by Melbourne to expand dating back to the 1920s. The first public discussion of municipal consolidation by the Greater Melbourne Chamber of Commerce appeared in the Orlando Sentinel on October 22, 1955. It was reported that Charles L. Herring, Executive Vice-President of the chamber had addressed the Melbourne Rotary Club to advocate for the consolidation of Melbourne, Melbourne Beach, Indialantic, and Eau Gallie. Herring explained that Brevard County had increased 96% in population between 1950 and 1955 and that the Melbourne area had the greatest percentage increase of any area in the state. The combined population of those cities would exceed 31,000 and would exceed 50,000 by 1960.

A 1956 referendum rejected Melbourne's attempt to annex an unincorporated area west and south of Melbourne. The Orlando Evening Star reported on September 13, 1956, that the proposed annexation had been rejected by a vote of 499 to 316.

On January 29, 1959, the Orlando Evening Star reported that the West Melbourne Chamber of Commerce had enacted a resolution praising the city councils of Melbourne and Eau Gallie for statements made in support of merging the two cities and combining all south Brevard County. The resolution said that the "West Melbourne Chamber of Commerce has long taken a position that all of the area of South Brevard should be formed together in one metropolitan form of government."

The Orlando Sentinel issue of April 1, 1959, reported that landowners west of Melbourne, headed by Cecil Platt, were circulating petitions to file a lawsuit opposing the renewed efforts of the City of Melbourne to annex areas west of Melbourne. This time, the area proposed to be annexed was a 22-square-mile zone that was the subject of an annexation election scheduled for April 18, 1959. The West Melbourne Chamber of Commerce was reported to be giving financial aid to the group opposing annexation. The West Melbourne Chamber of Commerce supported the consolidation of all south Brevard but opposed annexation solely by Melbourne. Melbourne's attempt at annexation was again defeated, this time by a vote of 1,319 to 1,200. In the area that was proposed to be annexed, only 42 favored annexation while 842 opposed it. The April 20, 1959, issue of The Miami Herald speculated that it was probable that Melbourne would make further attempts to annex land on its western border. To prevent such further attempts, residents secured special legislation setting a referendum to establish the City of West Melbourne. As reported by The Miami Herald on September 9, 1959, the referendum was approved by a vote of 189 to 153 and Brevard's ninth city was born. West Melbourne was created specifically to avoid annexation by Melbourne and to prevent the levying of ad valorem taxes.

The next mention of the possibility of consolidation by the City of Melbourne appeared in the_minutes of the Melbourne City Commission of July 26, 1960, which appointed a committee to study the advisability of consolidation of Melbourne with "Eau Gallie or other neighboring municipalities." Later, on December 13, 1960, the Melbourne City Commission appointed Elting Storms to serve on the "fact-finding consolidation committee." At the commission meeting of January 24, 1961, Commissioner Stan Koller suggested that the committee also collaborate with the communities of Indialantic and Melbourne Beach to explore consolidation.

The first mention of consolidation reported by the Eau Gallie City Commission appeared on August 22, 1960, when Commissioner Vance Bell expressed concern that it had been reported that he favored consolidation of Eau Gallie and Melbourne. Bell indignantly informed the commission that such reports were inaccurate. Bell would remain an opponent of unification continuously, up to and including the consolidation of Melbourne and Eau Gallie in 1969.

Homer Denius and George Shaw, the founders of Radiation, were the most prominent and consistent proponents of municipal consolidation during the 1960s. For them, dealing with the small towns in south Brevard County was inefficient and often led to uncoordinated strategic decisions. Moreover, they saw the benefits of having a larger city with more influence in Tallahassee and Washington, D.C. They felt that their quickly growing company required a larger city to continue to progress.

The Miami Herald revealed on December 18, 1965, that Shaw had convened a meeting of 150 industrial, political, and civic leaders of south Brevard County to discuss consolidation. The meeting participants agreed to "gather preliminary information for a professional analysis of consolidation." State Representative James H. Pruitt noted that Brevard County's considerable number of small municipalities had been a joke in Tallahassee.

The Melbourne Chamber of Commerce wasted no time in endorsing "immediate action" on a "feasibility study for the possible consolidation of the community of South Brevard." In reporting the chamber's endorsement on January 19, 1966, the Orlando Evening Star noted that the chamber's resolution would have "far-reaching implications for the overall economic development of South Brevard." The Orlando Sentinel noted on January 15, 1966, that the Eau Gallie Chamber adopted a similar resolution in favor of the study, saying that the chamber was "cognizant of the fact that many complexities and duplications of services and facilities have arisen as a result of the tremendous growth which has been experienced in South Brevard." The Orlando Sentinel reported on January 28 that the "newly reorganized" West Melbourne Chamber of Commerce had joined the Melbourne and Eau Gallie chambers in endorsing the study. The Orlando Evening Star reported on February 9, 1966, that the Palm Bay Chamber had unanimously endorsed the feasibility study.

In early 1966, Radiation retained the California firm of Griffenhagen-Kroeger, Inc. Edwin O. Griffenhagen, the founder of the firm, was a consulting management engineer with experience in management and public administration. The firm was commissioned to conduct a study of the feasibility of combining the municipalities of south Brevard County into a single municipality. At that time, the populations of the municipalities in south Brevard were as follows:

City	Population by 1960 Census
Eau Gallie	12,800
Melbourne	11,892
West Melbourne	2,266
Palm Bay	2,808
Indian Harbour Beach	not available
Satellite Beach	825
Indialantic	1,653
Melbourne Beach	1,004
Melbourne Village	458
Palm Shores	not available

The consultant spent several weeks in south Brevard County, meeting with municipalities, gaining information, and conducting public meetings.

The Melbourne and Eau Gallie Chambers of Commerce were strong proponents of consolidation. An article in the Orlando Evening Star by Frank Veale published on January 19, 1966, showed that both chambers had enacted a similar resolution endorsing the idea. The resolution called for "immediate action" on a "feasibility study for the possible consolidation of the community of South Brevard." The resolution noted that a merged community of more than 100,000 people would have political influence in Tallahassee, while the current small communities lacked the "strength of voice" in governmental matters.

On August 9, 1966, the Melbourne City Commission adopted Resolution Number 57-66 endorsing the unification of municipalities in south Brevard County.

The minutes of the Eau Gallie City Commission of November 14, 1966, reflect that the report was to be presented to the South Brevard Unification Education Committee. On November 15, 1966, the *Brevard Star*, a section of the *Orlando Evening Star*, reported that the report had strongly recommended that all the municipalities in south Brevard County be consolidated. The byline of the *Brevard Star* read: "Eleven Town Metropolis Urged by Unification Report." The report concluded that consolidation of these municipalities would not only result in improved government services and coordinated development but that the merged city would have increased political weight. Griffenhagen-Kroeger concluded that: "It can be a great city, where none of the eleven is apt to achieve greatness. It can provide a better, more uniform quality of service for all people. without a net increase in total cost, with tax reductions for many and only slight tax increases to a few not now bearing a fair share of their responsibility." (See *Florida Today*, June 20, 1969). That report provided the ammunition for the unification efforts which ensued. Although the opponents of unification desperately looked to discredit the report, that was difficult to do since the firm had consulted with governments throughout the world on a variety of public policy issues

Radiation continued to promote unification and made it clear that its continued growth in South Brevard County was contingent upon it. Harold O'Kelley, a senior executive of Radiation, told an assembled group of county and municipal leaders that there were several goals which he described as "necessary for optimum growth." He went on to explain that these goals "included better roads and bridges, area-wide planning and zoning, and unification of all or parts of South Brevard." Later, during the 1969 unification referendum campaign, O'Kelley joined in the door-to-door walking campaign undertaken by proponents of unification.

The immediate controversy in 1967 related to the way the referendum would be decided. Not surprisingly, the smaller cities advocated that there should be a city-by-city vote, meaning that a city would be included in the consolidation only if a majority of the voters in that city approved. Others, including the larger cities, advocated that the question should be decided by most of the people voting in the referendum, meaning that if a majority of the voters approved consolidation, a city could be included in the merged city even if a majority of its voters had rejected the proposal. The minutes of the Eau Gallie City Council of June 26, 1967, reflect that the City of Satellite Beach was vigorously lobbying for a city-by-city vote.

The *Cocoa Tribune* reported on June 30, 1967, that the bill to allow a referendum on municipal consolidation in south Brevard County had passed the Florida Senate and would soon pass the House. The bill initially included a provision creating an airport authority with the power to levy ad valorem taxes, but that provision was cut prior to passage. On July 7, 1967, the *Evening Tribune* reported that the House had passed the bill, and that the referendum would be held November 7, 1967. Even though the Brevard legislative delegation had a split four-two vote in favor of the bill, a majority of the House approved it. The bill provided that the outcome of the referendum would be decided by a majority of all voters. The news article noted that, if approved, the resulting municipality would be the sixth largest in the State of Florida. The article went on to say that: "Business, industrial and real estate interests appear to have been lined up solidly behind the consolidation proposal."

The *Evening Tribune* reported on October 5, 1967, that the Brevard Economic Development Council had pointed out that the proposed unification would result in Brevard County becoming a Standard Metropolitan Statistical Area (SMSA), because it would have a city with a population greater than 50,000. The SMSA designation would mean that the county would be included in census data that many businesses and industries use in determining where to consider investing.

The effort to convince voters to support the unification proposal was led by Joe Wickham, long-time county commissioner and President of the Metropolitan South Brevard Chamber of Commerce in 1967. Wickham had been a key leader in combining the five chambers of commerce in 1967, with lengthy experience in working to attract state and federal support for county infrastructure needs. He realized that a larger community working in a coordinated manner would give the community more influence with state and federal agencies. Wickham had a unique ability to foresee the development of the community and to understand what was necessary to foster growth. His leadership of the unification effort was consistent with his lifelong efforts to improve south Brevard County and his position as President of the chamber insured that the chamber would play a significant role in the consolidation efforts.

Tom Moldenhauer was another important official who also assured that the chamber of commerce was committed to consolidation. Moldenhauer was Mayor of Melbourne Beach at the time and served as President of the chamber in 1969. Moldenhauer was also head of community relations at Radiation.

On November 8, 1967, the *Evening Tribune* reported that the referendum had been defeated with 9,169 votes in favor of unification and 10,299 votes opposed. The opposition prevailed primarily because of its overwhelming rejection by Satellite Beach by a 1,464 to 290 margin. Only four of the affected cities, Melbourne, Eau Gallie, Indialantic, and Palm Shores, voted in favor of the proposal. The proponents of unification were undeterred, however, and at once began to plan a renewed effort.

On April 30, 1968, *Florida Today* reported that the "campaign is on again to unify area cities." On December 3, 1968, *Florida Today* editorialized: "Before this decade is over, the people of Brevard need to create at least one city of a size that will reflect the urban character of the county."

On December 12, 1968, the City of Melbourne adopted a resolution advocating further efforts to merge municipalities in south Brevard County. On December 14, 1968, *Florida Today* published an editorial discussing a new effort at unification, this time with a city-by-city vote. The editorial concluded that, if the cities of Melbourne, Eau Gallie, Indialantic, and Palm Shores voted for unification as they did during the last vote, the result would be a city with a population of 46,400. The editorial continued: "Unification leaders, of course, hope that other towns will join. But however, many (sic) decide to make the unity plunge, they will be better off than those that vote to maintain the costly divisiveness that characterizes South Brevard now."

On January 13, 1969, the City of Eau Gallie appointed Vernon Dicks and Elting Storms to serve on a committee to prepare a charter for a unified city. This time, the cities of Satellite Beach and Indian Harbour Beach were excluded from the effort. Each included city appointed a representative to serve on the drafting group. County Commissioner (later Judge) Dick Muldrew appointed me as the representative of the unincorporated parts of the county that would be included within the new city. Vernon Dicks, an Eau Gallie city council member, was elected chair of the group and I was elected vice-chair.

After the charter drafting committee completed its work, on May 9, 1969, the city councils of both Melbourne and Eau Gallie adopted resolutions requesting the Brevard legislative delegation to authorize a referendum to approve the charter and allow consolidation of the affected cities and surrounding unincorporated areas. One of the important provisions of the proposed charter was the notion that, if Melbourne were part of the unified city, the Airport Authority would continue as a semi-autonomous entity and that the chamber of commerce would continue to appoint one of its members.

The next challenge was to persuade the legislature to authorize another referendum. This time, it was proposed to have a city-by-city vote where the voters of each city would decide whether their city would be included in the new city. Walt Southworth, Ken Allen, and I spent several days in Tallahassee working with Brevard's legislative delegation. It was a very emotional matter for many people and some of the opposition was shrill and personal. I recall one legislator who was a former City Commissioner of Cocoa Beach berating me for the provisions for issuing bonds in the proposed charter that he claimed were unfair and unprecedented. I showed him that those provisions were identical to the those in the Cocoa Beach Charter. Another member of the legislature at that time was Bill Powell who was a surveyor from Eau Gallie. Powell had read the entire proposed legislation and had even tracked the legal description of the proposed new city and was able to show me several errors that I had made. Powell became a lifelong friend. He was an unusually competent surveyor who was a walking encyclopedia of historical data about the topography of Brevard County.

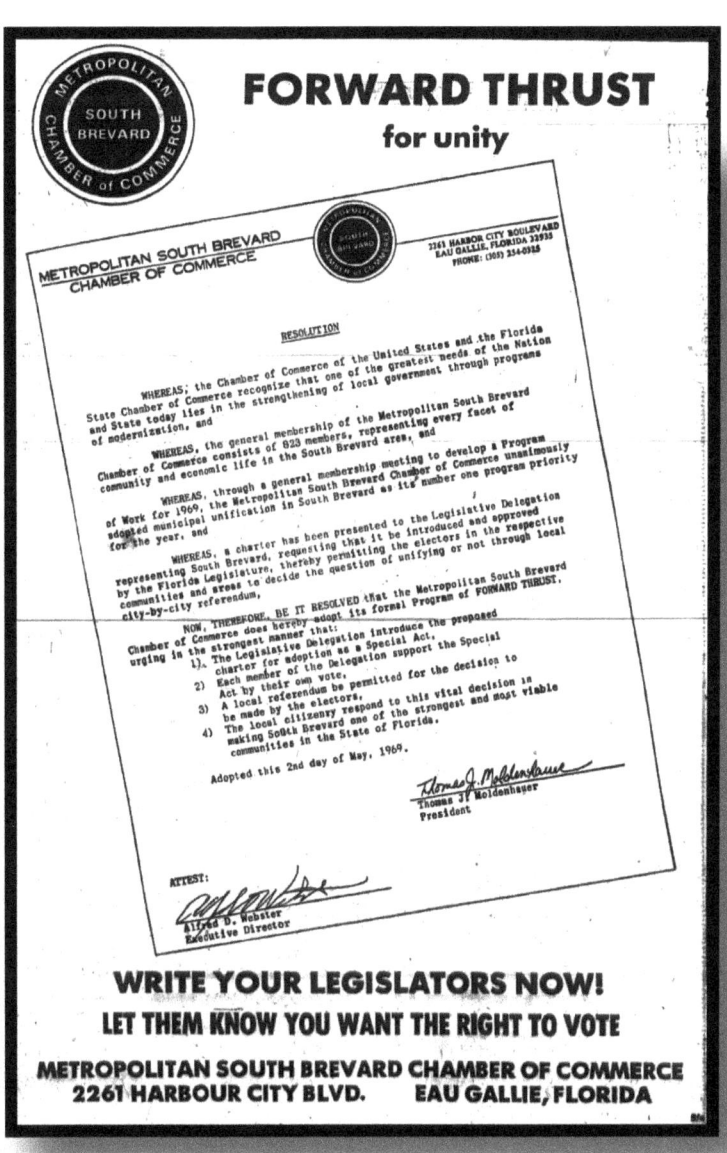

This 1969 ad sponsored by the chamber urged voters to contact their legislative representatives to urge them to support a referendum to decide whether municipalities in South Brevard would consolidate.

On May 4, 1969, the Metropolitan South Brevard Chamber of Commerce ran a large advertisement in Florida Today which was titled "Forward Thrust for Unity." The ad published a resolution adopted by the chamber on May 2 which recited that a general membership meeting of the chamber had unanimously adopted municipal consolidation as its highest priority and urged the Brevard legislative delegation to support the proposed referendum. The resolution proclaimed that a decision to consolidate would make "South Brevard one of the strongest and most viable communities in the State of Florida."

On May 13, 1969, *Florida Today* reported that the Brevard legislative delegation had agreed to introduce the bill allowing a referendum on the proposed eight city unification. An effort by Senator Beth Johnson to require the proponents to bear the cost of the referendum was included in the legislation. The bill was enacted and signed into law by Governor Kirk on May 30. 1969, thereby setting the stage for the campaign that followed.

The ensuing campaign was unusually bitter and some of the opposition tactics were a precursor to the scorched earth politics of the 21st Century. A *Florida Today* article on July 5, 1969, ten days prior to the referendum scheduled for July 15, appeared under the byline "Emotionalism due to increase as unification voting nears." The article described the tactics being used by opponents of unification. A Melbourne Beach activist circulated a campaign piece which purported to present the districts of the proposed new city and showed that Melbourne Beach would be in the same district as the African American area of Melbourne. When I told the newspaper that I considered this to be an appeal to racism, the activist called me at home and self-righteously proclaimed that it had nothing to do with race. Of course, it was all about racism. I also recall giving a speech in Palm Bay and having to have a police escort to leave the building due to threats of physical harm from the audience.

The most prominent and outspoken proponent of unification was the former airport director Ken Allen. Ken had left the airport to pursue personal business interests but had been elected as the Mayor of Melbourne in 1968. He pulled no punches in his mayoral campaign and made it clear that his motivation in running for mayor was to bring about municipal consolidation in south Brevard County. *Florida Today* reported on June 17, 1969, that "To Ken Allen, unification is a life-or-death fight. A battle for the economic and social survival of the area he helps lead." The newspaper noted that "Ken Allen has sapped himself financially and in every other way struggling for what he unequivocally (sic) believes will launch South Brevard into a new era: Unification."

Walt Southworth was the President of Operation Unity, Inc. (OUI), the primary group advocating for municipal consolidation. Walt was the Executive Director of the Y.M.C.A. in Brevard County and devoted tireless efforts to the unification effort. Florida Today reported on June 20, 1969, that Southworth guaranteed that a unified city could provide improved infrastructure and services.

After that bitter campaign, the referendum was only partially successful. Melbourne and Eau Gallie, the two largest cities, agreed to combine. The vote in Melbourne was 1,670 in favor and 374 against. In Eau Gallie, 1,620 voted for unification while 1,206 voted against. The effort failed in Palm Bay by 54 votes and in West Melbourne by 14 votes. Many believe that the consolidation of Melbourne and Eau Gallie has been essential to the economic growth and development that has occurred in the ensuing years. It is probable that without that consolidation, Harris would not have moved its headquarters to Melbourne, Grumman would not have established at the airport and Rockwell Collins would not have chosen to locate here. It was not surprising that the beachside cities did not want to join but the narrow losses in Palm Bay and West Melbourne were regrettable. Palm Bay has experienced spectacular growth, but that growth has brought many problems. Palm Bay has often experienced ineffective and sometimes corrupt government. If Palm Bay had been a part of the merged city, a lot of those problems might have been avoided. Although West Melbourne has not had all the same problems, it suffered for many years since it had no general ad valorem taxation and relied for revenue primarily on building fees. That caused West Melbourne to approve subdivision densities that resulted in demands for infrastructure that could not be supported by the tax base. It is possible that West Melbourne would have developed in a more orderly and sustainable manner had it joined the new city.

The narrow defeat of the proposal in Palm Bay was particularly vexing. Palm Bay had two precincts, one in Port Malabar and the other in the older section of the city. The proposed unification carried in Port Malabar but was soundly defeated in the older section. *Florida Today* reported on August 11, 1969, that officials of Radiation and General Development, the two largest businesses in Palm Bay, were exploring the possibility of separating Port Malabar from Palm Bay. The President of the homeowner's association in Port Malabar was quoted as viewing such a move positively.

Even though the referendum was only partially successful, the consolidation of Melbourne and Eau Gallie has been a remarkable success. The development of south Brevard's economic base, which is envied throughout the state and nation, would not have occurred without consolidation. The consolidated city has had the most stable and effective government in the county since the consolidation occurred. It is no accident that Melbourne has had such success in attracting aerospace and defense companies to the area.

There is one aspect of the consolidation that was a mistake. Following the vote to merge Melbourne and Eau Gallie, a committee was formed to recommend names for the new city as called for in the new city's charter. This group proposed five names to be considered by the voters: Melbourne, Eau Gallie, Harbor City, Brevard City and Riverside. The votes were reported in *Florida Today* on November 5, 1969, as follows: Melbourne 2,902, Eau Gallie 721, Harbor City 1,973, Brevard City 119 and Riverside 250. When the voters selected the name Melbourne, it created ill feelings that have persisted for many years. A new name would have made many people more accepting of the unified city. W. Lansing Gleason was a long-time civic leader and mayor of Eau Gallie. He was an influential leader of the unification movement. He said that "It would have been better to have a completely new name. Melbourne and Eau Gallie each has its own identity and sense of history. With the choosing of the name 'Melbourne,' that city's history has been imposed upon Eau Gallie." Even now, more than fifty years after unification, those sentiments ring true for some citizens.

The Metropolitan South Brevard Chamber of Commerce was a vital cog in the effort to unify South Brevard. Florida Today recognized that in an editorial on December 21, 1969, when it wrote: "The Metropolitan South Brevard Chamber of Commerce has been the most unifying influence in the area for the past couple of years. Its efforts were responsible for bringing Melbourne and Eau Gallie together. And it has been eminently successful in creating an atmosphere that encourages new business and industry and the expansion of existing firms. Without the chamber, in short, South Brevard simply would not be the prosperous, united community it is today."

CHAPTER NOTES

- The population data is from the Census of Population and Housing of the Bureau of Census of the U.S. Department of Commerce and can be found at Census.gov.
- The quotes from Harold O'Kelley are taken from *High Tech Among the Palmettos*, The *Story of Radiation, Inc., and How It Changed the Face of South Brevard County*, by Frank Perkins, ibid, at page 121.
- For discussion of the attempts to unify, see *A Tribute to Melbourne's Pioneers*, ibid, at pages 203 to 205.
- The quote from W. Lansing Gleason is taken from *Crossroad Towns Remembered: A Look Back at Brevard and Indian River Pioneer Communities,* by Weona Cleveland, ibid, page 149.
- All citations related to the meetings of the governing bodies of the cities of Melbourne and Eau Gallie are derived from either a review of the official minutes of those bodies or from a summation of those minutes prepared by Cathleen Wysor, who was city clerk of the Melbourne from 1994 to 2020. Both the minutes and Wysor's summary were provided to the authors by Kevin McKeown, the current city clerk of Melbourne.
- For further information about the merger of Melbourne and Eau Gallie see "Melbourne Orlando International Airport: A History from 1928 to 2022, "ibid.

CHAPTER SIX
The Consolidated Chamber Flexes its Muscles: 1969 To 1978

This public service announcement by Florida Today was published in support of the 1974 membership drive of the Melbourne Area Chamber of Commerce.

The increased influence of South Brevard's Chamber of Commerce's consolidation became readily clear. The Orlando Sentinel reported on May 24, 1969, that W. D. Webb, immediate past chair of the Metropolitan South Brevard Chamber of Commerce, had been appointed to the Board of Directors of the Florida State Chamber of Commerce, a clear sign that the new chamber was recognized as a significant actor at the state level. The news article also showed that Webb would serve as president of the East Central Florida Council of Chambers of Commerce, an organization that included presidents and executive managers of 35 Central Florida chambers of commerce. South Brevard was now playing in the chamber big leagues.

On December 2, 1969, The Miami Herald reported that the newly merged chamber was looking for an office nearer to the center of the newly combined city. The chamber's offices at the time were north of the Eau Gallie business district. The same news report said that the chamber would also soon consider changing its name to the Melbourne Area Chamber of Commerce to mirror the name of the new city. The chamber further disclosed to The Orlando Sentinel on December 5, 1969, that it would begin using "The Space Coast" as the official designation for Brevard County. This resulted from the fact that the state tourism office had divided the state into 12 areas for tourism promotion, giving Brevard County is own area and dubbing it "The Space Coast." That designation has continued for the ensuing 54 years.

The effectiveness of the newly combined chamber and city was the subject of some controversy, as shown by a news article in The Miami Herald on December 14, 1969. County Tax Assessor Clark Maxwell, Sr., it was reported, criticized the south Chamber of Commerce for boasting about the economic prosperity occurring in South Brevard at a time when the rest of the county was suffering economically because of cutbacks at the Space Center. Chamber President Beville Outlaw responded to Maxwell by saying: "The truth of the matter is that the picture in South Brevard is far better than the rest of the county. We should not be criticized for making the information available to residents and potential visitors." A couple of weeks later, on December 30, 1969, the Orlando Evening Star reported that the chamber was planning a movement to almost double its staff to eight members and increase services proportionately. The article also disclosed that the vote on a new name for the chamber would take place on January 9, 1970.

Betty Shepard wrote in the Orlando Evening Star on January 8, 1970, that the chamber was leading a "swelling tide" of support for the widening of U.S. 192 between Indialantic and Disney World. The article noted that Governor Claude Kirk, campaigning for re-election as the first Republican governor in Florida since Reconstruction, would be visiting the area in a few weeks, and business leaders would use the opportunity to promote the 192 expansion.

The Orlando Evening Star reported on January 14 that the proposed change of name for the chamber had passed unanimously. President Beville Outlaw promised "increased cooperation with the new city of Melbourne which the chamber worked to help create."

Florida Today reported on March 19, 1970, that the newly renamed Melbourne Area Chamber of Commerce would temporarily move to the east end of a building occupied by the First Federal Savings and Loan Association of Indian River County. This building was on the corner of U.S. 1 and Eau Gallie Boulevard on the east side of U.S. 1 between the eastbound and westbound lanes of Eau Gallie Boulevard. The building still stands today after many use changes following the demise of the savings and loan. A report in The Orlando Sentinel on March 19, 1970, affirmed that this was an interim move and that the chamber sought a permanent home.

The Orlando Sentinel issue of April 24, 1970, discussed another issue that would occupy the efforts of the Melbourne Area Chamber for many years. The chamber had led a local effort to cause a veteran's hospital to be built in South Brevard. The chamber, collaborating with Congressman Lou Frey, made a presentation at a hearing on the subject conducted by Congressman James Haley of Sarasota. Melbourne Mayor Adger Smith commended the chamber for "a splendid job on short notice" in making the presentation.

The chamber's aggressive actions continued to result in expansion and increasing influence. Florida Today reported on October 15,

1970, that the Melbourne Area Chamber of Commerce now had 540 business memberships.

The Melbourne Area Chamber undertook a newly invigorated effort to promote industrial development. Florida Today reported on April 15, 1971, that the chamber intended to raise $50,000 per year for the next three years to set up an industrial development department. The chamber pledged that its efforts would complement rather than conflict with those of the Brevard Economic Development Council, the county-funded agency charged with promoting industrial development.

The chamber newsletter of September 1971 (Vol. 2, No. 8) announced that the chamber's third annual Program of Work Retreat would be held in Freeport, Bahamas, from October 7 to 11. Shawnee Airlines would provide direct flights from Melbourne to Freeport. Even customs service in Melbourne would be provided.

The chamber's newly invigorated industrial development efforts kicked off with a meeting reported by Florida Today on October 2, 1971. Former Melbourne mayor Adger Smith was elected as chair of the Melbourne Area Committee of 100. The meeting showed that an agreement between the chamber and the Brevard Economic Development Council would result in Fran Tunstall, an employee of the council, acting in a dual role as manager of the chamber's new industrial development department. Later that year, The Orlando Sentinel would report on October 17, 1972, that Howard N. Hebert had been chosen to succeed Smith as chair.

On January 23, 1972, The Miami Herald reported that the chamber had set up several "special committees" to address organizational and management issues. Reidy A. Williams would head a committee to study the effectiveness of the services that the chamber provided to its members. The facilities committee, chaired by chamber president Howard Hebert, would seek a site for a permanent chamber building.

This newsletter of the Melbourne Area Chamber, published in September 1971, included a report of Congressman Lou Frey's visit to the chamber.

A significant effort undertaken by the chamber was reported in The Orlando Sentinel on April 9, 1972. The U.S. Air Force had decided to move a significant operation from Alexandria, Virginia, to Patrick Air Force Base. That operation, the Air Force Technical Applications Center, had a primary mission of monitoring nuclear testing around the globe and included more than 600 personnel. The center has remained in the community for over 50 years, performing its vital function. The Melbourne Area Chamber and other community groups traveled to Alexandria to welcome the group and aid its personnel in the logistics of the move. County Commissioner Hugh Evans led the county group while Al Webster took on most of the organizational tasks. I took part as chair of the Brevard Economic Development Council. It is indeed gratifying that the center is still a vital part of our community these many years later.

An article in the Orlando Evening Star on January 10, 1973, described the Melbourne Area Chamber's priorities for 1973, which were established based on a survey of its membership. Not surprisingly, roads and bridges topped the list. Unexpectedly, however, water resources were the next priority. Traffic safety, mass transportation, and industrial development were also high-priority issues. Tourism ranked only 10th. The news article noted that most of the chamber's "1,000-plus members" participated in the survey.

The chamber also renewed its efforts in consumer affairs matters. On March 18, 1973, the Orlando Sentinel reported that the chamber and its Better Business Division were processing about 100 consumer complaints per month.

Highway 192 continued to be at the top of the chamber's priorities. Florida Today reported on May 19, 1973, that a chamber delegation would meet with Governor Reuben Askew, Department of Transportation officials, and the local legislative delegation to discuss the matter. President Orlando Brillante would lead the delegation, joined by Executive Director Al Webster and Tom Moldenhauer of Harris Corporation, together with Gloria Biggs and Jim Jesse from Gannett Florida Corporation. I would join them as chamber president-elect. We had all been careful during the 1970 gubernatorial race between Askew and incumbent Claude Kirk to obtain pledges from each candidate about prioritizing 192. Brillante had worked on Askew's campaign for such a commitment while I had secured Kirk's support for the road. Imagine Brillante's surprise when he began to discuss the road and was at once cut off by the Governor, who heatedly protested that he was the first governor in history to be elected without a single promise regarding roads. The Orlando Sentinel issue of May 23 described the Governor as "visibly angered" by a statement by Orlando Brillante, president of the Melbourne Area Chamber of Commerce, that he had pledged new spans and four-laning." The Florida Today article of May 23 described how the Governor "visibly bristled" as he interrupted Brillante. To his credit, Brillante did not back down but continued to describe the meeting he had attended wherein Askew had discussed the road. Overall, it was not the kind of meeting you hoped to have with your governor.

The chamber's search for a permanent office led to the announcement in The Miami Herald on July 7, 1973, that the chamber and the Melbourne Area Board of Realtors had formed a corporation to buy the old A&P grocery store on Strawbridge Avenue in downtown Melbourne. Chamber Executive Director Al Webster said that the building was about 9,000 square feet, cost about $150,000, and would require renovations costing about $50,000. The news article stated that First National Bank of Melbourne had bought several buildings in the area, some for demolition and others for renovation. The article was mistaken in that it was the National Bank of Melbourne and Trust Company which was buying buildings in the area. I acted as trustee in these purchases in a futile effort to avoid a frenzy that would inflate prices. My hand in the process was also clear from the name I chose for the corporation set up by the chamber and the Board of Realtors, Melbourne Area Building Corporation, a demonstration of my complete lack of creativity.

The 1974 goals for the Melbourne Area Chamber of Commerce were reported in Florida Today on October 30, 1973, and in the Chamber Newsletter of November 1973. The six most urgent goals were established during a planning retreat conducted by chamber leadership during a weekend cruise to Nassau in October 1973. The chamber goals included a continued emphasis on improving U.S. 192 and water resources. Other goals included mass transportation, land use, industrial siting, and governmental organization. Following the planning retreat, the chamber surveyed its more than 800 members to determine their priorities. As reported by Chris Schausel in the Melbourne Times on December 10, 1973, governmental inefficiency and land use were among the top issues cited by the poll. Tom Myers, Business Editor of Florida Today, reported on December 14, 1973, that chamber members had been challenged to "defend our economic and political system."

Florida Today reported on February 1, 1974, that the chamber and Board of Realtors would begin moving into their newly renovated building on February 4 and 5. What was not shown in the news article was that cost overruns in the renovation of the building had created a budgetary crisis for the chamber. At the end of 1973, as I prepared to assume leadership of the chamber board, I discovered that the funds that had been allocated for the renovation of the building had been exhausted, and much work remained undone. We were able to borrow more funds to complete the work but the expense of serving the added debt would require the chamber to make substantial cuts in other expenses. Unfortunately, after analyzing the budget, Al Webster and I concluded that the only expense that could be cut that would be sufficient to offset the debt service was his salary. Al was, I think, embarrassed that the cost overruns had occurred and wanted to atone by resigning so that the chamber would be relieved of his salary. Al was beginning to experience health issues. Florida Today reported on July 31, 1974, that Webster had resigned as of August 15. Al Webster had been a highly effective chamber executive, leading the chamber through the consolidation of four chambers and the explosion in membership growth. Webster had headed the chamber since 1967 when the chambers merged and had been a leader in the effort which resulted in the merger of Eau Gallie and Melbourne. Florida Today quoted me as saying: "The chamber and the entire community are deeply indebted to him for his service. His knowledge and experience cannot be replaced." The chamber newsletter of August 1974, said: "It is fair to say that those things the Chamber has carried out would not have been accomplished without Al. The things that Al has put in motion will have a positive effect on Melbourne for many years to come. The Melbourne area should be grateful that Al Webster contributed his talents to the community." Tragically, Webster would not have much opportunity to enjoy retirement as he died of a heart attack on January 18, 1975. He was only 61 years old at the time of his death. Bob Bandy, Webster's assistant, would manage the day-to-day chamber operations, but would not be given the title of executive director.

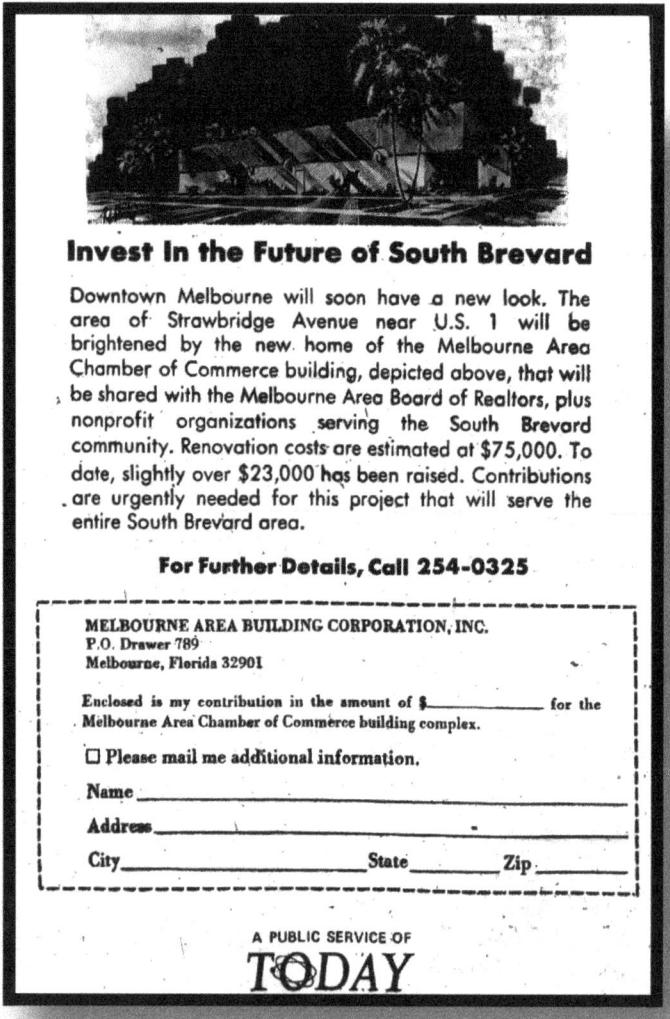

This advertisement in Florida Today on December 26, 1973, solicited funds for the renovation of the newly acquired chamber office building.

This article in Florida Today on December 27, 1973, described the renovations for the newly acquired offices of the chamber Florida Today reported on March 29, 1974, that the chamber had formed a water resources committee to address issues regarding potable water needs in south Brevard. In particular, the committee would look at the environmental impact of building a low-level dam in Lake Washington, as well as the need for buffer-land around the lake. The committee also acknowledged the newly created St. Johns Water Management District and the need for representation on the district board. Many of the recommendations of the committee, including the dam construction and establishment of buffer zones around Lake Washington were adopted.

To further its goal of promoting governmental efficiency, the chamber informed The Orlando Sentinel on April 19, 1974, that it would begin to identify areas of duplication of services by municipal and county government. Initial areas to be analyzed would include law enforcement, recreation, libraries, and fire protection. The study resulted in several recommendations which were adopted.

The May 10, 1974, newsletter of the chamber illustrated that the chamber was not ducking controversial public issues. The newsletter showed that the chamber had recently endorsed the proposed transfer of jai alai from Daytona Beach to Melbourne. The introduction of parimutuel gambling in Brevard County raised many emotions on both sides of the issue. The chamber board considered whether it should remain out of the issue but, in the end, decided that it should voice a view.

This news article in 1974 reports the visit of U.S. Senator (later Governor) Lawton Chiles' visit to the Melbourne Area Chamber. The visit occurred shortly after the chamber had moved into its new headquarters on Strawbridge Avenue.

The chamber's willingness to assert its views on controversial matters was again illustrated in an article by Jackie Reid in the Melbourne Times on March 18, 1974, that disclosed that the chamber would resist any efforts by the City of Melbourne to reduce the powers of the Melbourne Airport Authority. The mayor and one of the council members objected to a lease entered by the authority and reacted by suggesting that the airport should be brought under the control of the city. The chamber at once reacted in opposition to such a change and informed the city that any such move would "meet with firm resistance from the business community." As chair of the chamber, I stated: "If we get into the position where rentals are being set, leases and contracts are being negotiated based on politics, we will be back in the same boat we were in six years ago, and on the FAA blacklist."

Florida Today reported on May 19, 1974, in an article by Patsy Palmer, that a 20-person delegation from the chamber had returned from Tallahassee following a meeting with Secretary of Transportation Walter Revell and that it had been a "highly successful trip." Not surprisingly, the trip focused on expansion of the causeway and improvement of U.S. 192. Revell reported to the group that 192 rights-of-way would be acquired in 1975-76 and construction would begin in FY 1977-78. Right-of-way for the causeway would be achieved by September 1974 and construction bids would be reviewed in November 1974.

Chamber membership continued to grow. Florida Today reported on May 29, 1974, that the chamber's recent membership drive picked up 80 new members, taking the total membership past the 700-member mark.

The retreat to determine chamber goals for 1975 was held in New Falmouth, Jamaica. Among the goals created at that meeting were hiring a tourism and convention coordinator and ramping up efforts at downtown redevelopment.

On January 25, 1975, The Orlando Sentinel disclosed that the Melbourne Area Chamber of Commerce would celebrate its 50th anniversary at its annual dinner on January 25. As discussed earlier in this book, that anniversary celebration was proper only if one assumed that the chamber had not been founded until it was formally incorporated and a permanent, full-time executive director hired. To be correct, both the Melbourne chamber and the Eau Gallie chamber, being two of the progenitors of the Melbourne Area Chamber, had been active and effective several years prior to 1925.

Writing in The Orlando Sentinel on September 27, 1975, Sentinel reporter Hubert Griggs presented momentous news for the chamber. Griggs reported that money had been received by the Florida Department of Transportation from the Federal Highway Administration for the Melbourne Causeway bridge and widening project that would enable bids to be solicited by the end of the following week, with construction to begin with 90 days thereafter. For the Melbourne Area Chamber of Commerce, this announcement was the culmination of many years of tireless work. It is safe to say that in the history of the chamber, no single project has occupied more time, energy, and attention. The chamber used every weapon in its arsenal and enlisted the aid of anyone who could help, including governors, senators, congresspeople, state representatives, administrators, and local officials. The goals seemed within reach.

The 1975 chamber agenda also included efforts not related to transportation projects. On November 4, 1975, Florida Today reported that the Melbourne Area Chamber had teamed with the Brevard Public Schools to offer Brevard teachers a 5-week "adventures in business" program. Up to 50 Brevard teachers would attend a day-long class once each week for five consecutive weeks to "better understand why and how the free enterprise system works as it does."

Bob Bandy's departure as manager of the chamber was reported in The Orlando Sentinel on January 10, 1976. Bob had filled the role of manager while the board allowed the position of Executive Director to remain unfilled as a cost-saving measure. Although he had no prior experience as a chamber executive, Bob was a diligent worker with an engaging personality that made him an effective manager. He was reluctant to start programs on his own due to his interim status, but he conducted the board's initiatives well. Bob had been in radio work for much of his career and left the chamber to become the news director for a local radio station. With Bob's departure, it became imperative for the board to recruit a new Executive Director with alacrity and a committee was formed to conduct a national search to fill the position.

The year 1976 was, of course, the bicentennial for the United States. The chamber and the Melbourne Area Board of Realtors jointly undertook leadership of a program to celebrate this occasion. Florida Today reported on February 2, 1976, that the group had bought a 2,000-pound replica of the Liberty Bell which had been made by the same English foundry that cast the original bell. They persuaded the city to donate land west of the civic auditorium upon which a building to house the bell would be constructed. This committee eventually became an independent organization and incorporated as "Honor America, Inc." The Liberty Bell Museum that exists on that property today is the outgrowth of that chamber-led project.

On March 2, 1976, Florida Today reported that Eugene W. Patterson had been hired as chief executive of the Melbourne Area Chamber of Commerce with the title of executive vice-president. At the time, Patterson was serving as chief executive of the Meadville, Pennsylvania Chamber of Commerce. Patterson would serve the Melbourne Chamber for less than 2 years.

One of the initiatives undertaken by Patterson soon after assuming his role was the establishment of a tourism division. Florida Today reported on October 23, 1976, that Patterson would seek funds from the state Department of Tourism which would be matched by locally raised funds to set up the new division. He said that the tourism division would be a "semi-autonomous" arm of the chamber, like the Committee of 100, which was implemented to foster industrial development.

Another interesting issue tackled by the chamber during Patterson's tenure related to telephone service within Brevard County. At that time, a call from Melbourne to central or north Brevard was a long-distance call, requiring payment of a toll. Even though the cost was modest, it undoubtedly inhibited commerce between the geographic areas of the county. The Titusville and Melbourne chambers each adopted resolutions asking the Florida Public Service Commission to examine the economic feasibility of toll-free telephone service in the county. Florida Today reported on March 17, 1977, that more than 2,200 letters had already been received by the commission supporting such telephone service. The effort proved successful shortly after the request was made.

Florida Today showed on May 14, 1977, that the Melbourne Area Chamber of Commerce was undertaking a four-day membership drive. Patterson announced that the chamber presently had 650 members and had a goal of 1,000 members by the end of 1977.

Another significant issue being debated during 1977 was a bill in the state legislature that would allow counties to hold a referendum to decide whether a tax would be levied on hotel and motel bills, the revenues from which would be used for tourism promotion. Florida Today reported on June 1, 1977, that the Melbourne Area Chamber had endorsed the resort tax proposal, although several local hotel owners opposed it. Brevard's State Senator John Vogt said:" It's a relatively painless way to do a lot of good." The legislature then authorized the tax, Brevard County citizens held a referendum and approved the levy, and millions of dollars have been raised by the tax in the ensuing years. As the permissible uses of those revenues have been expanded over time, the county has reaped innumerable benefits for a wide variety of public needs.

Florida Today reported on September 3, 1977, that chamber president Davey Jones announced that Dictaphone Corporation had decided to build a large manufacturing facility in Melbourne. That announcement came only a few weeks after an announcement by Harris Corporation that it planned to move its world headquarters from Cleveland to Melbourne. Jones commented: "We can show them what we think is a great place to operate, but it is up to them to decide." He added: "It's the kind of activity that fits in with our area."

Gene Patterson's tenure as executive vice-president of the Melbourne Area Chamber ended in January 1978. Florida Today reported on January 19 that Patterson had resigned at the request of the executive committee. Chamber president Lanny Mauldin acknowledged that Patterson was an excellent administrator but saw that the chamber wanted to find a person "more public relations minded and more aggressive in making outside contacts." Mauldin's analysis is quite fair, and Patterson was, indeed, a competent administrator who was limited by his bland personality. Patterson's resignation resulted in the formation of a search committee that asked for applications from around the country and culminated a few months later with the selection of an executive who would raise the chamber to a new level of stability and influence.

A memorable event for the Melbourne chamber occurred on February 7, 1978, with the dedication of the new Melbourne Causeway. In announcing the dedication ceremony, Florida Today's issue of January 22 related that chamber president Lanny Mauldin advocated that the bridge be named for Ernest Kouwen-Hoven, who had constructed the original wooden bridge in 1920.

CHAPTER SEVEN

The Strawbridge Years: 1978 until 1988

William G. (Doc) Strawbridge was chamber president from 1978 to 1988. He led the organization to its accreditation by the U.S. Chamber of Commerce

The Orlando Sentinel reported on April 27, 1978, that William "Doc" Strawbridge had been selected as executive vice president of the Melbourne Area Chamber of Commerce. The news article related that Strawbridge had been selected by a 10-member search committee that had reviewed more than 180 applications and interviewed 16 of the applicants. I can attest as a member of the selection committee that Strawbridge was clearly the strongest candidate and the committee was unanimous in its recommendation. Strawbridge had been a successful businessman in Michigan prior to moving to Florida, where he became marketing director for the chamber of commerce in Pompano Beach. He was articulate with strong opinions but, at the same time, a good listener who valued the opinions expressed by others. As a former business owner, he was fiscally conservative and aware of the need to keep the chamber in sound financial condition. He was 52 years old at the time of his appointment.

Contrary to local legend, Strawbridge Avenue was not named after Doc. It existed long before Doc came to Brevard County, and no connection between Doc and the person for whom the street was named was ever discovered.

Immediately upon assuming his new responsibilities, Strawbridge, with the acumen and philosophy of a former business owner, undertook a goal for the chamber to establish cash reserves to fund a year's operating expenses. Although businesses often use such metrics to gauge their financial stability, it seemed a fantasy for the chamber to pursue such a goal. Nevertheless, within a brief time of assuming his new role, Strawbridge had achieved financial stability and kept such cash balances throughout his term of office.

Strawbridge hit the ground running at full speed. He began work on June 1. He wasted no time in assessing his new community. On August 17, he told The Orlando Sentinel that south Brevard's economy was "just terrific" and noted that "the strong foundation for the continuing growth is the increasing movement of electronics firms and other clean industries attracted in part by a highly trained technical labor pool of former space industry employees." On October 27, 1978, The Bradenton Herald reported that Strawbridge had boasted that south Brevard had attracted the corporate headquarters of Harris, as well as new facilities by Collins Radio, Documation, and Dictaphone. Strawbridge explained: "We have availability of good industrial property, a regional airport, we are midway between Jacksonville and Miami, and we have a tremendous community spirit." He noted: "You sense in the people here a feeling about doing things right."

Transportation needs were at the top of the chamber's agenda under Doc's leadership. Florida Today reported on January 31, 1979, that the chamber's transportation committee had developed a strategy to attack the funding problems delaying major road projects. First, the committee would ask executives of the largest employers in south Brevard to seek a personal meeting with Governor Bob Graham to convince him to help with the widening of Babcock Street and Eau Gallie Boulevard. Secondly, the committee would ask the Brevard County Commission to consider a bond issue to provide more funding for road needs. Florida Today reported further on May 9 that the Melbourne Area Chamber of Commerce was circulating two petitions addressed to the county commission and the State Department of Transportation. The petition to the commission urged the widening of Babcock Street south of 192 and the four-laning of Wickham Road north of 192. The petition to the state addressed the need to hasten the construction of high-rise bridges for the Melbourne and Eau Gallie causeways and to widen 192 through Melbourne and West Melbourne. The news article revealed that a chamber delegation had visited Tallahassee the previous month to promote these road needs. The chamber had also printed and distributed 3,000 copies of flyers titled "Tired of Crowded Roads?" The news article quoted Strawbridge as saying: "We see the chamber of commerce as the action arm of the community. We are the one catalyst outside of government that can get things done."

For many years, the chamber's efforts to improve transportation in the county were led by Clifton McClelland, Jr., a Melbourne attorney and my law partner for over 25 years. Clif had gained an extraordinary knowledge of the issues relating to roads, bridges, and transportation matters by standing for Brevard County on such matters during the years that our law firm represented the county.

He brought all that knowledge and experience to his role of chair of the chamber Roads and Transportation Committee. Clif described the committee's work as follows: "As Chairman of the Road and Transportation Committee (or later Infrastructure Committee), we lobbied for and supported the four lanes for the Causeways with the fly-over bridges; the construction of Eau Gallie Blvd; the widening of Babcock Street; expanding the lanes on 192 through Melbourne to the Osceola County line; installing six lanes for US 1 in Melbourne; providing four lanes on Wickham Road; the Aurora Road widening; the extension of Pineda from Wickham Road to I-95, and the St Johns Heritage Parkway."

Clif further explained: "A major transportation project requires planning and right of way alignment, public hearings, environmental permitting, right of way acquisition, preparation of construction plans and specifications, public bidding and contracting, construction, and construction inspection before final acceptance of the project. Each phase requires public funding. It can take 15 to 20 years between the time a project is conceived and the public rides on the road. There is a federal requirement that all major transportation projects must be approved by the metropolitan planning organization. In Brevard, this organization was called the Brevard Metropolitan Planning Organization (MPO), now known as the Space Coast Transportation Planning Organization."

An editorial in Florida Today on May 13, 1979, noted: "The history of the Melbourne Area Chamber of Commerce reflects, in many ways, the history of South Brevard itself." The editorial quoted Strawbridge as saying" "Our predecessors have done well giving us a plan and an economic base on which to build. We must now fine-tune our inheritance." The editorial noted that the chamber had created an impressive list of goals for the ensuing year, including greater support from governmental agencies in the development and reconstruction of roads and bridges, attracting more air carriers to the Melbourne Regional Airport, and continued solicitation of new industries to the area.

The chamber's leadership in the business community was recognized when Lanny Mauldin, immediate past chair of the chamber, was selected to represent the county at a White House Conference on Small Business. Florida Today reported on June 29, 1979, that, in preparation for the conference, the Melbourne chamber would host a meeting to discuss matters including governmental regulation, inflation, women in business, economic development policy, and government programs.

Bill Gray, Florida Department of Transportation project engineer, met with the chamber's transportation committee on July 30, 1979. As reported in Florida Today the following day, his report was quite positive. He reported progress on the widening and rerouting of U.S. 192, widening of the Eau Gallie Causeway, extension of Eau Gallie Boulevard, and the construction of a second high-rise span on the Melbourne Causeway. Although the news article discussed the disruption of traffic that was occurring because of these construction projects, it also confirmed the chamber's efforts to promote these transportation projects over many years. The optimism of Gray's report would be tempered, however, by a Florida Today article of February 27, 1980, which guessed that these projects would be set back by declining gas tax revenues at both the state and local level. Clif McClelland, chair of the chamber's Road and Bridge Committee, noted that gas sales for 1979 in Brevard County were four million gallons less than the previous year.

Melbourne celebrated its 100th birthday in 1980 and the chamber took the lead in organizing the celebrations, noting this milestone. Florida Today reported on January 23, 1980, that Doc Strawbridge had described a few events being planned to occur from mid-June until July 6 which would recognize the city's birthday. In addition to a fair, a parade of homes, fireworks and an interdenominational sunrise service, the chamber and its centennial committee would publish a book of the city's history.

The breadth of the chamber's activities was illustrated by an article in The Orlando Sentinel on January 27, 1980, which described a seminar to be conducted by the Business Education Committee of the chamber. The seminar would cover subjects as varied as targeted jobs, tax credits and tax law changes for small businesses.

Florida Today published a piece about Doc on May 10, 1981, which showed that the chamber had organized its industrial development efforts under two groups: The Melbourne Area Committee of 100 and the Major Industry Council. As Strawbridge explained it, the Committee of 100 would try to recruit new companies to the area while also dealing with problems facing existing employers. The Major Industry Council was limited to companies that employed more than 100 people and would deal with issues unique to those businesses. The news article noted that: "The Melbourne area has gained a reputation as one of the most attractive spots for new industry in the South."

The Orlando Sentinel noted on January 26, 1982, that construction of the second high-rise span of the Melbourne causeway was slated to begin in October of that year. District engineer William Gray gave that report at a meeting of the Melbourne Area Chamber.

On March 5, 1982, Florida Today reported that the Melbourne Area Chamber had instituted an arbitration board designed to resolve disputes between businesses and customers. Strawbridge noted that the chamber had received 1,900 telephone complaints about local merchants the previous year. He described the arbitration process as one that would protect businesses from unwarranted complaints while protecting customers from unethical practices.

On September 18, 1982, The Orlando Sentinel published contiguous announcements that illustrated the breadth and variety of the Melbourne Area Chamber programs. One announcement disclosed that the chamber would be sponsoring a seminar in conjunction with the Florida Department of Commerce and U.S. Department of Commerce designed to educate businesses on how to conduct international trade from Florida. Immediately below that announcement was a disclosure that the chamber was sponsoring a fashion show featuring men's and women's wear from a dozen area stores.

Another issue which stirred some controversy in 1982 had to do with the proposed development by Brevard Community College of a technical and vocational training center in the Melbourne-Palm Bay area. Representatives of Florida Tech and the Melbourne Area

Chamber put forth the idea of a joint BCC-FIT campus for such a center. Florida Today reported on October 21, 1982, that BCC was less than enthusiastic about such a joint venture. Although the idea was discussed for several months, BCC constructed the center at what is presently its Palm Bay campus.

Florida Today reported on November 5, 1982, that the chamber had changed its name to the Chamber of Commerce of South Brevard, despite opposition to the name from the Melbourne City Council and the Palm Bay Area Chamber of Commerce. The city councils of West Melbourne, Satellite Beach and Indian Harbour Beach all supported the change.

In 1983, a plan was put forth by a transportation consultant for Brevard County to construct a high-rise bridge from Malabar to the south beaches. As reported in Florida Today on May 26, 1983, the chamber's recently formed South Brevard Coordinating Council reviewed and considered the proposal. The chamber group unanimously endorsed the plan. This idea has never been pursued although it is periodically resurrected and always engenders a lively discussion.

Florida Today reported on July 23, 1983, that Strawbridge had completed a course at the Institute of Organizational Management at the University of Georgia. The course was sponsored by the U.S. Chamber of Commerce.

A significant chamber achievement was revealed in an article in the Vero Beach Press on November 23, 1983, which stated that the Pittsburgh Maulers of the United States Football League had decided that their training camp would be held at Florida Tech. The chamber and Florida Tech had worked together to entice the team to come to Melbourne. Not only would the Maulers train there, but they also committed to play at least two exhibition games in the county. For Florida Tech, it was an even bigger win because revenue from the Maulers would be used to construct more facilities in its gymnasium, facilities that would be available to the university when the Maulers were not training. The excitement surrounding the Maulers rose even higher when Florida Today revealed on January 10, 1984, that Mike Rozier, Heisman Trophy winner the previous year, had signed with the Maulers. The Maulers did train and play exhibitions in Melbourne that year but, unfortunately, the league disbanded soon afterward.

This article from Brevard Business News in 1984 describes the chamber's success in being accredited by the U.S. Chamber of Commerce.

The Chamber Newsletter of December 1984 revealed that the chamber had a staff of 22 employees with an operating budget of $400,000. It reported that it had achieved 86% of its goals for the year. One of its significant accomplishments was establishing the first chamber-based employee assistance plan in the nation. This plan would enable all chamber members to join a program managed by the chamber, allowing employees to help workers cope with personal and family crises. Florida Today reported on October 14, 1985, that the program was proving to be extremely popular with members. Dave Ashwell of Collins Avionics Division of Rockwell International reported that; "Every level of our organization has taken advantage of it. 'The chamber reported that 292 employees had used the program since it was inaugurated in August 1984.

The success of the Brevard County chambers was illustrated by an article in Florida Today on November 21, 1985, which said that Brevard County was the ninth fastest-growing area in the country. Ted Fuhrer, 1985 president of the South Brevard Chamber and general manager of the Rockwell Collins operations in Brevard, said: "It really does not surprise me. It has the right diversification of all the economic factors that make for a vibrant community."

Contrary to their expressions, these people are not being arraigned in a courtroom but, in fact, are being inducted as directors of the chamber in 1985. From the left are Harry Brandon, Dennis Meehan, Phil Gaarder, Joel Boyd and Tom Adams.

On January 28, 1986, Brevard County and the United States suffered a tragedy that would affect the county and nation for several years when the Space Shuttle *Challenger* broke apart 73 seconds into its flight, killing all seven crew members. This resulted in the grounding of the Space Shuttle fleet for more than two-and-a-half years while the disaster was investigated, and the program redesigned and restructured. The adverse impact on the county's economy was enormous. More than 2,200 employees at the Cape were laid off. The program did not resume until September 29, 1988, when *Discovery* was launched.

Although many people assume that chambers of commerce are focused on economic growth at any cost, it is fair to say that the Melbourne Regional Chamber has, for most of its history, taken a more balanced approach to economic growth. It has done a respectable job of recognizing the need to balance economic growth with the preservation of the quality of life in the community. Lloyd Behrendt, Chair of the chamber in 1989, described his efforts to achieve that balance by an initiative he took in 1986. Behrendt submitted the following recollection:

"In 1986, Mike McWilliams had to leave the Chair of the Growth Management Committee at the Chamber, due to the press of business. Doc Strawbridge asked me to take over. Having learned to repress my shyness, I did so as a favor to Doc. We were buds from the days when I was at TV-1, Ellie (Milford) Kristensen's TV operation 'behind' the Chamber in the old Huggins Hardware store that fronted on New Haven Avenue.

Someone on the Committee suggested we put together a Growth Management Symposium. I did not yet recognize that was the first community visioning process in south Brevard. It occurred shortly after Joe Duda started to develop Viera and they were one of the sponsors.

I remember three of the speakers I managed to lure to speak to a mixed group of developers and keep-it-the-samers:

Duane De Freese, who was completing his studies at FIT at the time, and, as of March 2024, is the Executive Director of INLNEP - the Indian River Lagoon National Estuary Program, a multi-million-dollar community-wide effort to keep our lagoon clean.

Linda Stewart, Orlando. former State Representative (D). She is now the Senator for Florida Senate District 13 in Central Florida.

Patrick Smith was recognized as a world-renowned author of especially Florida stories and what it took to settle wild Florida. His most noted historical novel is *'A Land Remembered.'*

We held the symposium at the brand spanking new 'Airport Hilton,' and I pushed my luck and would not let anyone attend unless they stayed overnight (it was all day on a Friday, and until 2 p.m. on Saturday), unheard of at the time. But there was a lot of interest, and we had a robust and diverse group.

The magic that format worked was this: As everyone had been so defensive and/or combative during the day session, they got to be great friends at the after-hours cocktail party with folks they often would not talk with much. Then as a result, they came to some solid conclusions during the Saturday session.

I sure wish we had Pat's talk on tape. He spoke of his awe at his first trip down Old Dixie Highway as a child with his folks in the 19-Teens. I can only imagine what a menagerie of birds he saw that still called this place home. He spun wonderful tales of beautiful plumage-bearing birds everywhere.

Managing that symposium got me noticed, and I am convinced it led to me becoming President/Chair. It was a change-over year in our nomenclature, with the former executive directors nationwide becoming presidents of their chambers mid-year, after a convention. As a result of that change of nomenclature, I have the distinction by accident of having been both president and chair of the Chamber.

I do not remember the meeting results, I can say I see many of the same issues on steroids today, the heavy lifting we pass on for our next group, to save the 'real' Florida. It will be a tougher journey, as now the numbers all the way around are much larger.

My experience here before the symposium in 1986? I had come to my own intuitive conclusion about balancing the natural environment and productive change to accommodate reasonable growth.

My hunch was that the beauty of the natural environment was the 'draw' that created a setting that people wanted to live, work, and sustain. The opposite side of the coin was that no one enjoys the environment without personal resources—which requires having a job, a house, and all the other things that go with reasonable growth.

> "It can be done; we all want the same thing: to live and enjoy the beauty here. It just requires a strong run at cooperation."
>
> Lloyd Behrendt
> March 24, 2024

The Orlando Sentinel reported on August 31, 1986, that Strawbridge had been elected as 1986-87 president of the Florida Chamber of Commerce Executives. That was a vivid illustration of the respect with which Strawbridge was held among chambers in the State of Florida.

In 1986, the leaders of what was then named the Chamber of Commerce of South Brevard and the Palm Bay Area Chamber of Commerce began discussions about the possibility of merging the organizations. By September of that year, they had hammered out a 14-point consolidation plan, which included several provisions designed to assure that the smaller Palm Bay organization would not be overwhelmed by the larger organization, and that Palm Bay would have a meaningful voice in the merged entity. Among those provisions were requirements that a stated percentage of directors would be from Palm Bay during the first years following the merger and a provision that required a minimum number of votes from Palm Bay to take certain actions, such as amending by-laws or articles of incorporation. In addition, all agreed that the first president of the merged organization would by Maxine Nohrr, the president-elect of the Palm Bay Chamber. In addition, the plan agreed that a search would be conducted to recruit the executive director for the new entity and that neither of the executives of the existing chambers would be assured of a position. Florida Today reported on September 5, 1986, that both chambers had called for a vote of their members in September and that both had approved it. The vote in favor of the merger was overwhelming in both groups. Of the approximately 1,600 members of the South Brevard chamber, only seven voted in opposition. In Palm Bay, only 18 of its roughly 500 members opposed consolidation. An editorial in Florida Today on September 7 was headlined: "Stronger Chamber Coming." The editorial continued: "The merger means the business community interests will be better served, and greater support and recognition will be forthcoming for most civic organizations. And South Brevard's interests will be better served and have a stronger voice through the consolidation. It is a solid move forward for the area and we look forward to the new group's accomplishments." Unfortunately, almost immediately, Palm Bay city officials began attacking the merger. Florida Today reported on January 3, 1987, that the City of Palm Bay would withdraw funding for the new chamber. The city also questioned the new chamber's use of the city-owned building which had been the headquarters for the former Palm Bay chamber. Carson Justice, the immediate past president of the Palm Bay chamber and a leader of the consolidation movement, noted: "But we as a business community felt we could better serve the south county with regard to all municipalities." Unsurprisingly, a new Palm Bay chamber was incorporated on April 20, 1989, thereby ending the effort to create a unified voice for South Brevard businesses.

The Indian River lagoon system is one of the highest-profile concerns today, which inspires extensive public discourse about how to restore it to its former condition. That discussion is, however, not new. An article in Florida Today on February 6, 1987, with a byline reading "Indian River Lagoon System is Worth It," showed that the chamber was aware of its economic value and aware of the threats to its health. Strawbridge was quoted as saying: "It certainly is a major amenity. Besides the direct economics, it is a lure to people who come here."

On April 1, 1987, Florida Today reported that Doc Strawbridge had been chosen from more than 70 applicants to serve as executive vice-president of the newly merged Greater South Brevard Chamber of Commerce. Strawbridge was quoted as saying:

"Although I effected the work of consolidating the chambers, being named officially to the position certainly is a much more comfortable feeling."

A significant step toward enhancing cooperation among the chambers in Brevard County occurred when the three chambers formed the Council of Chambers. The council looked to coordinate activities and pool resources of the chambers in several aspects of their work. Through its Better Business Council, it looked to resolve disputes between customers and businesses. Its Development Council planned to serve existing businesses and lure new businesses to the area. Its Visitor and Convention division sought to promote tourism and conventions. The Small Business Council provided counseling to small businesses. The council also promoted a drug-free workforce. One of its most ambitious goals was to support governmental efficiency to ensure a sound business environment.

The Miami Herald reported on June 17, 1987, that one of the newly combined chamber's most notable events would take place on June 22, 1987, when it would host the visit of President Ronald Reagan to Melbourne. Strawbridge told the newspaper: "It is my understanding that he will be here no more than a couple of hours and will be speaking on the economy and the budget." It fell to the chamber to organize the luncheon for the approximately 1,000 people who would meet with the president at the Melbourne Civic Auditorium. Reagan used the opportunity to promote various budget reforms, including the line-item veto and a Constitutional amendment requiring a balanced budget. He further implored the audience to support him in convincing Congress to agree to "a responsible budget deficit reduction package this year and to stay with it." He concluded by saying: "Well, the time has come for me to leave the good town of Melbourne and head back to Washington. But in closing, let me just say this: In these past few years, we have come so far together, restoring our nation to greatness. For love of liberty, let us work together once again to enact these budget reforms, to leave to our children a nation in which the people, and not the Government, truly rule. And then we will all have done our job. Because there are three of us alone that I know sitting here- the Governor, the Congressman, and myself-you know, you are really the boss. We work for you. And let us keep it that way."

Subtracting machine
President Reagan and Maxine Nohrr, president of the local Chamber of Commerce, get a kick out of the antique adding machine presented to Reagan as a gift Monday in Melbourne. Nohrr said the machine only subtracted and thus would work great at cutting the budget. Reagan, in the first of a series of planned trips to marshal support for his budget policies, opened a tough partisan campaign against Democratic budget and tax programs, vowing that "any tax bill that makes it into the Oval Office won't make it out alive." The Senate and House, both controlled by Democrats, are expected to approve a $1-trillion federal budget resolution this week calling for $65 billion in higher taxes over the next three years.

Published in many newspapers throughout the U.S., this photo of President Ronald Reagan with chamber president Maxine Nohrr was taken at the luncheon on June 23, 1987, when the chamber hosted President Reagan.

A report of the luncheon in The Orlando Sentinel on June 23 stated that the chamber had chosen 12 residents of the area to sit with the president, who regaled them with stories about his California ranch, his wife, and his experiences as an actor and governor of California. Florida Today reported on June 23 that the chamber had lost money on the event, including rent of $689 for the auditorium.

A report in Florida Today on August 2, 1987, noted with approval that the chambers of commerce in Brevard County were working together more than ever. The article noted that the Brevard Economic Development Council (BEDC) held a forum in April 1986 to discuss common goals among the three geographic areas of the county in attracting new businesses and industry. The newspaper credited the forum with fostering more cooperation and coordination between the chambers. However, all the chambers quickly noted that the idea of a countywide chamber was not likely to garner support soon.

Florida Today reported on February 18, 1988, that the Greater South Brevard Chamber of Commerce had organized a dinner the previous night to hear Florida Secretary of Transportation Kaye Henderson speak about road needs in Brevard County. Henderson noted that the county had 76 road projects totaling $306 million planned for completion by 2010.

Florida Today reported on September 15, 1988, that William G. (Doc) Strawbridge would retire as head of the chamber in February 1989. The article noted that, during Strawbridge's tenure with the chamber, membership had grown from about 600 to 2,002. The chamber budget, about $110,000 when he was first hired, had grown to more than $800,000. The chamber expressed its appreciation to Strawbridge at a dinner on February 3, 1989, reported by Florida Today on February 4. The dinner included a performance of "This is Your Chamber life," in which ten former chamber presidents for whom Strawbridge had worked paid a surprise tribute to Doc Strawbridge, who, with typical modesty, responded" "This is fabulous. I consider myself a lucky man. I never expected anything like this. I am just flattered to be given the opportunity to take part in this community."

Doc Strawbridge enjoyed retirement, traveling around the country collecting antiques and honing his wood refinishing skills. He passed away on May 19, 1996, at the age of 70, and all of South Brevard mourned his passing.

CHAPTER NOTES

- Information about the Council of Chambers was reported by Florida Today in an article of October 26, 1990. Although the article states that the Brevard Council of Chambers was created in May 1987, the only entity with a similar name shown by the records of the Florida Secretary of State is the Brevard County Chambers of Commerce Council, Inc. which was incorporated on November 11, 1977. This is the entity that evolved into the Council of Chambers.
- Reagan's speech at the Melbourne Civic Auditorium was found at https://www.reaganlibrary.gov/archives/speech/remarks-greater-south-brevard-area-chamber-of-commerce-luncheon-melbourne-florida.
- For information about Strawbridge's death, see:
- findagrave.com/memorial/85048335/william-gardner-strawbridge.
- For more information about the Challenger disaster see The Space Shuttle Challenger Disaster: The History and Legacy of NASA's Most Notorious Tragedy, by Charles River Editors, published by Greater Space Independent Publishing Platform, January 13, 2016.
- The quotes from Clifton McClelland, Jr. were provided to me by Clif in an e-mail of March 7, 2024.
- Lloyd Behrendt provided me with his narrative of his efforts at growth management by e-mail on March 24, 2024.

CHAPTER EIGHT

The Chamber as an Incubator

One of the valuable functions that the Melbourne Regional Chamber has performed during its history is to be an incubator for projects in their nascent stages, providing support for projects during their infancy before the projects reached maturity that enabled them to prosper as independent entities. There are many examples of such organizations that were birthed within the chamber and later spun off as important community groups. This chapter will describe several such organizations.

Honor America and Liberty Bell Museum

The year 1976 was the bicentennial for the United States. The chamber and the Melbourne Area Board of Realtors jointly undertook leadership of a program to celebrate this occasion. Florida Today reported on February 2, 1976, that the group had bought a 2,000-pound replica of the Liberty Bell which had been made by the same English foundry that cast the original bell. They persuaded the city to donate land west of the civic auditorium on which a building would be constructed to house the bell. This committee eventually became an independent organization and incorporated as "Honor America, Inc." The Liberty Bell Museum that exists on that property today is the outgrowth of the chamber-led project.

Economic Development Commission of Florida's Space Coast

The chamber's newly invigorated industrial development efforts kicked off with a meeting reported by Florida Today on October 2, 1971. Former Melbourne mayor Adger Smith was elected as chair of the Melbourne Area Committee of 100. The meeting agenda included an agreement between the chamber and the Brevard Economic Development Council (BEDC) would result in Fran Tunstall, an employee of the council, acting in a dual role as manager of the chamber's new industrial development department and as the BEDC's south Brevard office manager. Later that year, The Orlando Sentinel would report on October 17, 1972, that Howard N. Hebert had been chosen to succeed Smith as chair. Tunstall was later succeeded by Bruce Ingram who served in this dual role. From this concept of a public agency, BEDC, partnering with a private organization, the Melbourne Area Committee of 100, grew the concept that led to the creation of the present-day Economic Development Commission of Florida's Space Coast. An article in

Florida Today on July 9, 1989, described the efforts to create a public-private partnership that would unite the various economic development agencies in the county into a coordinated effort.

Junior Achievement of the Space Coast
Reidy Williams and John Wilson, both of whom were local managers of Southern Bell, convinced the newly consolidated chamber in 1968 to establish a Junior Achievement program in Brevard County, The Orlando Sentinel reported on June 14, 1968, that the Metropolitan South Brevard Chamber of Commerce had formed a steering committee with a goal of establishing the program in Brevard County schools. The news article described the program as: "A nationally franchised program" whose participants "learn the free enterprise system by setting up and operating their own miniature corporations." Florida Today reported on June 15, 1968, that the chamber would hire a part-time director of the program who would be trained by the national organization in Atlanta. A later article in The Sentinel on July 18, 1969, showed that Junior Achievement clubs would be introduced into four south Brevard County high schools in the fall of 1969, sponsored by the Metropolitan South Brevard Chamber of Commerce. Chamber Executive Director Al Webster revealed that 12 local businesses had shown support for the program. As a result of those first efforts of the chamber, the Junior Achievement program in the county became an autonomous organization which has experienced tremendous success in the ensuing 55 years and has positively affected thousands of young citizens.

Keep Brevard Beautiful
Keep Brevard Beautiful was instituted in Brevard County in 1981. The movement that resulted in that organization began in the Beautification Committee of the Melbourne Area Chamber of Commerce. Roberta (Bobby) Bechtel, a Melbourne city council member, and a leader of the chamber's Beautification Committee led the effort to form the organization and gain certification from Keep America Beautiful. Florida Today quoted Doc Strawbridge on November 2, 1981, as saying:" It's one of the finest things we could do to make our community a cleaner place to live in." Keep Brevard Beautiful continues to work to beautify the county even today.

Business Voice
In 2008, in an effort spearheaded by Joel Boyd and Travis Proctor, the chamber formed Business Voice of East Central Florida as a not-for-profit nonpartisan committee of continuous existence. The new organization was quite effective in vetting and endorsing candidates for local elective offices and taking stands on local public policy issues. As explained in a Florida Today article on January 17, 2016, some people were uncomfortable with a chamber organization issuing endorsements and taking positions on issues. Others, however, were determined that Business Voice could have a greater impact if taken beyond the single chamber and broadened to include the central and north areas of the county. Thus, it was decided in 2015 to broaden the composition of Business Voice beyond the Melbourne chamber and become a separate organization. Larry McIntyre, past chair of the Cocoa Beach Chamber and an active member of the Melbourne Regional Chamber was chosen as the first chair of the expanded Business Voice. Business Voice has continued to provide an effective means to express the voice of businesses on political matters. The bylaws of Business Voice provide that each chamber in the county may have a representative on the board of Business Voice but, thus far, Cocoa Beach and Palm Bay have declined to take part.

Community Foundation for Brevard
On February 11, 1983, the Melbourne Area Chamber incorporated the Melbourne Area Chamber Foundation, Inc., a Florida corporation not for profit. The chamber then applied for and received tax exemption under Section 501(C)(3) of the Internal Revenue Code for the foundation. An article in Florida Today on August 3, 1986, outlined the history of the foundation. The article showed that the idea for the foundation came out of discussions by a strategic planning committee of the chamber which showed the need for a tax-exempt organization that could solicit and receive charitable gifts and bequests to be used for future general community charitable needs. Jack Scott and Dan O'Connell of Gannett had approached the chamber about a year after formation of the foundation and suggested that it might qualify for a grant from the Gannett Foundation that would enable the foundation to hire a full-time executive director and pay other operating expenses. Scott and O'Connell made it clear that the grant would be possible

only if the foundation were freed of control by the chamber and expanded to help all of Brevard County. As a result of those discussions, on June 29, 1983, the name of the foundation was changed to The Community Foundation of South Brevard, Inc. The grant was received, and an executive director was soon employed. On August 27, 2010, the name of the foundation was changed to The Community Foundation for Brevard County, Inc. to reflect the countywide nature of its mission. Today, the foundation is thriving and has collected and distributed millions of dollars that have been spent for a wide variety of community needs.

Melbourne Downtown Redevelopment
Efforts to revitalize downtown Melbourne did not begin with the Melbourne Chamber of Commerce but it is fair to say that the first tangible steps were taken by the chamber. As reported by Florida Today on December 13, 1974, the chamber hired Jack Mason as a part-time employee in 1974 and charged him with responsibility to find ways to draw businesses and customers to the downtown area. The newspaper reported that the first efforts included the establishment of a farmers' market and an art fair. As reported by Florida Today on August 6, 1979, the chamber's downtown committee conducted surveys to gather information for more plans. Those initial efforts were successful enough that the Downtown Melbourne Association, a dormant organization of downtown business owners, hired Mason to expand those effort, which led to the creation by the City of Melbourne of the Melbourne Downtown Redevelopment Committee. As reported by Florida Today on May 30, 1982, the chamber remained a key player in the redevelopment effort and communicated with downtown merchants to counter false rumors that caused many merchants to resist the redevelopment efforts. The Melbourne Downtown Redevelopment Committee has been the primary impetus for the revival of downtown Melbourne into the vibrant, rapidly growing area it is today, bustling with new restaurants, retail businesses, hotels, apartments, condominiums, and entertainment venues. The success of downtown redevelopment is another example of an effort that was not the primary responsibility of the chamber, but it was the chamber that brought together the people who made the effort succeed.

King Center for Performing Arts
It would be an exaggeration to say that the Melbourne chamber was responsible for the Maxwell King Center for Performing Arts. The King Center became a reality over 30 years ago due primarily to the efforts of Dr. King, members of the Brevard state legislative delegation, and State Senator Clark Maxwell, Jr. The King Center has been improved and sustained since its construction by the efforts of dozens of volunteer board members and other associates, and generous donations from the community. However, it is fair to say that the chamber played a key role in motivating Dr. King and Senator Maxwell to vigorously pursue state funding for the facility. As related above, in 1983 the chamber formed the Melbourne Area Chamber Foundation. Part of the charge of the foundation was to fulfill the role of a strategic planning committee to identify critical community needs. Dr. Maxwell C. King, President of what was then Brevard Community College, was a member of the board of directors of the foundation and an active participant in its work. Among other things, the committee had lengthy discussions and brain-storming sessions about the need for a large venue for public events and performances. State Senator Clark Maxwell, Jr., who had an office in the chamber building, was also privy to those discussions. Maxwell held several unusually influential positions in the state senate and was later appointed as head of the now abolished office that managed all public community colleges in the state. Maxwell was able to secure funding for the planning, design and construction of the Maxwell C. King Center for the Performing Arts. It is impossible to say how much the chamber influenced this project, but it is likely that it had some positive impact.

Space Coast World Trade Council
A Florida Today report on December 2, 1981, disclosed that the Melbourne Area Chamber of Commerce would hold an inaugural meeting of the Space Coast World Trade Council the following week. The speaker for this first meeting would be the regional managing director of the U.S. Department of Commerce's International Trade Administration. The newly formed council was open to members of any chamber of commerce in Florida. The purpose of the council was to promote export trade from the Space Coast The council would become an independent organization

when it filed Articles of Incorporation on April 13, 1988. It remains active today.

CHAPTER NOTE

- Information about the expansion of Business Voice beyond the Melbourne Regional Chamber was provided to me by Brent Peoples who took part in those decisions on behalf of the chamber. The information was provided in an e-mail on November 27, 2023.

CHAPTER NINE
Accreditation

Since 1964, the United States Chamber of Commerce has offered a program to accredit state and local chambers of commerce. The accreditation process was designed to cause state and local chambers to engage in a continuous self-analysis of their growth and development. According to the U.S. Chamber's website it is "an opportunity for the organization to reassess its objectives and resources, program of work, procedures, and achievements." Further, the U.S. Chamber says: *"Accreditation means that a local or state chamber of commerce has been recognized by the U.S. Chamber of Commerce for having sound programs and organizational procedures and for continually creating and maintaining positive change in the community."*

See https://www.uschamber.com/chambers-of-commerce/accreditation-self-analysis-survey-for-locl-chambers-of-commerce.

In 1984, Chamber president executive director Doc Strawbridge urged the chamber to undertake the process of accreditation. Only 500 chambers in the nation were accredited at that time. I was serving as president that year. We set up six task forces which included 29 chamber members. We examined the strengths and weaknesses of all aspects of the chamber, including operations, organization, programs, finance, staff, communications, and plant equipment and facilities The effort resulted in the accreditation of what was then named the Chamber of Commerce of South Brevard in November 1984 The December 17, 1984, issue of Brevard Business News reported that Harry Cowan, manager of the southeast region of the U.S. Chamber of Commerce, had presented the certificate of accreditation at the chamber's annual luncheon two days before.

By 2005, the accreditation process of the U.S. Chamber had evolved so that there was a hierarchy of accreditation, ranging from simply being accredited to achieving a 3-, 4- or 5-star chamber designation. The Melbourne chamber achieved a 4-star rating that year. According to an article in Florida Today by Patrick Peterson on February 27, 2010, as soon as the chamber received the 4-star rating, it resolved to pursue a 5-star rating.

Under the leadership of 2009 Chamber Chair Joel Boyd and President Christine Michaels, the chamber initiated a 5-star accreditation application under the watchful eye of 2005 Chair Jim Ridenour, a recognition achieved only by the top 1% of chambers in the United States, met with success. Ninety-seven percent of all chambers are not accredited at any level. To reach 5-star ranking, the U.S. Chamber of Commerce must review and evaluate the chamber in eight areas: governance, finance, human resources and staff, government affairs, program development, technology, communications, and facilities. On February 23, 2010, during the term of office of Chair Dorothy Allen, the Melbourne Regional Chamber was awarded recognition as a 5-star chamber. Florida Today's report of February 27 showed that only 63 chambers in the country had reached that top rating. That designation must be reexamined at five-year intervals thereafter and the chamber has subsequently been re-accredited as a 5-star chamber in 2015 and 2020.
See https://www.melbourneregionalchamber.com/accredtations.

As of November 2016, there were 7,022 chambers in the U.S. Of those, only 206 were accredited at any level. Only 105 achieved 5-star ranking. That means that those chambers with 5-star ratings were among the top 1.49% of all chambers in the country.

The Florida Association of Chamber Professionals (FACP) also has a review process FACP accredits chambers at two levels: a Certified Chamber level and a Certified Plus Chamber level Chambers that operate at the "highest level of proficiency" are accredited at the Certified Plus Chamber level. The Melbourne Regional Chamber was accorded designation as a Certified Plus Chamber in September 2010, a designation which was reaffirmed in September 2016.
See https://www.facponline.com/chambers-of-commerce.

The process of accreditation is rigorous and requires compiling, analyzing, and presenting an enormous amount of data. However, the process provides significant benefits for the organization. It has the benefit of improving and promoting good business practices, recognizing leadership, and proving best practices for the organization. The Melbourne Regional Chamber is proud to be recognized as one of the top chambers of commerce in the United States as evidenced by its accreditation.

CHAPTER TEN

Chamber-Airport Relations

The relationship between Melbourne Orlando International Airport and the chamber has been mutually supportive for most of the airport's existence. At times, the chamber's support has been critical to the airport's success.

On February 8, 1966, the city council of Melbourne began development of a semi-autonomous Airport Authority. The FAA encouraged the creation of an independent authority due to its displeasure with some of the efforts of the city to divert airport revenues, and failures of the city to follow applicable deed restrictions and grant assurances. At that meeting, there was a first reading of Ordinance 66-1 creating the Melbourne Airport Authority. This ordinance was approved after its second reading on February 22, 1966. That ordinance created authority in the form that it exists today.

The ordinance provided that the Airport Authority would be *a "body corporate"* with the power to sue and be sued It created a seven-person governing board, three of whom would be members of the City Commission, appointed by the commission The Chamber of Commerce was given the power to appoint one of the members and the tenants of the airport industrial park were given the power to appoint another member The reasoning for that composition of the authority was a recognition that the airport needed to be run as a business rather than as a political organization By having the chamber and the industrial tenants appoint members, it became highly likely that some appointees would have solid business experience, would advocate that the airport adhere to business principles, and bring business experience and business logic to the management of the facility. At times, it has been asserted that the chamber and industrial tenant appointees were chosen to represent the organizations that appointed them. In fact, those appointees were there to represent all users of the airport, just as the other members of the authority do. The Airport Authority was granted broad powers to maintain, manage and develop the airport.

The chamber's willingness to assert its views in support of the Airport Authority was illustrated by an article by Jackie Reid in the Melbourne Times on March 18, 1974, that disclosed that the chamber would resist any efforts by the City of Melbourne to reduce the powers of the Melbourne Airport Authority The mayor and one of the council members objected to a lease entered into by the authority and reacted by suggesting that the airport should be brought under the control of the city The chamber immediately reacted to oppose the change and informed the city that any such move would *"meet with firm resistance from the business community."* As chair of the chamber, I stated: *"If we get into the position where rentals are being set, leases and contracts being negotiated based on politics, we will be back in the same boat we were in six years ago, and on the FAA blacklist."*

There was another attempt to alter the composition of the Airport Authority. In 1979, a group of residents of Trailer Haven approached the City Commission and asked that a resident of the mobile home park be included as a member of the Airport Authority. The commission was divided in its response to that request but decided to place the question on the ballot for a vote of the electorate. A vigorous campaign ensued with proponents of the proposition arguing that the residents of Trailer Haven should be represented on the authority to look after the interests of the residents. Joe Mullins, who was then a member of the City Commission and would later serve as mayor, was particularly vocal in his support of the measure. A couple of other commissioners were silent on the matter since they recognized the sensitivity of the issue. Opponents of the proposal argued that the Airport Authority had been an unusually effective public body and that the inclusion of a member for the purposes of promoting the interest of a particular group would be detrimental to the overall interests of the airport. The Chamber of Commerce and several major employers in the area took the lead in opposing the change. The referendum took place in November 1979 and the proposed change was rejected by fifty-seven percent of the voters, losing in all but one precinct of the city. Bob Johnson, a former city council member, was quoted in *Florida Today* on November 8, 1979, as saying: *"I think the voters just want to keep politics out of the airport."*

Relationships between the airport and the chamber were not always ideal. When Jim Johnson succeeded Ed Foster as airport director, the relationship soured almost at once. Johnson saw no need to seek the help of the chamber, consistently maintaining that the aviation industry was unique and that no one from outside the industry could offer information of value. When Lee Bohlmann became the chamber executive, her marketing expertise led her to conclude that Johnson knew nothing about marketing and that she could quickly improve airline service at the airport if Johnson would allow her to direct the marketing of the airport. For several years, the dispute between Johnson and Bohlmann inhibited progress at the airport.

Despite the ego battles between Johnson and Bohlmann, the chamber and airport managed to work together effectively on airline service. An article in Florida Today on January 23, 1997, described the efforts of a community coalition, formed through the leadership of the chamber, to support the airport. The article described the Airport Coalition as a sub-group of the Governmental Affairs Committee of the Melbourne-Palm Bay Area Chamber of Commerce.

A successful joint effort occurred when the community came together to lure Spirit Airlines to serve Melbourne. As described in a Florida Today article on May 22, 1998, the Airport Coalition had taken the lead in attracting this new air service. The coalition and the airport collaborated with Spirit to obtain a slot at New York's LaGuardia Airport that enabled Spirit to begin service between Melbourne and LaGuardia. Bohlmann was quoted as saying: *"Good things come to those who wait, great things come to those who are proactive."*

Another joint effort between the chamber and airport quickly followed when, as reported by Florida Today on August 5, 1998, Delta Airlines raised the possibility that it might reduce or curtail service at Melbourne due to declining profit margins. Bohlmann noted that an extraordinary community effort would be needed to prevent action by Delta. The chamber again played a lead role in putting together the Delta Task Force to suggest methods to increase Delta's margins at the Melbourne airport. The Task Force met with Delta officials on October 8 and as reported by Dwight R. Worley in Florida Today on October 9, 1998, Delta was impressed. Delta spokesperson Bill Berry said: *"The airport did an excellent job of identifying new revenue sources for us."* Bohlmann commented: *"They asked a lot of questions, especially about the cruise industry, and we had the answers."*

I recall trying to mediate the disputes between Bohlmann and Johnson. In 1999, I had been called to active duty for 6 months with the Air Force and returned to find that communications between the airport and chamber had broken down altogether. I suffered from an inflated confidence in my mediating skills and thought that I could repair the damage by sitting down with Johnson and Bohlmann and encouraging them to communicate. That meeting lasted for about 10 minutes before Johnson and Bohlmann were shouting insults at each other and making it clear that neither party had anything to learn from the other. Relationships between the airport and the chamber were repaired only after Bohlmann had retired from the chamber and Johnson had left the airport authority in 2005. The appointment of Richard Ennis as interim airport director resulted in an immediate improvement in the relationship.

In 2007, the airport was negotiating a transaction with a German-based tour operator. The deal was in jeopardy because of a lack of U.S. Customs and Border Protection (CBP) agents to process passengers from the proposed flights. As reported in Florida Today on June 23, 2007, the chamber once again came to the aid of the airport when it wrote to Ralph Basham, CBP commissioner. Shannon Meyer's letter said: *"Without these agents, we are sure to lose this very beneficial piece of business."* Unfortunately, the German carrier determined that its financial condition would not support the transaction.

CHAPTER NOTES

- The quote from Jamie Dwight was taken from an e-mail he sent to me on October 7, 2023.
- For more information about the relationship of the airport and the chamber, see Potter, William C., *"Melbourne Orlando International Airport: A History from 1928 to 2022."* Independently published in 2022 in Melbourne, Florida.
- All citations related to the meetings of the governing bodies of the cities of Melbourne and Eau Gallie are derived from either a review of the official minutes of those bodies or from a summary of those minutes prepared by Cathleen Wysor, who was city clerk of Melbourne from 1994 to 2020. Both the minutes and Wysor's summary were provided to the authors by Kevin McKeown, her successor as city clerk of Melbourne.

CHAPTER ELEVEN

The Malta Years:
1989 until 1995

Following Doc Strawbridge's notice that he would retire, the Greater South Brevard Chamber of Commerce undertook a nationwide search to identify his successor. The search effort drew 60 applicants from 23 states. On January 24, 1989, Florida Today disclosed that the chamber had selected Larry Malta to be executive vice-president of the group. Malta, age 38, was then serving as executive vice-president of Cocoa Beach Chamber. This surprised many people in the community. Some members in each of the chambers thought that it was wrong to have recruited Malta without having received permission from the Cocoa Beach Chamber. Some in the Cocoa Beach Chamber were secretly relieved to see Malta move on. The optimistic view in both chambers was that Malta might improve relations between the two organizations. On its face, it was a good hire since Malta was an experienced chamber executive with a solid education.

Shortly after Malta took over, the South Brevard Chamber changed the titles of the leaders. As reported in Florida Today on June 12, 1989, the by-laws were changed so that the chief administrative officer would have the title of president while the head volunteer would have the title of Chair. The change was made to be consistent with a nationwide trend among chambers.

By 1989, the development of Viera by the Duda organization had caught the attention of the chamber. Lloyd Behrendt, 1989 chair of the chamber, told Florida Today on July 2, 1989: "They (Duda) have a clean slate that they can plan something to begin with. They are putting together a hell of a community. We are looking forward to collaborating with them."
In an affirmation of Malta's strong credentials as a chamber executive, Florida Today revealed on August 12, 1989, that he had recently taught two courses at the U.S. Chamber of Commerce's Institute for Organization Management. The courses were held at the University of Colorado where Malta instructed 54 chamber executives in "Marketing Your Chamber and Community" and "Building Community Leadership Programs."

Almost immediately upon assuming the position in south Brevard, Malta was thrust into a controversy with the newly formed Palm Bay Area Chamber of Commerce which had been formed following the merger of the original Palm Bay Chamber and the Melbourne Chamber. On November 4, 1989, Florida Today reported on the new Palm Bay group. As indicated in Chapter Seven, the Palm Bay Area Chamber and the Chamber of Commerce of South Brevard voted overwhelmingly to merge, effective on January 1, 1987. However, another group in Palm Bay was incorporated as a new Palm Bay Chamber of Commerce on April 20, 1989. Thus, after lengthy negotiations and yeomen's efforts, we were back in the same situation. The new chamber next went to the City of Palm Bay and urged the council to cease support of the South Brevard Chamber and support only the new group. Florida Today reported on November 4, 1989, that a representative of the new Palm Bay Chamber argued that Palm Bay needed its own representation. Shortly thereafter, Florida Today reported on December 26, 1989, that a representative of the new Palm Bay Chamber had urged the Palm Bay council to evict the South Brevard Chamber from the building that it had used since the merger, even though the South Brevard Chamber had recently spent $40,000 improving the property that housed the chamber's Better Business Bureau. Despite all these provocations, officials at both chambers told Florida Today on April 6, 1990, that they were eager to work together.

The next controversy that faced the chamber arose from its Better Business Council. As reported by Tony Boylan in Florida Today on June 17, 1990, there were three Better Business Bureaus in Brevard County, each one affiliated with the chambers of commerce in the geographic sections of the county. The chambers reacted to defend their turf when the Maitland-based Central Florida office of the Better Business Bureau began recruiting members in Brevard County. The three Brevard bureaus sent a letter to the president of the Council of Better Business Bureaus asking that they order the Central Florida group to cease its expansion. The council claimed to have no authority to stop the expansion and suggested that the groups learn to coexist.

Despite the several controversies in which the chamber was engaged, there were positive developments. On October 22, 1990, Florida Today reported that the Melbourne, Titusville, and Palm Bay area had been ranked 20th among the 151 cities as the best retirement communities in the nation. Malta told the newspaper that the chamber had sent out between 5,000 and 6,000 packets with relocation information the previous year and was sending out more than that in the current year.

Water continued to be a subject of great debate within the county and a high priority for the Greater South Brevard Area Chamber of Commerce. The creation of the South Brevard Water Authority had been the beginning of an effort to create wells in the Bull Creek Wildlife Management Area in Osceola County. This proposal was vehemently opposed by the City of Melbourne, the primary provider of water in south Brevard County. The chamber worked diligently to find common ground between the city and the authority. Cheryl Reed reported in Florida Today on November 10, 1990, that a compromise had been reached whereby the authority would seek groundwater in Osceola County while the city would build a five million-gallon-per-day purifying plant. These issues became moot when the water authority lost a lawsuit that decided that it had no right to extract groundwater in Osceola County.

A guest editorial by Larry Malta in Florida Today on October 22, 1991, revealed that the chamber had created a 20-year transportation plan. The plan included 16 Florida Department of Transportation projects and nine county road projects.

An article by Tony Boylan in Florida Today on November 7, 1991, explained how the Melbourne-Palm Bay Chamber collaborated with the Florida Chamber of Commerce on legislative issues that affected chamber members. Malta asserted that health care, taxes and education were the highest concerns of his members.

In early 1992, the Brevard Public Schools (BPS) were under fire from their accrediting body, the Southern Association of Schools and Colleges (SACS). An investigating committee of SACS had threatened to place BPS on probation, due not to any academic shortcomings but rather to the irresolvable disputes between the school board and BPS's senior leaders. Larry Malta was quoted in Florida Today on February 16, 1992, as expressing the chamber's concern over the possibility of probation. Malta noted: *"The placement of our school system on probation will reflect negatively on the reputation of schools and threaten the vitality of our economy, which relies upon a high-tech workforce."*

JOE WICKHAM, third from left, receives the Melbourne-Palm Bay Area Chamber of Commerce's Outstanding Community Service Award from Larry Malta, left, chamber president; Tom Mills of Mills Contstruction and Mike Means, director of Holmes Regional Medical Center. Wickham served on the Eau Gallie City Council and as a Brevard County commissioner.

This news article in 1991 reported that the Melbourne-Palm Bay Area Chamber of Commerce had awarded its Outstanding Community Service Award to Joe Wickham. Wickham (known as "Papa Joe") had been a long-time county commissioner for whom Wickham Road and Wickham Park are named. He had also been active in the chamber for decades, including service as chair.

Under Malta's guidance, the local chambers formed a *"Brevard-First Task Force."* As reported by Florida Today on April 12, 1992, Malta described the task force as "designed to enlighten our self-image, educate our populace on the wealth of expertise and products we have here in Brevard, *and ultimately improve our market share within our county.*"

Later that year, the Melbourne-Palm Bay Chamber took on less parochial issues. In a guest editorial in Florida Today published September 2, Malta made an impassioned plea for tort reform. He argued that the then-existing tort system had "*introduced a new element of risk to long-term business planning.*" It is fair to say that efforts at tort reform since publication of that editorial have not mitigated that risk.

An issue that consumed much of the chamber's time and resources in 1992 and early 1993 had to do with the county government center, which had been constructed in Viera. Although Titusville stayed the official county seat, as the center of population shifted south, sentiment increased in favor of constructing courts and other government facilities that were more conveniently located for the bulk of citizens. In response to that sentiment, the county undertook a study in 1986 to determine its need for office space. In March 1989, Duda Lands made a proposal to the county for the development of a central office complex west of I-95 and north of Wickham Road. The proposal included a complex financing mechanism involving "*lease-purchase financing*" and the sale of certificates of participation. In June 1989, the county commission approved the proposal and sale of the certificates. In September 1989, a group of citizens formed The Brevard Citizens for Better Government and began a series of efforts to protest construction of the government center. The actions included calls upon Governor Bob Martinez and the U.S. Attorney to investigate the county's actions. Despite the protests, the county went ahead, the center was built, and the county began occupying the facility in January 1991. In September 1991, the county commission gave a nod to the protesters and voted to hold a referendum in March 1993 to decide whether to abandon the complex. This became a significant public issue with national repercussions as well as a local issue that unleashed unusually heated emotions and rhetoric. On a national basis, if the county were to abandon the building, it would call into question the validity of a financing mechanism that was being increasingly used throughout the country. The concern was so great that 22 bond marketing firms publicly warned the county against the move and told the county that such a move would impair its credit rating. Locally, abandonment of the facility would mean the end of the move to centralize facilities at a place proximate to the population center.

The referendum was in two parts: First, it asked voters if the county should remain in the complex; and second, if the vote favored remaining in the complex, voters were asked whether the facility should be refinanced by using traditional government bonds rather than a lease-purchase.

The Melbourne-Palm Bay Area Chamber of Commerce, along with other organizations and firms throughout the county, jumped into the issue with both feet, because of the national repercussions, the threat to the county's credit rating, and the need for a central complex. On February 27, 1993, a letter in Florida Today from Larry Malta commented on the added financing expenses the county would face if it abandoned the complex. Florida Today reported on March 9, 1993, that the Melbourne-Palm Bay Chamber's political action committee had sent 25,000 mailers in support of keeping the facility intact. Malta was quoted as saying that chamber volunteers were speaking "anywhere people want us to. People are hungry for information."

Florida Today reported on March 17, 1993, that on the previous day the referendum had rejected the idea of abandoning the facility as well as the proposal to refinance. The vote on the proposal to vacate was 52% to 48%. The vote on refinancing was 56% to 44%. Given a light turnout and a close vote, the efforts of the chamber may have been critical on an issue which could have caused severe long-term damage to economic development in the county.

Another county-wide issue took center-stage for the chamber in 1994 related to a proposed county charter to be voted on by the electorate in November of that year. The Melbourne-Palm Bay Chamber held its first meeting on the charter during a breakfast reported in Florida Today on July 8, 1994. During that meeting, Gary Cunningham, an active leader in the chamber, raised an issue that business leaders had advocated for and would continue to advocate to no avail. Cunningham argued that some county commissioners should be elected on a county-wide basis rather than from a district.

He argued that when a commissioner is responsible only to voters in a district, he/she tends to be parochial and only cares about issues affecting that district. Proponents of districts argued that county-wide elections are more expensive and favor wealthy candidates and interest groups. Unfortunately, Cunningham's views did not prevail. Although at-large districts were not included in the charter approved by voters in November 2004, the chamber did not abandon its views on the matter. An article in Florida Today on January 1, 1995, noted that the charter became effective that day. The article quoted Pat Tweed of the Melbourne-Palm Bay Chamber's legislative committee as noting: "I know the overall feeling is that at-large commissioners would be less parochial, as a general overall theory." As this book is written and looking back on actions of the Brevard County Commission in recent years, anything that would have broadened the vision of the commissioners would have been a notable improvement.

Another issue facing the chamber that year related to the Economic Development Commission. John McCauley, director of the Brevard Economic Development Commission, an agency of county government, retired in 1988. After his retirement, community leaders worked with the county to create a public-private partnership, the Economic Development Commission of East Central Florida, which would be funded not only by the county but also by private businesses. Unfortunately, the new entity got off to a rocky start with five different executive directors in six years. An article in Florida Today on July 31, 1994, announced the hiring of Lynda Weatherman as president of the commission and reported the thoughts of various leaders as to how the commission could be more effective. Malta, speaking for the chamber, offered his opinion that the mission of the organization was unclear.

On October 19, 1995, Florida Today reported that Larry Malta would leave his position as president of the Melbourne-Palm Bay Area of Commerce as of December 31, 1995. Rodger Ingram, chair of the chamber board, declined to comment on the reason for Malta's departure but did note that membership had grown by more than 25% during Malta's tenure. Although Malta's departure was not altogether amicable and there were issues leading to his departure other than those disclosed in the news article, a detailed recitation of those issues would seem to be of little value 28 years later. Malta later became executive director of the Largo Chamber of Commerce. The Tampa Bay Times reported on March 1, 1997, that he had resigned that position after a year on the job.

On December 16,1995, an article in Florida Today said that Steve Dickinson, a former manager for Florida Power and Light, would function as interim president of the chamber. A permanent replacement for Malta was expected to be selected during the first quarter of 1996. Dickinson initially applied for the permanent position and was included in the list of finalists. However, Florida Today reported on February 10, 1996, that Dickinson had withdrawn his name from further consideration for the position.

CHAPTER NOTE

- The information about the decision to build the Viera government center, the ensuing protests and the referendum are taken from several news articles published in Florida Today on October 27, 1991.

CHAPTER TWELVE

The Bohlmann Years:
1996 To 2005

Florida Today reported on March 12, 1996, that Lee G. Bohlmann had been appointed as president of the Melbourne-Palm Bay Area Chamber of Commerce. Bohlmann had previously served as executive-vice president of the Carlsbad, California, Chamber of Commerce. Chair Brian Lightle noted: "She's very qualified and serves as one of 17 women throughout the United States to have earned the Certified Chamber Executive designation." Bohlmann had been selected from a large applicant pool of candidates from across the country. The article noted that the chamber had 2,000 members and a budget of approximately $800,000.

I served on the search committee that selected Bohlmann and found she had the requisite experience. Her interview showed that she was knowledgeable, energetic, and articulate. Her only weakness as noted later was that she was not always a willing listener, but most hiring processes are not structured to show whether the applicant is a good listener. Bohlmann was introduced to the community by an article in Florida Today on March 31, 1996, in which she said: "I am not here to send edicts from on high. I am here to help the community meet its goals and objectives." Bohlmann's tenure with the chamber began with a flurry of activity. Her efforts with the Airport Coalition during this time are described in Chapter Ten.

An early initiative of Bohlmann was the creation of The Academy of Business and Finance at Melbourne High School in 1997. The academy was a three-year academic program run in partnership with the Melbourne-Palm Bay Area Chamber of Commerce in association with the National Academy Foundation. The aim of the program was to provide high school students with business, finance, leadership, teamwork, and technical skills. The program, with about 75 students per year, would prove to be unusually effective in preparing students for business success.

Bohlmann was particularly energetic and effective in dealing with governmental matters. When Brevard County began a major rewriting of its zoning code, Bohlmann followed it closely to ensure that it did not adversely affect businesses. In an article in Florida Today on July 4, 1999, she expressed her concern that the new regulations might slow economic growth. The county was considering a performance-based zoning system whereby a plot of land could be put to any use so long as it met specific air quality, water quality, noise, lighting, odor, and traffic guidelines for a specific area. Bohlmann noted that this radical change was "being rushed."

The chamber prepared to celebrate its 75th anniversary in 2000. As explained earlier in Chapter Three of this book, the chamber had been formed no later than 1919 but was not formally incorporated with a full-time director until 1925. The chamber has chosen to mark its anniversaries from the date of incorporation. On October 3. 1999, Wayne Price authored an article for Florida Today that said that Bohlmann was preparing for the chamber's diamond anniversary to take place the following year. Bohlmann noted that the chamber in 1999 was addressing many of the same issues that the chamber faced in 1925, including attracting more commerce to the area and providing more parking downtown.

A few weeks later, on October 30, 1999, Florida Today reported that Bohlmann had been awarded a five-year recertification as a Certified Chamber Executive. It was noted that she was one of a few women in the country who held this certification.

Bohlmann had a particular interest in work force issues and vigorously pursued opportunities to provide a solid work force in Brevard County. A significant accomplishment was reported by Tony Manolates on February 24, 2000. The Melbourne-Palm Bay Chamber was one of four organizations in Florida to share a $2.25 million grant from the state aimed at increasing the number of entry-level jobs. The chamber would work with the Brevard Workforce Development Board to place at least 200 entry-level employees with program participants.

Bohlmann continued to make her mark at the state level. Victoria Reid wrote in Florida Today on July 6, 2000, that Bohlmann had been appointed by Governor Jeb Bush to a new state board designed to help build the state's work force. The 20-member board of Workforce Florida, Inc. would make policy recommendations to the Agency for Workforce Innovation. Bohlmann disclosed that among the issues she would like to pursue were the barriers that kept some people from working, including a lack of childcare, transportation, and training.

An article in the Fort Myers News-Press on March 28, 2001, reviewed Brevard County's population gains between 1990 and 2000 and noted that Palm Bay and Melbourne had grown 26% and 19%, respectively. Chuck Galy, vice-president of the Melbourne-Palm Bay Chamber was quoted as saying: "We still have a feeling of mid-size America as opposed to metropolis America. People like that."

Of course, one of the exciting questions for the new Millenium was the "Y2K" concern that there might be a digital Armageddon caused by computers crashing everywhere. When I questioned Jamie Dwight, 2001 chamber chair, about his term in office, he noted the initial relief when Y2K fears proved to be harmless only to have that relief shattered by the events of 9/11. Jamie added: "In hindsight, it is clear our collective shock, fear, anger, determination, condolence, and genuine patriotism were unifying forces. The American flag lapel pins became immediately ubiquitous, though the healing and recovery of that time is still an ongoing part of us."

The chamber had an unusually ambitious program of work for 2002. Lee Bohlmann wrote a guest editorial for Florida Today on January 20, 2022, in which she described the top five chamber priorities 0f 2002 as: 1. Economic development and creation of new jobs; 2. Education; 3. Business assistance and advocacy; 4. Tourism and conventions; and 5. Traffic and transportation. Among the other legislative priorities of the chamber, one that stood out related to health care which Bohlmann described as "one of the highest expenses for an employer." In an early hint of a fight that would culminate nine years later with the passage of the Affordable Care Act, Bohlmann promised to oppose "mandated health benefits at the federal level."

The business community in Brevard County suffered a huge blow with the *Columbia* disaster on February 1, 2003. The *Columbia* disintegrated as it reentered the atmosphere over Texas and Louisiana, killing the seven-member crew and once again throwing the space program into chaos, wreaking economic havoc in Brevard County. Space Shuttle operations were suspended for more than two years, and construction of the International Space Station was halted until flights resumed in July 2005. Bohlmann reacted to the tragedy by telling Florida Today on February 1: "It is going to be scary. We are going to go into an investigative mode, which usually shuts down everything else."

In early 2003, a proposal was put forth to add one cent to the sales tax payable in Brevard County. The revenue from this proposed increase would be divided between the county and the Brevard Public Schools. The Melbourne-Palm Bay Chamber studied the issue closely. At the May 2003 meeting of the Brevard County Council of Chambers, the council committed funds to urge voters to approve the proposed increase. On September 21, 2003, Bohlmann wrote a letter to Florida Today informing readers that the chamber's board had voted to support the tax. She revealed that a straw poll of chamber members showed support by an almost three to one margin. The tax was approved by voters on November 4 by a comfortable margin.

The versatility of the chamber was clearly proven on June 30, 2003, when the Brevard County Manatees faced the Fort Myers Miracles at Space Coast Stadium. As reported in Florida Today on that day, not only did chamber chair Doug Mead throw out the ceremonial first pitch, but even more astoundingly chamber President Lee Bohlmann sang the national anthem.
Another accolade for the chamber in 2003 was reported in Florida Today on October 19 when Marj Bartok chair-elect of the chamber received the 2003 Woman-Owned Small Business Subcontractor of the Year Award from Kennedy Space Center. Bartok, owner and president of Spherion Staffing, had been nominated by Boeing Company for the prestigious award.

The following year, 2004, will be long remembered for Hurricanes Charley, Frances, Ivan and Jeanne. Estimates of damage in Brevard County from the three hurricanes were $796 million. An article in Florida Today on October 8, 2004, described Highway A1A in Satellite Beach as looking "like a chamber of commerce nightmare." Bohlmann noted: "I've never seen anything like this before."

In February 2005, Bohlmann met with Jim Ridenour, then serving as chair of the chamber. Jim, a retired Air Force fighter pilot who had flown many combat missions during the Vietnam War, was a particularly interesting leader. Jim had retired from the Air Force as an 0-6 but quickly tired of retirement and, to relieve his boredom, took a job as a night clerk at a Marriot Hotel. Predictably, Jim's leadership skills soon propelled him into a management position, and he became manager of three Marriot properties in south Brevard County. When Bohlmann approached Ridenour with a request that she be allowed to take a leave of absence for a year to travel, Jim was ready with an answer founded on his uncommon, good sense and denied the request. The result was that on March 3, 2005, Florida Today reported that Bohlmann would step down as president of the Melbourne-Palm Bay Area Chamber of Commerce on April 1 to "redirect her life to focus on speaking engagements, travel and consulting work." The newspaper noted that Bohlmann was "known throughout the community for her snappy wit, sense of humor and pro-business savvy."

On March 14, Florida Today reported that the board of directors of the chamber had voted to appoint Chuck Galy as acting president of the organization. The board also authorized the executive committee to function as the search committee to recruit a new CEO. On April 25, Ridenour told Florida Today that more than 60 candidates had applied for the position. Ridenour affirmed that the job paid $70,000 to $95,000 per year and "we're looking for people with experience, but, more importantly, we're looking for a good leader."

CHAPTER NOTES

- As to the effects of the Challenger disaster, see" The Space Shuttle Challenger Disaster: The History and Legacy of NASA's Most Notorious Tragedy" by the Charles River Editors, published by Create Space Independent Publishing Platform in 2016.
- For more about the Academy of Business and Finance, see the article in Florida Today on May 10, 2005.
- Jamie Dwight's quote was taken from an email he sent to me on October 7, 2023.
- As to the effects of the Columbia disaster, see "Return to Flight: Inside NASA's Space Shuttle Missions in the Wake of the Columbia Disaster" by Dr. James F. Peters, published by CreateSpaceIndependentPublishingPlatform in 2015.
- I am not certain how long Bohlmann traveled following her resignation, but it was less than she had envisioned when she requested a leave of absence. On November 7, 2005, Florida Today reported that she had founded her own company, Building Better Organizations, which was described as a "workplace consulting business."

CHAPTER THIRTEEN

Meyer, Michaels, and Malesic: 2005 until 2017

On August 24, 2005, Florida Today reported that Shannon Meyer had been named as president and CEO of the Melbourne-Palm Bay Area Chamber of Commerce. Meyer, age 30, had been the CEO of the Twin Cities North Chamber in Mounds View, Minnesota. She was selected from a pool of 76 applicants. Jim Ridenour said: "She's extremely enthusiastic and knowledgeable about chamber workings."

In an article in Florida Today on February 4, 2006, Meyer set forth the chamber's priorities for 2006. One priority was to work with state and local transportation officials to advance the Palm Bay beltway and widening of Wickham Road as well as the extension of the Pineda Causeway west to I-95. Meyer also boldly set a goal to increase chamber membership by at least 10 percent.

Brevard County commissioners considered holding a referendum in 2006 to increase local sales taxes by a penny. The idea was that this extra revenue would be used primarily to fund critically needed road projects but also for schools, jail expansion and recreation projects. However, the Melbourne-Palm Bay Chamber told the commission that it was not workable to conduct such a referendum in 2006. As Meyer told the Vero Beach Press Journal on March 23, 2006: "Our members agree that transportation is critically underfunded, but there are a lot of steps to take before we would advise a referendum."

Meyer was a vocal proponent of a regional approach to problems with all stakeholders having a role in planning and prioritizing needed improvements. On March 30, 2006, Meyer explained to Wayne T. Price at Florida Today: "It is critical for us to have success in smart-growth planning; to think on a regional basis. Even more important is that we in the county need to work together on this regional vision."

However, the chamber also knew that there is a delicate balance between regional coordination and the competition between chambers that is inevitable. That dilemma was illustrated by an article in Florida Today on June 29, 2006, which said that the Melbourne-Palm Bay Chamber was setting up a satellite office on Spyglass Hill Road in Viera. Meyer acknowledged that the chamber already had "a significant presence in Viera, but Viera is a dynamic, growing area, and the businesses there need additional representation." She also said that the chamber was working with Brevard Public Schools to set up an Academy of Business and Finance in the new Viera High School. These moves by the Melbourne-Palm Bay Chamber at once generated questions from the Cocoa Beach Area Chamber of Commerce. Cocoa Beach Chamber president Kathi Schillo noted:" We have many, many business partners in that area."

The Melbourne-Palm Bay Area Chamber also came to the aid of a "sister" chamber during the year. A news article in Florida Today on November 18, 2006, showed that the chamber had donated $5,400 to the chamber in Biloxi Bay, Mississippi to help in rebuilding from Hurricane Katrina. The three hurricanes that had swept through Brevard County in 2004 had heightened the chamber's empathy for hurricane victims.

Chuck Galy provided a "fascinating timeline" of the chamber to Bylynn Pickett which was published in Florida Today on November 21, 2006. Among the documents which Galy shared with the newspaper was a 1928 chamber publication of "Melbourne Statistics." The publication listed a lumber company, a poultry farm, and a manufacturer of concrete blocks as among the most important industries of the Melbourne area.

Regional planning continued to be a priority in 2007. Myregion.org had been formed in 2001 to bring together leaders from throughout Central Florida to address future planning needs on a regional basis. Florida Today reported on August 11, 2007, that myregion.org had put forth its plan that referenced the notion of areas of increased density of development, including the concept of taller buildings. Shannon Meyer was cited as saying: "It is a great plan for regional planning. Because we are part of a seven-county coalition, it means we will have a stronger voice in Tallahassee on issues that are important to Brevard, such as transportation and affordable housing.

Shortly after that, Meyer was appointed to the Chamber of Commerce Committee of 100, a national group of chamber executives that stands for the viewpoints, needs of chambers throughout the country, and presents those ideas to the U.S.

Chamber of Commerce. Jacob Stuart, president of the Orlando Regional Chamber, nominated Meyer for this role and noted to Florida Today on August 23, 2007, that it was "a good opportunity to gain experience from a powerful assortment of outstanding colleagues."

On November 8, 2007, Meyer told Florida Today that the highest priority for the chamber during the ensuing year would be to better serve its members. She said: "We will do so by continuing to focus on: business advocacy and strengthening the voice of our members; education, both for our members and through our academy involvement in the local schools; recruiting and retaining good businesses in this area; and finally, by working collaboratively with other organizations to promote the interests of our business community." She went on to argue that the four chambers in Brevard County had shared interest in "creating, promoting and sustaining a strong business economy – locally, regionally and globally."

Another issue that gained the attention of the chamber during this time was the proposed property tax reform to be decided by a referendum on January 29, 2008. The proposed Constitutional Amendment would increase the homestead tax exemption from $25,000 to $40,000, cap appraisal hikes for second homes and commercial properties and allow homeowners to transfer their Save Our Homes tax savings to a $500,000 limit. Florida Today reported on December 5, 2007, that the Melbourne-Palm Bay Area Chamber of Commerce had convened a special meeting at which it decided to endorse the proposed amendment. The amendment would easily pass with over 60% of voters statewide approving the measure.

A significant innovation of the chamber in 2008 was the establishment of the Women's Business Council. Florida Today reported on June 15, 2008, that Sally Shinn, executive director of the Space Coast Early Intervention Center, was the recipient of the Woman of Excellence Award presented by the Women's Business Council. This award has been given to many extraordinary women during the ensuing years and the council, now known simply as "Women of Excellence" is an important part of the chamber. The mission of the organization is "To empower the diverse working-women of our community to achieve their highest potential through collaborative initiatives focusing on networking, professional development and community outreach."

On October 15, 2008, Florida Today reported that Shannon Meyer had resigned as president of the Melbourne-Palm Bay Area Chamber of Commerce and that she had accepted a job as president of the chamber of commerce in Cedar Rapids, Iowa. Travis Proctor, then serving as chamber chair, related that he and Joel Boyd, incoming chair, would be part of a search committee to recruit a new president.

On January 24, 2009, Florida Today reported that Christine Michaels had been hired to be the new president and CEO of the Melbourne-Palm Bay Chamber. Michaels was then serving as president of the Alexandria, Virginia, Chamber of Commerce.

Michaels obviously understood the importance of the space industry in Brevard County. On May 22, 2009, Florida Today published a letter from Michaels reacting to attempts from other states to lure space related activities. Michaels urged federal and state financial support to expand space activities in the county.

A big day for Michaels, the chamber and chair Joel Boyd was described in an article in Florida Today on June 10, 2009, under the by-line "Chamber's new look." The article described how the chamber had completed a $200,000 renovation of its headquarters. The project, renovating the building and improving technology, coincided with the grand opening of the nearby new city hall.

Another innovation of the chamber for 2009 was described in Florida Today on July 11, 2009, as the chamber debuted its "Chamber 2040" group. This sub-group of the chamber was designed to attract members between the ages of 20 and 40 and focused on "career growth, professional development and issues of interest to partners under the age of forty." This group has been an active part of the chamber since its founding. At the time of this writing, it is known as "Space Coast Young Professionals."

Under the leadership of 2009 chair Joel Boyd and 2010 chair Dorothy Allen, the chamber made a noticeable shift to regionalism during those years. On October 15, 2009, in an article by Keilani Best and Wayne T. Price, Florida Today reported that the Melbourne-Palm Bay Area Chamber of Commerce would change its name to Melbourne Regional Chamber of East Central Florida, effective as of January 1, 2010. CEO Michaels told the newspaper that the new name reflected the more regional focus of the chamber. Regionalization was reemphasized when Florida Today reported on December 28, 2009, that the chamber had entered a partnership with myregion.org. An element of that partnership was that the chamber would have a representative on the board of advisers of myregion.com. According to Michaels, this signified that the chamber would "support regional issues and inform and influence southeast Central Florida, an area that stretches from Indian River County to Orlando."

Travis Proctor, who had been chair of the chamber in 2008, was appointed as Vice-Chair for Regionalism and appointed as the chamber's delegate to myregion.org and the chamber's representative on its board of advisors. The chamber's involvement with myregion.org continued from 2010 through 2012. By the end of 2012, myregion.org had curtailed its activities due to lack of funding.

An example of the kind of issue which merited regional support was the subject of a letter from Jacob Stuart as president of the Central Florida Partnership published in The Orlando Sentinel on October 6, 2011. Stuart's letter addressed NASA's plans for crewed space exploration following the end of the space shuttle program. He applauded NASA's announcement of its design for heavy-lift rockets and noted that the Central Florida Partnership, "collaborating with the Florida Chamber of Commerce, Space Florida, and others" supported policies, investments and advocacy that name Florida as the best location for the next generation of federal and commercial aerospace opportunities."

Myregion.org had been started in 1999 with the goal of encouraging regional collaboration. It began as a partnership between the Orlando Regional Chamber of Commerce and the East Central Florida Regional Planning Council. An article by Larry Pino in The

Orlando Sentinel on November 25, 2016, chronicled the efforts of Jacob Stuart, former president of the former Orlando Chamber of Commerce, to drive cooperation among seven counties-Brevard, Lake, Orange, Osceola, Polk, Seminole and Volusia- to address a variety of issues, including highway infrastructure, public transportation, smart growth and water resources as well as numerous other issues of public concern. Stuart's efforts bound those seven counties to a regional model titled the Central Florida Partnership. In 2017, the Central Florida Partnership was merged with the Metro-Orlando Economic Development Commission.

In addition to promoting regional cooperation during this period, the chamber, under the leadership of Boyd and Proctor, engaged in substantive discussions with the other chambers of commerce in Brevard County about the possibility of creating a unified chamber for the entire county. These discussions were more than preemptory and fostered lengthy discussions about both the merits and the mechanics of such a consolidation. In the end, however, fears that the Melbourne Chamber was trying to usurp the authority of the other chambers resulted in the termination of the discussions.

Another significant action by the newly renamed chamber during this time was the creation of a chamber sub-group to be christened the Nonprofit Council. Florida Today reported on November 9, 2009, that this group would enable nonprofit organizations to network, exchange information and take part in training sessions. Remarkably, more than 100 members of the chamber were nonprofit organizations. The Nonprofit Council is still an important subgroup within the chamber as of the writing of this book with a stated mission as "Dedicated to providing nonprofit organizations with the tools they need to succeed through leadership training, information sharing, and review of best practices."

The Melbourne Regional Chamber placed renewed emphasis on tourism in 2009. Florida Today reported on December 17 that the chamber had produced a video marketing the area which would be featured on Delta Air Lines flights worldwide during that month. In addition, the chamber had produced a new guidebook and website touting tourism in the Melbourne area. Tom Poehailos, general manager of the Crowne Plaza Oceanfront noted that the video might reach three million viewers and said: "We really tried to put the Space Coast on the map, especially the Melbourne coast, in terms of establishing an identity."

An exceptionally significant accomplishment of the chamber occurred in early 2010 when it was awarded a 5-star rating by the U.S. Chamber of Commerce. The enormity of that accomplishment was described in Chapter Nine above.

The issue of tax abatements for new and expanding businesses was a hot issue for 2010 and drew the attention of the chamber. The discretion to grant tax abatements to new and expanding employers was expiring in both Melbourne and West Melbourne and the question of whether to extend that discretion for another 10 years would be put before the voters of both cities in November 2010. The program had proven to be a worthwhile investment. According to a Florida Today article on March 12, 2010, during the previous 10 years, Melbourne had granted 17 abatements to businesses which had invested $119 million in new construction and created 2,300 jobs. In that article, Michaels reiterated the chamber's support for the program and said: "We want them to have as many tools as they can to help an existing business expand or to bring in new businesses." Florida Today reported on May 5 that West Melbourne had called upon the chamber to help promote a favorable vote. On October 29, Michaels told Florida Today: "For the amount of abatement, the investment that resulted is staggering." Voters in both cities renewed the abatement authority by a healthy margin.

The Melbourne Regional Chamber undertook a major new venture in 2011 by agreeing to hold the Florida 2011 TechXpo, an event which would feature, according to an article in Florida Today on July 11, exhibits of "emerging technologies and leading-edge innovations. Exhibitors would include alternative and renewable energy biotech and life sciences, defense, resilient technology, composites, and robotics. The TechXpo was held on the campus of Florida Institute of Technology on October 11, 2011. Florida Today reported on October 12 that more than 80 companies took part in the show, including several from as far as Canada and South Korea. Christine Michaels told the newspaper that she was hopeful TechXpo would spawn permanent tech industry collaboration.

Michael's outlook for tech collaboration was more than idle talk. Shortly after the conclusion of TechXpo, the chamber began planning an organization designed to bring together people from "all aspects of tech industry." The Space Coast Tech Council was formally launched in January 2014. Florida Today reported on February 28 that the council had held its first meeting the previous day and 130 people had attended the event. An article in Florida Today on March 17, 2014, described the council as "an organization that invites all tech-related companies and supporting groups to join forces and focus efforts on the growth of the tech community." Among the founders of the council were Artemis, GE Transportation and Florida's High Tech Corridor Commission. Space Coast Daily reported on October 7, 2015, that the council was preparing to hold its second TechXPo, to be held at Melbourne Orlando International Airport and Eastern Florida State College Aviation Center. The council expected that as many as 100 companies would take part. The chamber employed a person whose primary responsibility was to manage the Tech Council and TechXpo. As the council and TechXpo grew in prominence, that staff member began to act autonomously, thereby creating some conflict with Michaels. When the staff member in charge of the council resigned, the council slowly withered.

On May 12, 2014, Michaels authored an article in Florida Today on behalf of the Women of Excellence committee. She noted that the committee had grown during the past few years from a small group of 30 women in the community to over 175 business leaders in 2014. She indicated that the meetings were open to both women and men.

On September 11, 2014, Florida Today reported that Christine Michaels had resigned as CEO and president of the chamber. The chamber issued a terse statement as follows:" As chamber president, Michaels represented Melbourne's business community by working with chamber members and other civic leaders to help facilitate economic development in our region." There was obviously some dissatisfaction among the chamber leaders as to Michael's leadership and her management skills. Problems that became clear during the last leadership retreat conducted under her administration culminated with her decision to resign.

With the departure of Michaels, once again Chuck Galy stepped in, providing a steady hand to steer the ship while a new CEO was recruited. On July 30, 2015, an article in Florida Today presented that the Melbourne Regional Chamber of East Central Florida had hired Christian Malesic as its CEO and president. Malesic had taken office as president in June. Prior to coming to Melbourne, Malesic had been an "executive officer" at the Home Builders Association of Berks County in Pennsylvania. He had also lived in Brevard County prior to his position in Berks County when he worked as an "engineering liaison" to Northrop-Grumman on the Joint STARS program. Malesic's tenure would prove to be short and unsatisfactory.

One of the initiatives that Malesic promoted was Small Business Saturday, a movement designed to entice people to eschew internet shopping and buy from local merchants. Malesic told Florida Today on November 27, 2016, that Small Business Saturday was a growing national movement based on the Black Friday shopping phenomenon. Malesic explained that: "The concept of 'Shop Small' and Small Business Saturday is intended to bring that business back home. Go to your neighbors. Go to your friends. Go to people that are paying taxes in your community, just like you are, who are raising their kids in your neighborhood, just like you are."

Malesic resigned as chamber president in June 2017. He had served in that position for almost 2 years. Several chamber leaders felt that Malesic worsened the existing problems rather than improve them. Also, a decline in membership occurred during his tenure.

CHAPTER NOTES

- The discussion about the chamber's interest in regionalism and its affiliation with myregion.org is based upon the author's conversations with Joel Boyd and Travis Proctor, the chamber leaders primarily responsible for trying to promote regional cooperation.
- The discussion about negotiations to create a consolidated chamber of commerce for the county is based upon the author's conversations with Travis Proctor.

- The idea of councils within the chamber evolved during this time. As explained on the chamber website, the board of directors of the chamber may, from time to time, establish a council to focus on a "particular niche of partnership." See https://www.melbourneregionalchamber.com/councils/. If interest in that niche later declines, the board may elect to disband the council. Memberships in some councils are included in the standard chamber dues while other councils may have added annual dues. As of the time of writing this book, the chamber councils are the Nonprofit Council, the Space Coast Young Professionals, the Viera Regional Business Alliance, the Small Business Council, the Business Advocacy Committee, and the Women of Excellence.
- For more about the Women of Excellence, see https://www.melbourneregionalchamber.com/women-of-excellence/.
- For more about the Nonprofit Council see https://www.melbourneregionalchamber.com/nonprofit-council/.
- Meyer would remain with the Cedar Rapids chamber for only about 2 years before leaving in December 2010 to become CEO and president of the Fox Cities Chamber of Commerce and Industry in Wisconsin.
- Information about Michael's decision to resign was conveyed to me verbally by several of the chamber officers who confronted her to express their dissatisfaction.
- Michaels became CEO and president of the Greater Brandon (FL) Chamber of Commerce shortly after leaving Melbourne. From Brandon, she moved on to become CEO of the Greater Fayetteville (NC) Chamber of Commerce. She was appointed CEO and president of the Oak Ridge (TN) Chamber of Commerce in September 2020. She is still in that position at the time this book is written.

CHAPTER FOURTEEN

AYERS:
2017 until Present

On December 14, 2017, Wayne T. Price authored an article in Florida Today that revealed that Michael Ayers had been appointed as the president and CEO of the Melbourne Regional Chamber of East Central Florida. Ayers, 38 years old, had been selected after a nationwide search. A graduate of the University of Illinois at Champaign-Urbana, Ayers had most recently served as Director of Government Relations for Sanford Burnham Prebys Medical Discovery Institute in Lake Nona. Ayers promised: "My tenure will focus on improving the value of a chamber membership, so the Melbourne chamber is that organization that companies choose to invest in."

Brent Peoples was the chair in 2018. He characterized 2018 as the "Year of the Blue Flame," meaning that at the beginning of 2018, the chamber was a disorganized fire, and the aim was to get the chamber burning like a hot blue flame. As Peoples described it: "In 2018, the Melbourne Regional Chamber of Commerce embarked on a transformative journey under the leadership of Michael Ayers. With a vision to ignite a powerful, purposeful, and impactful presence in the community, the Chamber set out to redefine its role, instilling a sense of pride and purpose. Formerly a disorganized entity, the Chamber underwent a significant cultural shift, adopting a forward-thinking approach and shedding the burden of trying to cater to everyone. Michael Ayers' appointment as President marked a turning point after a period of lackluster leadership. His emphasis on professionalism and collaboration spurred improved relationships with various key community entities such as the EDC, TDC, Homebuilders, other Chambers, the Brevard County Legislative Delegation, and Melbourne Main Street. This enhanced collaboration generated a notable positive buzz within the community."

Several chamber leaders, including Peoples, Ayers, Todd Pokrywa, Kim Agee and Michael Melhado, visited the Manatee Chamber of Commerce to explore things that had worked well for other chambers. From this was conceived the idea of a Chamber/Community Leadership Retreat which would be an "outward-looking" retreat replacing the more introspective Board of Directors retreats.

Several committees were reinvigorated and rebranded, including the Government Affairs and Women on the Rise Committees. Additionally, the Viera/Suntree Business Council was revamped into the Viera Business Alliance, creating a more inclusive and dynamic platform for local businesses. This change was the result of the recognition by the chamber leadership of the extraordinary growth, both residential and commercial, that was occurring in Viera and the desire of the chamber to influence and encourage that development. In recognizing that opportunity, the chamber was influenced by the example of Lakewood Ranch, a large development east of Bradenton and Sarasota on Florida's Gulf Coast. The chambers of commerce in Bradenton and Sarasota, although both effective organizations, had ignored the explosive growth of Lakewood Ranch and missed the opportunity to expand their sphere of influence by serving that area. The Melbourne Regional Chamber was determined not to make that mistake with Viera, and the Viera Business Alliance was its response. As set forth on the chamber website: "The very definition of "Alliance" is what we are all about; merging efforts and interests, joining together for a common cause, and creating a group of people who support each other. The Viera Regional Business Council wants to be the champion of Viera area businesses." Among the annual activities of the alliance are the "Spring Fling," a tabletop event designed to highlight the businesses of Viera, Suntree and Rockledge. Another annual event of the alliance is the "Mix, Mingle and Jingle" event that, aside from the networking opportunities, provides Michael Ayers with the opportunity to show off his children while wearing what is undoubtedly the most garish Christmas sweater in the county.

The Chamber played a significant role in several key community events, such as the Kickoff event for new Superintendent Dr. Mark Mullins and the attendance of Governor Rick Scott at the Valor Awards. Notable developments included the creation of ex-officio positions among the Economic Development Commission, County Government, the Tourism Development Council, and the Chamber Board of Directors, strengthening partnerships with these important local entities.

The Trustee Program was revitalized to align with the goal of adding value to both the Chamber and the community. Furthermore, the

Chamber focused on recruiting impactful board members to drive strategic initiatives forward.

As part of rebranding its events, the Thursday morning breakfast was transformed into the more inclusive "Good Morning Space Coast."

These initiatives collectively propelled the 2018 Chamber's transformation into a dynamic, community-focused organization, igniting the "Blue Flame" of positive change and progress envisioned by Peoples.

Downtown redevelopment is an issue that would prove to be at the forefront of chamber activities throughout Ayers' term as president. On May 3, 2018, the Melbourne City Council faced the issue of granting a variance to the height limitations in the downtown area to accommodate a proposed hotel that wanted to construct a building 123 feet tall while the zoning only allowed 90 feet. According to a Florida Today article on that day, Ayers lobbied long, hard, and successfully in favor of the change.

Not surprisingly, given Ayers' background as a Director of Government Relations, business advocacy has played a key role in chamber activities during his tenure. Each year in February or March, the four chambers of commerce in Brevard County travel to Tallahassee together to hold meetings and briefings with legislators, state agencies and business associations. The joint effort entails a detailed list of legislative actions to be addressed which make up the legislative priorities for each of the four local chambers. Not only does the priorities list include the number of each bill but also includes the sponsor of each bill. The coordination between the chambers and the level of detail in the legislative priorities is impressive. The impact on the legislative delegation has been unusually effective.

On June 3, 2018, Ayers wrote as a guest columnist in Florida Today about the tight labor market in Brevard County and suggested recruiting techniques for employers. Ayers saw: "The need for skilled, quality workers, particularly in the high-tech and engineering fields, is stronger than ever before. We now must hunt for talent. To do that successfully we need to know how to express our employee brand, which requires an integrated approach with the company's marketing team. It is more than a product sales strategy; It is now a people sales strategy."

The chamber did its best to help its members as they struggled to deal with the impact of COVID-19. On March 30, 2020, Ayers wrote a guest column in Florida Today suggesting steps that could be taken by consumers to aid Brevard businesses during the coronavirus. Ayers first saw how quickly society had changed with the virus. Ayers outlined several steps that consumers could take to help local businesses as they struggled to adapt to the restrictions of the virus. Among his suggestions was: "When you support a local business, shout it from the rooftops via social media. Take a photo, tag the business, and let your friends and family know how they too can help during this time of uncertainty."

On April 29, 2020, the presidents of the four chambers in Brevard County, Ayers from Melbourne, Marcia Gaedcke from Titusville, Nancy Peltonen from Palm Bay, and Jennifer Sugarman of Cocoa Beach, jointly penned a column for Florida Today addressing economic recovery from COVID-19. Their conclusion was: "The restart will require methodical planning, new processes and limitations for which there simply are no mandates to reference. The great news is that we are building on a solid foundation, one created when the space shuttle program was retired, and local leaders made the conscious decision to diversify our economy." The four presidents went on the say: "By uniting the Brevard business community, we will relaunch our economy and work toward our common goal: recovery and prosperity for all of the Space Coast."

Bailey Gallion authored an article in Florida Today on June 26, 2020, describing how a surge in COVID-19 cases in Florida had forced many businesses which had reopened to rethink the decision to do so. The article described how several Brevard restaurants had reopened and were being forced to close their doors again. The article quoted Michael Ayers as advising: "People need to continue to practice the same guidelines of social distancing. Businesses should be encouraging face masks wherever possible or wherever necessary, taking all the necessary precautions so they can avoid a blanket shut down where their income is at once going to stop."

In early 2021, then Chair-elect Neal Johnson and the chamber board appointed a task force to present the board with options for the chamber's office building. The task force examined four alternative possibilities: 1. Renovating the building; 2. Engaging a development partner to redevelop the property; 3. Retaining a fee simple interest in the land and selling the air rights to a developer; or 4. Selling the property and relocating to new leased or purchased space. The report of the task force set forth the pros and cons of each of these alternative courses of action.

Ayers wrote another guest column for Florida Today on February 15, 2022, this time addressing the tax on aviation sales and rentals. Ayers pointed out that Florida was losing aviation business to other states because of its six percent tax on aviation sales and rentals. Ayers talked about how this adversely affected Embraer in Melbourne and Piper in Vero Beach. Ayers argued that by ending the tax "Florida could position itself as a more desirable location for investment and jobs in the general aviation industry."

As COVID-19 abated and society learned to live within the restrictions imposed by the virus, the Melbourne Regional Chamber returned to its more traditional concerns including its historical leadership role on transportation issues. Now the attention turned to Ellis Road and the 1.7-mile stretch between Wickham Road and John Rodes Boulevard. The chamber had been instrumental in the creation of the interchange at I-95 and Ellis and the extension of St. Johns Heritage Parkway south to Malabar Road. However, the narrow 1.7-mile stretch of two lanes created a huge bottleneck for the 20,000 people per day going to work at the airport as well as passengers traveling to fly from the airport. Articles in Florida Today on June 4 and June 9, 2022, said that Ayers had written a letter on behalf of the chamber to Florida Department of Transportation Secretary Jared Perdue requesting a meeting to discuss what Ayers described as an "artery that is a critical component for the continued growth and economic expansion of our community." The news articles affirmed that this project was ranked by the Space Coast Transportation Planning Organization as its top strategic priority.

For 2023, the joint chamber trip to Tallahassee included the following priorities: 1. Talent supply and education; 2. Innovation and economic development; and 3. Business climate and competitiveness. Within each of these priorities, the chambers identified specific proposed legislation which would affect the priorities, together with the legislative sponsors of such legislation.

In 2023, the chamber's attention turned again to downtown redevelopment as well as its own building and how it might fit within the ongoing redevelopment of the area. An article in Florida Today on February 19, 2023, showed that in August 2022 the chamber had pursued a proposal whereby it would partner with a developer and build an 11-story building incorporating parking and a new headquarters on its property. However, as the article revealed, that proposal had been delayed due to "economic conditions" and the chamber was continuing to explore sale of its existing property. An article in Florida Today on July 10, 2023, reported that the chamber had listed its property for sale at $2 million. The developer of The Drift, a proposed eight level, 337-unit apartment building to be built on the site of the former National Bank of Melbourne and Trust Company between Melbourne and New Haven avenues, said that the chamber might consider taking space in that building, however the chamber did not finalize the suggested agreement.

One of the chamber's highlights of 2024 was awarding the Legacy Award to Ted Fuhrer, who had been chair of the chamber in 1985. Ted had been manager of the Rockwell Collins operations in Melbourne from 1976 to 1995, when he was promoted to a senior executive position at Rockwell's headquarters. Ted was a key leader in Brevard County and had exerted an enormous influence through his leadership of several civic organizations, including United Way, Junior Achievement, the Melbourne Airport Authority, and the Brevard Economic Development Council. Ted retired to Georgia but was delighted to return to Melbourne to be recognized by the chamber at its annual impact awards dinner.

Speaking of legacies, another 2024 highlight was Mark Boyd becoming the chair of the board. Mark's father, Joel Boyd, had chaired the chamber in 2009. The only other father and son to lead the chamber were the author and his father, Dave Potter, who led the Greater Melbourne Chamber of Commerce in 1965.

On February 21., 2024 The chamber filed an amendment to its Articles of Incorporation which changed its name to Melbourne Regional Chamber of Florida's Space Coast, inc.

On May 28, 2024, the Chamber closed the sale of tits building for a purchase price of $1,900.000. At the same time, the Chamber entered into a lease with the Airport Authority to rent a building located at 1135 West NASA Boulevard in the midst of the airport industrial park. The intent of the Chamber is to lease this building while searching for a more permanent home. Wisely, the Chamber leadership segregated the funds received from the sale of the building and will hold those funds in an account separate from its operating account and will separately account for those funds. The intent is that these funds not be used for operational expenses but be retained for capital expenditures.

Michael Ayers resigned as President of the chamber at the end of July 2024 in order to assume a position as a senior executive of a manufacturing business which his family has owned for many years. Fortunately, Michael plans to remain in the community and to remain active in civic affairs.

On August 14, 2024, the Chamber announced that it had selected Anne Conroy-Baiter to be its President and CEO. This selection was the culmination of a thorough process that solicited applicants from throughout the U.S. as well as local candidates. The Chamber received more than 100 applications. Virtual interviews were conducted of the top 8 candidates and in person interviews were conducted with the final 3 candidates. Conroy-Baiter was widely perceived to be a brilliant selection, having previously served as President and CEO of Junior Achievement of the Space Coast where she led that organization to unprecedented accomplishments and respect. Upon announcement of her selection, Conroy-Baiter said: "My career has always been fueled by a mission to enhance and enrich the communities we call home, so my commitment to making the Space Coast even more successful and vibrant as we navigate growth and change is unwavering."

CHAPTER NOTES

- As to the Central Florida Partnership and MyRegion.com, see https://issuu.com/centralfloridapartnership/docs/brochure_myregion.org.
- For more about the chamber's advocacy efforts, see https://www.melbourneregionalchamber.com/tallahassee-fly-in/. https://www.melbourneregionalchamber.com/advocacy-program/.
- https://www.melbourneregionalchamber.com-business-advocacy/.
- The quote from Brent Peoples and the information about the initiatives that were taken in 2018 were in an e-mail from Peoples to me dated November 27, 2023.
- For more about the Viera Regional Business Alliance see https://www.melbourneregionalchamber.com/viera-regional--business-alliance/.
- The information regarding the resignation of Ayers and the hiring of Conroy-Baiter is taken from a press release of the Melbourne Regional Chamber on August 14, 2024.

EPILOGUE

I have enjoyed writing this book as it has enabled me to revive some pleasant memories and to recall some interesting people with whom I had the privilege to interact. I think that together we had some positive influence on our community.

The process of researching and writing this book left me with three overriding conclusions. First, when one views the development of south Brevard County from the macro-level, the evolution during the time of the chamber's existence has been truly remarkable. Our community has evolved from a village with an economy based upon fishing, citrus and lumber to a center of aerospace and defense industries. When one considers that communities throughout the country have shrunk in population, lost much of their core industries, and suffered from economic and social blight during this time, we have much to appreciate in the development of our community.

The second conclusion has to do with the role of the chamber in the evolution of our community. While it would be presumptuous to claim that the chamber has been responsible for the evolution of the area, it is not immodest or inaccurate to say that the chamber has been one of the institutions that contributed substantially to the way the community has evolved. It is fair to say that without the chamber the conditions to foster positive development would have been far less favorable.

The chamber has been effective because of the altruistic dedication of several talented individuals who have recognized the organization as a vehicle for community benefit. Certainly, the chamber offers its members many benefits, and many join the chamber to take advantage of the networking opportunities. However, those leaders of the chamber who have had the greatest impact in enabling that chamber to make a substantial difference are those who genuinely believed that it is possible to make the community a better place for everyone. Their altruism is what shines the brightest in this rich history. As I conclude writing this book, Mark Boyd has assumed the chairmanship of the Melbourne Regional Chamber. Mark embodies the spirit of community service established by his grandfather, Dr. Joe Boyd, and his father, Joel Boyd. Mark's decision to contribute some of his community service through the chamber confirms the importance of the role of the chamber in influencing the development of our community. He is one example of what drives leaders to create today and envision tomorrow in concrete, achievable terms.

One final thought: The chamber has not done a creditable job of keeping records of its plans and accomplishments over the years. As you will see from reading the book, I relied primarily upon newspaper archives, personal recollections, and oral interviews to compile this history. I often wished I could speak to those who are no longer here but were crucial to the chamber's growth throughout the early formative years, to gain their perspectives on the future. I hope that this history, which I offer as a legacy to the chamber, will serve as a chronological baseline that current and future leaders will continue over time. It illustrates the true metamorphosis of a special organization that helped build this community in positive ways, and clearly shows how the visionary commitment of a few people working together on a dream can change the world.

AFTERWORD

By: Michael Ayers

As my tenure comes to a close as the President and Chief Executive Officer of the Melbourne Regional Chamber, I reflect on my time and the age-old question of what is the value of the chamber? Having never worked for a chamber prior to this role, I had no idea what I was getting into or what to expect. Now, I can say without a doubt the chamber is the heartbeat of a community, and a strong chamber means a strong, pro-business climate where organizations, large and small, thrive.

The 'value' of a chamber can mean different things to different people. It might be a way to gain more customers in the market through networking, it might be because it is "good for the community" to have a strong chamber, or it may be a way for those new to the area to meet people and get involved. Chambers must continue to evolve to meet the needs of their community partners. The landscape has changed over the last few decades. It used to be the chamber of commerce was the only opportunity when it came to networking and connecting with your community. In modern times, though, people have options ranging from other social/civic clubs to networking groups to engaging with others online, so the chamber must continue to adapt to remain relevant and valuable.

The most consequential chambers are the ones that take substantive action in their community to improve it. The Melbourne Regional Chamber has done this countless times in its history, whether it was advocating for the Melbourne Causeway to be completed, the widening of US 192 or the merger of the cities of Eau Gallie and Melbourne. Each of these items were important to the growth and success of the Space Coast. Those of us who live here now benefit from the hard work that was done before us. Chambers have the bird's eye view to recognize gaps in their communities and then work to fill them. Evidence of this exists in the Chamber's leading role in the creation of the Community Foundation of Brevard, Keep Brevard Beautiful and the eventual formation of the countywide Economic Development Commission of Florida's Space Coast.

One of the greatest accomplishments of my tenure was the transformation of the Chamber's "board" retreat into a "community leadership" retreat. The primary motivation for this was for the Chamber to increase its visibility in the community on significant issues facing our community as we continue to grow and mature.

The Chamber should be the convener of community leaders to talk about the issues that will impact us and what role the Chamber can and should play to proactively shape the outcomes that are best for our business community.

It is my strong opinion that advocacy remains a lynch pin for the success of chambers going forward. While chambers always have and will continue to be the "connectors" in their community, chambers must continue to evolve and lead the way as change agents in their communities. There are many items where leadership in our community is needed and the Chamber must remain engaged in those, including: improving the health of the Indian River Lagoon, supporting crucial upgrades to infrastructure including the expansion of Ellis Road, and continuing the push to ensure our schools have the resources needed to produce students that are ready for work.

While my time at the Melbourne Regional Chamber is now behind me, I look back with fond memories of the people I have met and the accomplishments we achieved together. I am proud of the nearly 100 years of success it has had in our community and remain bullish on the future of the Chamber.

ACKNOWLEDGEMENTS

I appreciate the encouragement and cooperation I have had from the chamber management team in this book. Michael Ayers and Melody Buller have been particularly helpful. Melody is a fount of knowledge about chamber history.

I also spoke and corresponded with several past chairs of the chamber to ask for ideas and recollections. Joel Boyd provided a great deal of information about his term as chair as well as information about noteworthy events in other years. Neal Johnson and Dorothy Allen also provided some valuable information. Jim Ridenour spent time with me relating developments during his term.

Brent Peoples has been unusually active with the chamber during the past decade or so and has taken part in developing much of the chamber's strategy during that time. Brent was able to not only explain what had occurred in the development of that strategy but also provide insight into the factors that caused decisions to be made as they were.

Ted Fuhrer, Brian Lightle, Marj Bartok, Jeff Godwin, Travis Proctor, Tom Mills, Jack Ryals, Jamie Dwight, Julie Braga, and Deb Harmon were also helpful in relating information about their terms as chairs. I appreciate the piece submitted by Lloyd Behrendt describing the efforts of the chamber to promote a balanced growth agenda for the community. Don Nohrr reviewed the manuscript and provided several suggestions.

My friends and former law partners Pat Healy and Gene Cavallucci also loaned their lawyer's eyes to this project in reviewing the manuscript and making useful suggestions. They were both great partners and skilled lawyers and the help they rendered on this book reflected those traits.

Dorothy Allen was indispensable in editing this book and making several valuable suggestions for improving my draft. She volunteered her help and spent many hours which contributed greatly to the accuracy and thoroughness of the book. It was Dotty who suggested the title, a suggestion that I readily accepted given my complete lack of creativity.

This is the fourth book for which Lois Deveneau has done the formatting and cover design for me and guided me in self-publishing. I appreciate the fact that I have not exhausted her patience and that she continues to help me so effectively. She has always made big improvements in my work.

My good friend Harry Deffebach provided me with a couple of publications from Harris Corporation, now L3 Harris, which were useful in relating the history of Harris in the area.

Finally, as with all the books I have written, I appreciate the fact that my wife Wendy tolerates it when I retreat to my office which is littered with news articles and publications while I isolate myself to write.

APPENDICES

APPENDIX A: Population Growth in South Brevard County

City	1920	1940	1970	2000	2020
Melbourne (pre-consolidation)	533	2,622			
Eau Gallie (pre-consolidation)	507	1,114			
Melbourne (consolidated)			40,236	71,382	84,678
Palm Bay (Tillman)	110	349	6,927	79,413	120,181
West Melbourne			3,050	9,824	25,924
Indialantic			2,685	2,944	3,010
Melbourne Beach			2,262	3,335	3,231
Indian Harbour Beach			5,371	8,152	9,019
Satellite Beach			6,558	9,577	11,226
Grant-Valkaria			97	140	4,509
Malabar	201	422	634	2,622	2,949
Micco			119	1,941	9,574
Melbourne Village				597	681
Palm Shores			202	790	1,200
Viera					28,375
Brevard County	8,505	16,142	230,006	476,230	616,628

APPENDIX A NOTES

- The census data was obtained from the United States Census Bureau at census.gov/en.html.
- Some of the information is incomplete since census tracts changed from one census to another and the fact that some of the cities or populated areas have only recently been formed.
- The purpose of the table is to illustrate the population boom which has occurred during the time in which the Melbourne Regional Chamber and its predecessors have existed. Although incomplete, the data sufficiently serves that purpose.

APPENDIX B: Chief Executives of the Melbourne Regional Chamber and its Predecessors

Melbourne Chamber of Commerce
Elton Hall	1919-1920
Leroy W. Cooper	1921
Joseph Masch	1924-1925
Fred Wedler	1925
B.E. Ingham	1927
Harry Goode	1929-1932
W.E. Fitch	1935
F.M. Sawyer	1937
H.B. Fielding	1942
Harry C. Cooke	1943
Arthur C. Cundy	1944
Frank H. Little	1947
Sarah W. Knight	1948

Eau Gallie Chamber of Commerce
R.E.L. Niel	1926-27
Bernice Werley	1952-1954
Polly McAdam	1955
Hazel Turpin	1960
Barbara Madden	1962-1965
Lois Frye	1965-1966

Greater Melbourne Chamber of Commerce
Henry F. Harris	1948-1950
Charles R. Herring	1950-1959
Gary Marco	1959
Robert Manning	1960

West Melbourne Chamber of Commerce
Lonnie Coker	1960
Harlan Manweiler	1960
Paul Schubert	1963
Earl Abbott	1964

Palm Bay Chamber of Commerce
A.J. Knecht	1960

Greater Melbourne Chamber of Commerce
Robert W. Bruce	1962
William A. Moore	1964-1966
Billie Matson	1966

South Brevard Beaches Chamber of Commerce
Elmer H. Haupt	1963-1966

Metropolitan South Brevard Chamber of Commerce, *later Melbourne Area Chamber of Commerce*
Alfred D. Webster	1967-1974

Melbourne Area Chamber of Commerce

Eugene Patterson	1976-1977

Melbourne Area Chamber of Commerce,
later The Chamber of Commerce of South Brevard,
later The Greater South Brevard Area Chamber of Commerce

Willliam G. (Doc) Strawbridge	1978-1988

The Greater South Brevard Area Chamber of Commerce,
later Melbourne-Palm Bay Area Chamber of Commerce

Larry Malta	1988-1995

Melbourne-Palm Bay Area Chamber of Commerce

Steve Dickinson (interim)	1995-1996
Lee Bohlmann	1996-2003
Chuck Galy (interim)	2005
Shannon Meyer	2006-2008

Melbourne-Palm Bay Area Chamber of Commerce,
later Melbourne Regional Chamber of East Central Florida

Christine Michaels	2009-2014

Melbourne Regional Chamber of East Central Florida

Christian D. Malesic	2015-2017

Melbourne Regional Chamber of Florida's Space Coast

Michael S. Ayers	2018-2024
Anne Conroy-Baiter	2024 to present

APPENDIX B NOTES

- The Chief Executive Officer has been known by various titles over the years. In the early years, the highest full-time employee was sometimes known as the secretary or executive secretary. At other times, that employee was referred to as the executive director or executive vice-president. That position currently is given the title of president. Florida Today reported on June 12, 1989, that the chamber had altered its organizational documents to provide that the chief administrative officer would henceforth have the title of president while the volunteer head of the board of directors would have the title of chairperson. Those titles have been used consistently since then.
- From August 1974 until March 1976, the Melbourne Area Chamber of Commerce had no one with the title of Executive Director. Due to financial constraints, the chamber did not hire a replacement for Alfred D. Webster when he retired in August 1974. Bob Bandy, who had been Webster's deputy assumed many of the duties of an executive director from August 1974 until January 1976 and proved to be an effective manager but never was given the title of manager nor a title signifying that he was the chief executive officer.

- It is highly probable that this list is incomplete, but it represents those for whom I could find records.
- Florida Today reported on December 10, 1995, that Steve Dickinson had been appointed interim president of the chamber following the resignation of Larry Malta in September 1995. Dickinson held that interim position until Lee G. Bohlmann was selected for the permanent position as president in March 1996.
- Florida Today reported on March 14, 2005, that the chamber had appointed Chuck Galy as acting president of the chamber. Galy held that interim position until September 2005 when Shannon Meyer was named president of the organization. Galy has been one of the unsung heroes whose dedication to the chamber provided stability to the organization during the ever-changing circumstances in which the chamber operated. Galy was initially hired by the chamber as a marketing representative in April 1990. During the ensuing 28 years, Galy would hold every management position within the organization, including Interim President, Executive Vice-President for Operations, Marketing Director, and head of the Better Business Bureau. Galy's steady presence, calm demeanor and enthusiastic promotion of the chamber's goals provided a reliable and stable base for the organization for many years. Galy, a long-distance runner whose feats included running in the Boston Marathon, retired in November 2015.
- The years during which these executives served are not necessarily complete but merely indicate those years that I could verify they held the office. In many cases, the tenures of these officials would have been more extensive than in the years shown.
- The various names given to the Melbourne Chamber of Commerce during the 1950s, 1960s and 1970s did not signify a change in the organization, but only different names given the organization. Until the merger of the chambers in 1967, the entity continued without change. On September 1, 1967, four chambers of commerce in south Brevard County (Eau Gallie, Melbourne, South Brevard Beaches, and West Melbourne) dissolved the existing chambers and incorporated as the Metropolitan South Brevard Chamber of Commerce, Inc. The Palm Bay Chamber of Commerce declined to join the combined chamber at that time. On February 6, 1970, the Metropolitan South Brevard Chamber of Commerce changed its name to Melbourne Area Chamber of Commerce, Inc. On November 18, 1982, the Melbourne Area Chamber of Commerce,

Inc. changed its name to The Chamber of Commerce of South Brevard, Inc. On December 23, 1986, The Chamber of Commerce of South Brevard, Inc. merged with the Palm Bay Chamber of Commerce to form The Greater South Brevard Area Chamber of Commerce, Inc. On August 12, 1991, the name was once again changed to Melbourne-Palm Bay Area Chamber of Commerce, Inc. On July 16, 2010, the name was changed to Melbourne Regional Chamber of East Central Florida, Inc. Finally, on February 21, 2024, the name was changed to Melbourne Regional Chamber of Commerce of Florida's Space Coast, Inc.

APPENDIX C: Chairs of the Melbourne Regional Chamber and its Predecessors

1925 - 1966

Melbourne Chamber of Commerce
1925	Albert Vorkeller	1947	Locke Davison
1942	W.W. Kerr	1949	Ernest L. Blackburn
1944	H.H Guerin	1952	Walter H. Fordyce
1947	Victor Robbins		

Eau Gallie Chamber of Commerce
1927	Dr. Willam J. Creel	1959	Garrett Quick
1943	Howard G. Blake	1961	Bert N. Pooley
1952	James T. Chapman	1962	Milton McGrath
1953	Van G. Werley	1963	Adger Smith
1954	Aubrey Bates	1958-59	Hal Hagenwald
1955	Ernest L. Johnson, Jr.	1965-1966	Ken Sanders

Greater Melbourne Chamber of Commerce
1954	Charles E. Price	1962	Jim Perrine
1955-56	Richard A. Lawrence	1963	Dr. J. B. Winton
1959	Richard B. Muldrew	1964	John H. Wilson
1960	Ralph Bickford	1965	E. Davison Potter
1961	Hal Curry	1966	Clifford W. Higgins
1962	J. Edward Lyons	1966	William Kercher

Palm Bay Chamber of Commerce
1959	Alex Lindsay	1963-1964	A.O. Eckwall
1960	Herschel Pence	1965	Anne Florin
1962	J.J. Finnegan	1966	Warren F. Foster, Jr.

South Brevard Beaches Chamber of Commerce
1958-59	James R. Allan	1965-1966	Arthur Proulx
1961	Paul Knox	1962	Charles Neimeyer
1963-1964	Roy C. Warner		

West Melbourne Chamber of Commerce
1957	Harland F. Manweiler	1963	William W. Newcomb
1959	Norman Lund, Jr.	1964	Earl Abbott
1960	Lonnie Coker	1965	Dr. Cliff C. Heiner
1961	Charles J. McVey	1966	Harvey Huggins, Jr.
1962	William Hickman		

Metropolitan South Brevard Chamber of Commerce
1968	W.D. Webb
1967	Joseph H. Wickham
1969	Thomas J. Moldenhauer

APPENDIX C, continued: Chairs of the Melbourne Regional Chamber and its Predecessors

1970 - 1990

Melbourne Area Chamber of Commerce
1970	Beville Outlaw	1976	Adger Smith
1971	T. Maurice Rouede	1977	David M. Jones
1972	Howard N. Hebert	1978	Lanny E. Mauldin
1973	Orlando Brillante	1979	Joe E. Glover
1974	William C. Potter	1980	Mike Gatto
1975	Jack E. Burklew	1981	Joseph Brett

The Chamber of Commerce of South Brevard
1982	Jim Whitley	1984	William C. Potter
1982	Yvonne Bixby	1985	Ted Fuhrer
1983	William Sullivan	1986	Sam Bockman

Greater South Brevard Area Chamber of Comm
1987	Maxine Nohrr	1989	Lloyd Behrendt
1988	Ed Silberhorn	1990	Judy Hornsby

1991 - 2025

Melbourne-Palm Bay Area Chamber of Commerce
1991	Tom Mills	2001	James Dwight
1992	Mike Means	2002	Jim Blevins
1993	Wendy Brandon	2003	B. Doug Mead
1994	Gene McCarthy	2004	Marj Bartok
1995	Rodger Ingram	2005	Jim Ridenhour
1996	Brian Lightle	2006	John Hopkins
1997	Donald Nohrr	2007	Kim Brown
1998	David Dugan	2008	Travis Proctor
1999	Dr. Jeff Godwin	2009	Joel Boyd
2000	Bob Stuhlmiller		

Melbourne Regional Chamber of East Central Florida
2012	Franck Kaiser	2019	Kim Agee
2010	Dorothy Allen	2020	Todd Pokrywa
2011	Tom Poehailos	2021	Jeff Robison
2014	Katherine Cobb	2022	Neal Johnson
2015	Glen Chaney	2013	Jack Ryals
2017	Dale Howlett	2016	Julie Braga
2018	Brent Peoples	2023	Deborah Harmon

Melbourne Regional Chamber of Florida's Space Coast
2024	Mark Boyd
2025	Natasha Spencer

APPENDIX C NOTES

- It is highly probable that this list is incomplete, but it lists those for whom I could find records.
- On September 1, 1967, four chambers of commerce in south Brevard County (Eau Gallie, Melbourne, South Brevard Beaches, and West Melbourne) dissolved the existing chambers and incorporated as the Metropolitan South Brevard Chamber of Commerce, Inc. The Palm Bay Chamber of Commerce declined to join the combined chamber at that time. On February 6, 1970, the Metropolitan South Brevard Chamber of Commerce changed its name to Melbourne Area Chamber of Commerce, Inc. On November 18, 1982, the Melbourne Area Chamber of Commerce, Inc. changed its name to The Chamber of Commerce of South Brevard, Inc. On December 23, 1986, The Chamber of Commerce of South Brevard, Inc. merged with the Palm Bay Area Chamber of Commerce to form The Greater South Brevard Area Chamber of Commerce, Inc. On August 12, 1991, the name was once again changed to Melbourne-Palm Bay Area Chamber of Commerce, Inc. On July 16, 2010, the name was changed to Melbourne Regional Chamber of East Central Florida, Inc. Finally, on February 21, 2024, the name was changed to Melbourne Regional Chamber of Florida's Space Coast, Inc.
- The Chair has been known by various titles over the years. In the early years, the highest volunteer, non-paid official was most often known as the president. That position currently is given the title of chair. This list includes the individuals who held the highest non-paid volunteer position in the organization regardless of the title given to their position at the time of their service.
- With all due respect to my fellow former chairs of the Melbourne Chamber, without question the most notable chair was Davy Jones, who was chair in 1977. David M. Jones was a retired Air Force Major General at the time he served as chair, having retired in 1973 as Commander of the Air Force Eastern Test Range and as Department of Defense Manager for Manned Space Flight Support Operations. Maj. Gen. Jones had begun his military career by earning his wings in the Army Air Corps. In early 1942, Jones volunteered for the Doolittle Project, a secret bombing raid to be launched against Japan. On April 18, 1942, Jones and his fellow Doolittle Raiders bombed Tokyo and, lacking fuel to make a safe landing, bailed out

over China. He was aided by Chinese citizens in evading capture and went next to India where he spent three months flying bombing raids against the Japanese. In September 1942, Jones was sent to North Africa to develop low-level bombing techniques. On December 4, 1942, his plane was shot down over North Africa, and he was imprisoned in Stalag Luft III for the next two and a half years. In the prison camp, he was selected to serve on the escape committee and led the work on the tunnel used in the Great Escape. After the war, Jones became a test pilot and, at one point in time, had flown more supersonic jets than any other pilot in the Air Force. The Charles Bronson character, the "Tunnel King," in the 1963 film *The Great Escape* was based upon Davy Jones. In the film about the Doolittle Raid, *Thirty Seconds Over Tokyo*, actor Scott McKay played Jones. Davy died in 2008 at the age of 94. For more about Jones, see "Biographies: Major General David M. Jones" on the official website of the U.S. Air Force, United States Air Force. I retrieved this information from that site on June 21, 2023.
- Another notable chair was Norman Lund, Jr. who was chair of the West Melbourne Chamber of Commerce in 1957. Alas, Lund's notoriety was markedly less desirable. The Orlando Sentinel of August 8, 1967, reported that Lund had been arrested and charged with first degree murder of his wife. Charges against Lund were later reduced to second degree murder, and he went to trial on these charges in December 1967. The Miami Herald reported on December 21, 1967, that Lund had been acquitted following jury deliberations of less than an hour.
- Yvonne (Beck) Bixby became the first female chair of the combined chamber in 1982. Yvonne was a remarkable woman who broke many glass ceilings in Brevard County. Yvonne had emigrated to the U.S. from the Netherlands in the early 1960s and had moved to Brevard County in 1968 to become the manager of a travel agency owned by the National Bank of Melbourne and Trust Company. When the bank decided to sell the agency, Yvonne scraped together sufficient resources to buy it and created a successful business. Although Brevard County was a very conservative area at that time and hardly at the forefront of the feminist movement, Bixby's intelligence, charm, and diligence enabled her to assume leadership roles in several local organizations, including terms as president of the local chapter of the American Cancer Society and the Eau Gallie Rotary Club. She proved to be an exceptional chair of the chamber. An article about Yvonne written by Gayla Schaefer

published by Florida Today on February 28, 2006, was headlined "Immigrant Charms the Space Coast." Yvonne died in 2010 after struggling with breast cancer for several years.
- The only spouses to have each served as chairs of the chamber were Maxine and Don Nohrr. Maxine served as chair in 1987 while Don served in 1997. Don would agree when I assert that Maxine's term as chair was more notable than his term. Not only was Maxine the first chair following the 1986 merger between the Palm Bay and South Brevard chambers, but Maxine presided over one of the most prominent events in the chamber's history when it hosted the luncheon for President Ronald Reagan.

APPENDIX D: Chamber Financial Performance: 2004 To 2022 (USD)

YEAR	REVENUE	EXPENSES	NET ASSETS	MEMBERSHIP DUES REV.	PROGRAM SERV. REV.
2022	$742,154	$687,004	$212,145	$691,362	$2,710
2021	$751,549	$671,406	$156,431	$347,971	$179,810
2020	$603,380	$567,370	$27,092	$409,689	$27,097
2019	$691,256	$668,438	-$8,718	$469,800	$37,536
2018	$616,941	$658,557	-$31,736	$414,039	$38,085
2017	$686,279	$761,706	$9,536	$406,845	$72,192
2016	$677,696	$784,763	$106,439	$461,796	$32,257
2015	$721,483	$731,074	$213,506	$473,450	$45,015
2014	$660,738	$731,926	$223,097	$500,552	$26,982
2013	$635,423	$683,988	$294,285	$475,797	$47,478
2012	$631,226	$674,125	$342,850	$478,074	$36,844
2011	$629,644	$663,665	$385,749	$502,076	$63,186
2010	$659,483	$657,917	$429,770	$482,549	$97,528
2009	$701,474	$752,242	$418,204	$503,146	$68,599
2008	$842,921	$877,082	$468,972	$576,593	$80,365
2007	$901,339	$871,305	$503,133	$595,939	$118,130
2006	$828,857	$824,766	$473,099	$570,695	$50,173
2005	$764,379	$683,815	$469	$544,527	$72,007
2004	$709,666	$695,362	$388,444	$536,017	$50,333

APPENDIX D NOTES

- These data are taken from the IRS Form 990 filed by the chamber per applicable IRS regulations. These returns are published by Pro Publica and were retrieved from the website at propublica.org. I was unable to find Form 990's for the chamber prior to 2004.
- The numbers in the 990's as to the chamber's net assets have little practical meaning. The Financial Accounting Standards Board (FASB) issued Standard Number 93 in 1987, which required exempt organizations to recognize depreciation of capital assets. By far, the chamber's key asset is its office building; the value reflected on

Form 990 filed by the chamber reflects the depreciated value of the building, which bears little or no relationship to its fair market value. Thus, the chamber's actual net assets as of 2022 are understated on Form 990.
- It is impossible to ignore the data that show that membership dues have declined during the period shown. What is not clear, however, is the reason for that decline. There has been a very substantial increase in the number of businesses in south Brevard during that time. However, there has also been an explosion of growth in the number and variety of business organizations in the area. My speculation is that the decline in dues revenue results from the increased number of business organizations competing to be the advocacy group for businesses. The revenue decline in 2020 is undoubtedly largely due to the pandemic. Chamber leaders who have looked at this issue periodically have found these trends in membership to be consistent with national trends among chambers and other business membership organizations.
- The fluctuation in revenues from program services is another unclear item. The widely disparate income figures result from the intermittent and unforeseeable opportunities for programs that generate substantial revenues.
- It is notable that the chamber has done a respectable job of controlling expenses during the time shown. Unfortunately, controlling the costs in such an organization usually relates to tight control of the staff size.
- The building bought by the chamber in 1973 has provided financial security for the organization. It has been an asset that the chamber has used as collateral to borrow operating capital during lean times. In 2021, under the leadership of Neal Johnson, the chamber appointed a task force to make recommendations about the building. By that time, the building was direly needing some critical repairs. The building was also substantially larger than the space needed for chamber operations. On the other hand, land values in downtown Melbourne had exploded, and the building had become very valuable. The task force, composed of past and current chamber leaders, identified four options for consideration by the Board of Directors: 1. Renovation of the building; 2. Redevelopment of the building through a joint development effort with a private developer; 3. Retaining the land and development of the air rights with a private development partner; and 4. Selling and purchasing another building. After receiving and considering the report of the

task force, the Board of Directors decided to sell the building and, as noted above, sold the property in May 2024.

- The chamber has done a remarkable job in maintaining its effectiveness despite dramatic shifts in its revenue. It has done so by managing its finances closely and adopting prompt changes in reaction to revenue fluctuations. One of the reasons it has been able to do so is that it has had a financial manager who has provided unusual stability and experience. Melody Buller has been the financial manager of the chamber since March 1987. Florida Today reported on April 18, 2004, that her title had been changed to chief financial officer. Florida Today reported on August 26, 2007, that she had been recognized for her 20 years of service by the Florida Association of Chamber Professionals Leadership Conference. Chamber CEO Shannon Meyer commented on that award by saying: "It is a great honor to have someone as dedicated to the chamber as her on our staff. She is an integral part of our team, and she is well deserving of this distinguished honor." Melody's continued presence, historical knowledge, financial skills, and profound dedication to the chamber have been and still are today an essential element in the organization's stability.

BIBLIOGRAPHY

Books

Amis, A. B., and John G. Johnson. "Radiation, Inc.: An Anthology of Defining Stories." 2nd ed., George P. Burdell Publishing, 2019.

Charles River Editors. "The Space Shuttle Challenger Disaster: The History and Legacy of NASA's Most Notorious Tragedy" Create Space Independent Publishing Platform, 2016.

Cleveland, Weona. "Crossroad Towns Remembered: A Look Back at Brevard and Indian River Pioneer Communities." Florida Today, 1994.

Cleveland, Weona. "Mosquito Soup." The Florida Historical Society Press, 2014.

Ellis, William D. "The Harris Story." Published by Harris Corporation. 1972.

Melbourne Area Chamber of Commerce Centennial Committee. "Melbourne: A Century of Memories." 1980.

Melbourne Centennial Committee. "A Tribute to Melbourne's Pioneers." 1989.

Patterson, Gordon. "Florida Institute of Technology." Arcadia Publishing, 2000.

Perkins, Frank. "High Tech Among the Palmettos: The Story of Radiation, Inc. and How It Changed the Face of South Brevard County." Oak Publishing, 2014.

Peters, Dr. James F. "Return to Flight: Inside NASA's Space Shuttle Missions in the Wake of the Columbia Disaster." Create Space Independent Publishing Platform, 2015

Potter, William. "Melbourne Orlando International Airport: A History from 1928 to 2022." Self-published, 2022.

Raley, Karen, and Ann Raley Flotte. "Melbourne and Eau Gallie (Images of America)." Arcadia Publishing, 2002.

Stone, Elaine Murray. "Brevard County: From Cape of the Canes to Space Coast." Windsor Publications, 1988.

Periodicals

Patterson, Gordon. "Countdown to College: Launching Florida Institute of Technology." Florida Historical Quarterly, Volume 77, Number 2, Fall 1998

Patterson, Gordon. "Space University, Lift-Off of Florida Institute of Technology." Florida Historical Quarterly, Volume 79, Number1, Summer 2000.

Websites

https://www.melbourneregionalchamber.com/.
https://www.uschamber.com/.
https://www.melbourneregionalchamber.com/tallahassee-fly-in/.
https://www.melbourneregionalchamber.com/advocacy-program/.
https://www.melbourneregionalchamber.com-business-advocacy/.

ABOUT THE AUTHORS

William C. Potter is a graduate of Brown University and the University of Michigan Law School. He practiced law in Florida from 1965 until 2002, serving as president of the firm of Potter, McClelland, Marks, and Healy and, later, as a partner in the firm of Holland & Knight. In 2002 he moved to Europe to serve as Head of the Rule of Law Department of the Office of the High Representative (OHR) in Bosnia and Herzegovina. OHR handled administering the Dayton  Peace Agreement which ended the brutal war which had taken place in the Balkans during the early 1990s. He served as a director of what is now the Melbourne Regional Chamber for more than 25 years, serving as chair in 1974 and 1984. He served on the board of directors of several banks and businesses, including a publicly traded defense contractor and an insurance company. He served as legal counsel for the Melbourne Airport Authority for more than 25 years and has now served as a member of the authority for 18 years. He is currently serving as chair of the authority. He served as a Trustee of Florida Institute of Technology from 1980 to 2022, including serving as Chair from 1990 to 1997. He currently serves as Trustee Emeritus. He was inducted into the Florida Tech Sports Hall of Fame in 2017. He was inducted into the Space Coast Business Hall of Fame in 2016. He is the author of the book *A Bosnian Diary: A Floridian's Experience in Nation-Building*, published by the Florida Historical Society in 2005 and the book *Melbourne Orlando International Airport: A History from 1928 to 2022*, self-published in 2022. Potter is also the co-author of *A History of Intercollegiate Athletics at Florida Institute of Technology: 1958 to 2023*, published in 2023, and author of *Ramblings*, self-published in 2024. Potter is a retired officer of the Florida Air National Guard, where he served as Judge Advocate General for Florida. He and his wife Wendy are the parents of three children and grandparents of three grandchildren. They divide their time between Indialantic and Montana.

Michael Ayers was President and CEO of the Melbourne Regional Chamber from January 2018 to July 2024. From 2015 to 2017, Ayers was the Director of Government Relations for Sanford Burnham Prebys Medical Discovery Institute in Lake Nona. Prior to that time, Ayers served as Chief of Staff for three agencies in the State of Florida, the Agency for Persons with Disabilities, the Department of Economic Opportunity,  and the Agency for Workforce Innovation. Prior to coming to Florida, Ayers worked on Capitol Hill, serving as a legislative assistant to Congressman Robin Hayes and working for the House Committee on Government Reform. Ayers earned a Bachelor of Science in Business Administration degree from the University of Illinois in 2001. He lives in Melbourne with his wife Kaite and their two children.

INDEX

A

A&P grocery store, 6, 135
Abbott, Earl, 227, 231
Adams, Tom, 27, 28, 154
Agee, Kim, 208, 232
Air Force Missile Test Center, 18, 69
Alexandria, 134, 200
Allan, James R., 231
Allen, Balaam, 9
Allen, Dorothy, 173, 201, 223, 232
Allen, Ken, 108, 122, 125
American Automobile Association magazine, 101
American technological education, 18, 69
Amherst College in Massachusetts, 56
Amis, A. B., 39, 240
Ann Raley, 17, 39, 240
Apollo Program, 30-32, 35
Arlington, 9
Ashwell, Dave, 153
Askew, Reuben, 134
Associated Chambers of Commerce of Brevard County, 55-57, 65
Association of Chamber of Commerce Executives (ACCE), 44
Atlantic Gulf Communities, 30
Atlantic Ocean, 11, 56, 64
Aurora Road, 149
Ayers, Michael, iii, 7, 208, 209, 211, 214, 219, 223, 242
Air Force Eastern Test Range, 110, 233

B

Bahama Beach Club, 76
Banana River Expressway, 101, 102
Banana River Naval Air Station, 14, 17, 18, 62, 69
Bandy, Bob, 138, 142, 228
Barnes Engineering Company, 98
Bartok, Marj, 193, 223, 232
Basham, Ralph, 178
Bates, Aubrey, 231

BCC-FIT campus, 152
Bechtel, Roberta (Bobby), 166
Beechcraft, 31
Beeline Highway, 101, 103
Behrendt, Lloyd, 155, 157, 163, 181, 223, 232
Bethpage, 36
Better Business Bureau, 88, 93, 94, 111, 182, 229
Bickford, Ralph, 231
Big orange, 19, 83
Biggs, Gloria, 134
Bixby, Yvonne, 232
Blackburn, Ernest L., 75, 76, 231
Blake, Howard G., 62, 231
Blevins, Jim, 232
Blue-green Indian River, 58
Bockman, Sam, 232
Bohlmann, Lee, 177, 192, 193, 228
Bosnia, 242
Boston Tea Party, 44
Boyd, Dr. Joe, 21, 217
Boyd, Joel, 154, 167, 173, 200, 201, 205, 213, 217, 223, 232
Boyd, Johnny, 72
Boyd, Mark, 213, 217, 232
Boykin, Marshall, 108
Boylan, Tony, 182, 184
Braga, Julie, 223, 232
Brandon, Harry, 154
Brandon, Wendy, 232
Brett, Joseph, 232
Brevard business community, 211
Brevard Community College, 108, 151, 169
Brevard Council of Chambers, 107, 162
Brevard Country, iii-240
Brevard County Board of Commissioners, 48
Brevard Economic Development Agency, 88
Brevard Economic Development Council (BEDC), 161, 165
Brevard Engineering College (BEC), 24
Brevard Hospital Association, 34, 41

Brevard Junior College, 108
Brevard Museum of Natural History, 97
Brevard Public Schools (BPS), 184
Brevard Sentinel-Star, 3
Brevard Ship Canal, 56
Brevard World Fair Authority, 98
Brevard-Osceola County line, 86
Brevard's legislative delegation, 122
Bridgeport Engineering Institute (BEI), 23
Briggs, W. R., 57
Brillante, Orlando, 134, 135, 232
Bronson, Charles, 234
Brown, Colvin, 57
Brown, Frank B., 85
Brown, Kim, 232
Brownlie Hall, 29
Brownlie, V.C., 26
Bruce, Robert, 27
Bryant, Farris, 27, 95
buffer zones, 140
Building Community Leadership Programs, 181
Buller, Melody, 223, 238
Bumper 8, 18, 69
Burdell, George P., 39, 240
Burklew, jack E., 232
Burton, O.L., 83
Business Education Committee of the chamber, 150
Butt, Noah B., 59

C

C. Potter, William, i, iv, 40, 232, 242
Callahan, Pat, 72
Caloosahatchee River, 55
Campbell Point, 51
Campbell, J.O., 48
Canada, 29, 203
Canaveral Harbor, 13, 61
Canaveral Harbor District, 61
Canova Beach, 13, 54
Canova, C.C., 54
Cape Canaveral, 5, 13, 18, 20, 23, 24, 27, 34, 39, 61, 69, 74, 85, 87, 97
Cape Canaveral Auxiliary Air Force Base, 18
Cape Canaveral Hospital, 34
Carolina route, 64
Carr, Marjorie Harris, 66
Cary-Elwes, Reverend H., 48
Cavallucci, Gene, 223
Cedar Rapids, Iowa, 31, 200
Census Bureau, 92, 93, 226
Central and Southern Flood Control District, 100
Central Florida, 7, 18, 20, 28, 31, 58, 61, 62, 69, 77, 97, 102, 103, 130, 156, 167, 182, 187, 198, 201, 202, 205, 208, 215, 228, 230, 232, 233
Certified Plus Chamber, 173
Chaney, Glen, 232
Chapman, James T., 231
Charleston, 44
Chemical, Dow, 28
Chiles', Lawton, 139
China, 234
Christ church, 27
Chubb, 37, 41
Circuit Court Judge, 34
City of West Melbourne, 20, 91, 116
Clark Maxwell, Jr, 169
Clark, Milton, 10
Cleveland, Weona, 40, 240
Cobb, Katherine, 232
Cocoa Beach, 14, 87, 102, 122, 167, 181, 198, 211
Cocoa Ranch, 38
Cocoa Tribune, 5, 26-28, 48, 50, 56, 57, 60-62, 70, 72, 76, 77, 79, 80, 82, 87, 89, 97, 98, 112, 120
Coker, Lonnie, 91, 227, 231
Collins Pro Line avionics, 31
Collins Radio company, 31, 41
Collins, Arthur, 31
Collins, LeRoy, 86
Community Foundation for Brevard, 3, 6, 167, 168

Community Foundation of South Brevard, 6, 168
Conroy-Baiter, Anne, 7, 214, 228
Cooke, Harry C., 227
Cooper, Leroy W., 50, 227
Coordination Council of Brevard County, 77
Couch, Roy O., 64
counties-Brevard, 202
Country Club Drive, 26
County Agricultural Agent, 57
County, Berks, 205
Courthouse extension facilities, 83
South Brevard county, iii, 2, 8-11, 13, 17, 20, 23, 29, 30, 34, 35, 38, 39, 41, 61, 69, 70, 73, 78, 80, 91, 93, 96, 99, 100, 102, 111, 115, 117, 118-121, 125, 128, 166, 183, 194, 217, 226, 229, 233, 240
COVID-19, 211, 212
Cowan, Harry, 172
Cowles, Gardner, 30
Crane Creek, 9, 10, 58, 108
Creel, Dr. W.J., 56, 83
Creel, Dr. Willam J., 231
Cross Florida Barge Canal, 65, 66
cross-state highway, 49
Crowne Plaza Oceanfront, 202
Cundy, Arthur C., 227
Cunningham, Gary, 186
Curry, Hal, 231
Customs and Border Protection (CBP), 178

D
D.C, Washington, 117
Dandridge, Marty, 37
Dania, 59
Darden, Woodrow, 24
Davison, Locke, 231
Daytona, 51, 58, 60, 140
Daytona Beach, 60, 140
Deepwater port, 13, 61, 63
Deffebach, Harry, 40, 224
Deltona Corporation, 30
Denius, Homer, 20, 25, 39, 117

Department of Commerce's International Trade Administration, 169
Development of Regional Impact (DRI), 38
Deveneau, Lois, 223
Dibble, Harold, 23
Dickinson, Steve, 187, 228, 229
Dicks, Vernon, 122
Dixie Highway (now U.S. Highway One), 50, 51
Dixon, Donya, 23
Downtown Melbourne Association, 168
Dr. James F. Peters, 195
Duda, A., 38, 42
Duda, Joe, 155
Dugan, David, 232
Dwight, James, 232
Dwight, Jonathan, 101

E
East Central Florida Regional Planning Council, 102, 103, 201
East Coast Association, Inc., 60
East Coast Canal, 56
East Coast Highways Association of Florida, 84
Eastern Florida State College Aviation Center, 204
Eastern's Silver Falcons, 80
Eau Gallie (pre-consolidation), 226
Eau Gallie Boulevard, 131, 148, 150
Eau Gallie Bridge, 54
Eau Gallie Causeway Boulevard, 54
Eau Gallie Chamber of Commerce, 5, 19, 50, 52, 54-56, 59, 62, 79, 80, 82, 83, 86, 227, 231
Eau Gallie Civic Center, 88
Eau Gallie Record, 54
Eau Gallie Rotary Club, 94, 234
Eau Gallie's harbor, 56
Eckwall, A. O., 99, 231

Economic Development Commission of Florida's Space Coast, 88, 165, 220
Edge, Walter, 72-74
Edmundson, Woody, 72
Ellis, William D., 240
Elton Hall, 48, 49, 61, 227
Ennis, Richard, 178
Evans Library, 26

F

Fielding, H.B., 62, 227
Financial Accounting Standards Board (FASB), 236
Finnegan, J.J., 94, 231
Fishing haven, 92
Fishing Rodeo, 80
Fitch, W.E., 227
Florida, i-242
Florida 2011 TechXpo, 203
Florida Association of Chamber Professionals (FACP), 173
Florida Association of Colleges and Universities (FACU), 26
Florida Canada Corporation, 29
Florida Chamber of Commerce, 157, 184, 201
Florida Christian Churches, 96
Florida Cross State Canal, 59
Florida Department of Environmental Protection, 74
Florida East Coast Railroad, 9, 10, 59
Florida Flying Alligator Club, 70
Florida Flying Alligators, 74
Florida Greenway, 66
Florida Inland Navigation Commission, 56
Florida Institute of Space Technology, 27
Florida Institute of Technology, 1, 23, 28, 29, 40, 84, 97, 203, 240, 242
Florida Power, 70, 187
Florida Presbyterian College, 27
Florida Technological University (FTU), 28
Florida Today, 21-240
Florida Turnpike, 91
Florida's East Coast, 58, 77
Florida's High Tech Corridor Commission, 204
Florida's Space Coast, i, 7, 65, 88, 99, 165, 214, 220, 228, 230, 232, 233
Florin, Anne, 231
Fogg, Jack, 81, 98
Fordyce, 80, 81, 231
Fordyce, Walter H., 231
Fort Lauderdale, 21, 58-60
Fort Lauderdale News, 58
Fort Myers News-Press, 55, 192
Fort Pierce News-Tribune, 58
Fort Pierce-Orlando, 91
Forward Thrust for Unity, 124
Foster, Ed, 36, 176
Foster, Edward L., 32
Foster, Warren, 107
Foster, Warren F., Jr., 231
Fourth District Court of Appeals, 102
Freese, Duane De, 156
Frey, Lou, 131, 133
Friedland, Nate, 108
Front Street Park, 51
Front Street south of the Indialantic bridge, 51
Frye, Lois, 227
Fuhrer, Ted, 41, 154, 213, 223, 232
FY 1977-78, 141

G

Gaarder Phil, 154
Gaedcke, Marcia, 211
Gallion, Bailey, 211
Galy, Chuck, 192, 194, 198, 205, 228, 229
Gatto, Mike, 232
General Development Corporation (GDC), 29
Gilbert A, Colonel, 56
Giles, James, 55
Gleason, Lansing W., 52, 126, 128
Gleason, William Henry, 9
Glenn, John, 5
Glover, Joe E., 232

Godwin, Dr. Jeff, 232
good roads committee of the Melbourne Chamber of Commerce, 51
Goode, Harry, 227
Goode, John, 9
Goode, Richard W., 9
Patterson, Gordon, 40, 240
Governor's Chamber of Commerce Merit Award program, 95
Graham, Bob, 148
Grant-Valkaria, 226
Graves, Cyrus, 11
Gray, Bill, 150
Gray, William, 151
Great Depression, 12, 13
Greater Cocoa Chamber of Commerce Mosquito Control Committee, 62
Greater South Brevard Area Chamber of Commerce, 6, 183, 228, 230, 233
Green, Harry, 50
Griffenhagen, Edwin O., 117
Grissom, Gus, 28
Growth Management Symposium, 155
Grumman 6F Hellcat, 15
Grumman Corporation, 35, 37, 40
Grumman F4F Wildcat aircraft, 15
Guerin, H.H, 231
Gulf Atlantic Ship Canal, 65
Gulf Coast, 65, 209

H

Hagenwald, Hal, 231
Haley, James, 131
Hardee, Cary, 51
Harmon, Deborah, 232
Harris, H. E., 77
Harris, Henry F., 227
Haulover Canal, 13
Haupt, E.H. Jr., 99
Haupt, Elmer H., 227
Hayes, Robin, 242
Healy, Pat, 223
Hebert, Howard N., 132, 165, 232
Hector, Cornthwaite John, 9
Heiner, Clif, 103
Heiner, Dr. Cliff C., 231
Mike Rozier, 152
Heisman, 152
Henderson, Kaye, 162
Herald, Bradenton, 59, 147
Herlong Jr, Sidney S., 77
Herlong, Syd, 92
Herring, Abbott, 108
Herring, Charles L., 85, 88, 115
Herring, Charles R., 227
Herzegovina, 242
Hibiscus Boulevard, 22
Hickman, William, 231
Hickory Street, 34
Higgins, Cliff, 106, 107
Higgins, Clifford W., 231
high-rise bridge, 50, 148, 152
Highway A1A, 65, 106, 193
Holmes Regional Medical Center (HRMC), 34
Home Builders Association of Berks County in Pennsylvania, 205
Honest John's Fish Camp, 11
Honor America, Inc., 143, 165
Hopkins, George Washington, 10
Hopkins, John, 232
Hornsby, Judy, 232
Houston IV, John Carol, 9
Howlett, Dale, 232
Jr, Huggins Harvey, 231

I

Immigrant Charms the Space Coast, 235
Inc, Griffenhagen-Kroeger, 117
India, 234
Indialantic, 11, 13, 39, 48, 49, 51, 54, 59, 60, 75, 76, 84, 87, 94, 112, 115, 116, 118, 121, 131, 226, 242
Indialantic-By-The-Sea, 13
Indian Harbour Beach, 118, 122, 152, 226
Indian River Area, 9
Indian River Bluff, 78
Indian River lagoon system, 158

Ingham, B.E., 227
Ingram, Bruce, 227
Indialantic Hotel, 11
Indialantic Casino, 11
Ingram, Rodger, 187, 232
Inlet Committee, 54
INLNEP - the Indian River Lagoon National Estuary Program, 156
Inside the Iron Works, 36, 41
Institute of Management Studies, 27
Institute of Organizational Management, 152
Internal Revenue Code, 45, 167
IRS, 236

J

J-STARS program, 36, 41
Jacobus, Bruce, 70
Jacobus, Curt, 70
Jacobus, Dale, 70
jai alai fronton, 93
Jane Green Penna-Wah, 10
Jefferson Mammoth elephant, 55
Jesse, Jim, 134
John Rodes Boulevard, 87, 212
Johnson, Beth, 124
Johnson, Bob, 176
Johnson, Ernest L., Jr., 231
Johnson, Jim, 176
Johnson, John G., 39, 240
Johnson, Neal, 212, 223, 232, 237
Joint Long-Range Proving Ground (JLRPG), 18, 69
Jones, Davey, 144
Jones, David M., 232-234
Jorgensen, John, 78
Joseph, Williams B., 107
Jurgens, Bill, 1

K

Kaiser, Franck, 232
Karen Raley, 17, 39
Kelly, Robert, 23
Kennedy Space Center, 30, 193
Kercher, Bill, 108
Kercher, William, 231
Kerr, W.W., 231

Keuper, Jerome, 23, 96
King, Dr. Maxwell C., 169
Kirk, Claude, 131, 134
Kissimmee, 48-51
Knecht, A.J., 227
Knight, Sarah W., 72, 227
Knox, Paul, 231
Koller, Stan, 116
Kouwen-Hoven, Ernest, 11, 48, 145

L

L3Harris, 20
Labor Day celebration, 77
Lake Washington, 9, 80, 140
landlocked harbor, 82
Latham, Charles, 11
Lawrence, Richard A., 231
Leesburg Watermelon Festival, 72
Liberty Bell Museum, 143, 165
Lichty, Stanley S., 48
Light Company, 70
Lightle, Brian, 190, 223, 232
Lindsay, Alex, 231
Little, Frank H., 73, 225
Loan Association of Indian River County, 131
lower east coast, 49
lunar excursion module (LEM), 36
Lund, Norman, 87, 231, 234
Lyons, J. Edward, 231

M

Madden, Barbara, 227
Malabar, 15, 17, 29, 30, 34, 75, 89, 94, 126, 152, 212, 226
Malesic, Christine D., 228
Malta, Larry, 181, 184, 186, 187, 228, 229
Manatee Chamber of Commerce, 208
Manned Orbital Laboratory, 104
Manning, Robert, 227
Manolates, Tony, 191
Manweiler, Harland F., 231
Marathon, Boston, 229
Marco, Gray, 227
Martinez, Bob, 185

Masch, Joseph, 51, 52, 227
Mason, Jack, 168
Mason, Thomas, 9
Massachusetts Institute of Technology, 23
Mathers, Al, 59
Matson, Billie, 227
Mauldin, Lanny E., 232
Maxwell King Center, 169
Maxwell, Clark, 130, 169
McAdam, Polly, 227
McCarthy, Gene, 232
McCauley, John, 187
McCauley, John E., 32
McClelland, Clif, 150
McGrath, Milton, 102, 107, 231
McIntyre, Larry, 167
McKay, Scott, 234
McKeown, Kevin, 38, 64, 128, 179
McNulty, C. H., 62
McVey, Charles J., 231
McWilliams, Mike, 155
Mead, B. Doug, 232
Means, Mike, 232
Meehan, Dennis, 154
Melbourne (consolidated), 226
Melbourne (pre-consolidation), 226
Melbourne Airport, 21, 22, 25, 29, 35-37, 40, 71, 72, 78, 81, 95, 98, 103, 108, 140, 175-177, 213, 242
Melbourne Airport Authority, 22, 37, 140, 175, 176, 213, 242
Melbourne and Eau Gallie chambers, 48, 81, 95, 106, 117, 118
Melbourne and Piper in Vero Beach, 212
Melbourne Area Board of Realtors, 135, 142, 165
Melbourne Area Chamber Foundation, 6, 167, 169
Melbourne Area Chamber of Commerce, 6, 39, 129, 130-132, 135, 141-143, 147-149, 166, 169, 227-229, 232, 233, 240

Melbourne Beach, 11, 39, 75, 77, 115, 116, 118, 121, 124, 226
Melbourne Beach Investment Company, 11
Melbourne Business and Professional Association, 73
Melbourne Centennial Committee, 13, 39, 240
Melbourne Chamber of Commerce, 3, 5, 12, 48-53, 55-57, 59-63, 68, 70, 71, 73, 75-81, 84, 86, 87, 96, 98, 102, 105, 115-117, 168, 214, 227, 229, 231, 234
Melbourne Chamber's transportation, 50
Melbourne City Council, 51, 52, 58, 64, 78, 152, 166, 210
Melbourne Civic Auditorium, 6, 161, 163
Melbourne Downtown Redevelopment Committee, 168
Melbourne High School Stadium, 100
Melbourne Municipal Airport, 15, 70
Melbourne Naval Air Station, 15, 17
Melbourne Orlando International Airport, 1, 40, 41, 57, 128, 175, 179, 204, 240, 242
Melbourne Railway, 50
Melbourne Regional Chamber, i, iii, 1-3, 7, 9, 42, 45, 48, 69, 155, 165, 167, 170, 173, 201-203, 205, 208, 209, 212, 214, 215, 217, 220, 221, 226-228, 230-233, 242
Melbourne Regional Chamber of Commerce, i, 1, 7, 208, 230
Melbourne Regional Chamber of East Central Florida, 7, 201, 205, 208, 228, 230, 232, 233
Melbourne Regional Chamber of Florida's Space Coast, 7, 214, 228, 232, 233
Melbourne Rotary Club, 115
Melbourne Times, 14, 52, 54, 136, 140, 175

Melbourne Village, 118, 226
Melbourne Vocational School, 79
Melbourne-Cocoa, 60
Melbourne-Eau Gallie Airport, 14, 15
Melbourne-Indialantic bridge, 48
Melbourne-Kissimmee Road, 49, 50
Melbourne-Palm Bay Area Chamber of Commerce, 6, 7, 177, 183, 185, 190, 194, 197, 199-201, 228, 230, 232, 233
Melbourne-Palm Bay Chamber, 184, 186, 191-193, 197, 198
Melbourne's Beaches of the Sea Island, 72
Melhado, Micheal, 208
Melpar, 20
Melton, C. E., 51
Merritt Island, 13, 62
Merritt Island Launch Area, 13
Methodist Church, 25
Metro-Orlando Economic Development Commission, 202
Metropolitan Planning Organization (MPO), 149
Metropolitan South Brevard Chamber of Commerce, 5, 6, 30, 110-112, 120, 124, 127, 130, 166, 227, 229, 231, 233
Meyer, iii, 178, 196-200, 206, 228, 229, 231, 238
Meyer, Shannon, 178, 197, 198, 200, 228, 229, 238
Miami, 16, 21, 35, 48, 50-54, 58-60, 62-65, 69, 70, 72-81, 84, 88, 89, 91-93, 95-103, 107, 109, 110, 116, 117, 130, 132, 135, 148, 161, 234
Miami Herald, 16, 35, 48, 50-54, 59, 62, 65, 69, 70, 72-75, 77-80, 84, 88, 89, 91-93, 95-97, 99, 100-103, 107, 109, 110, 116, 117, 130, 132, 135, 161, 234
Michaels, Christine, 173, 200, 203, 204, 228
Michigan, 10, 21, 147, 242
Midway City, 53

Mills, Tom, 223, 232
Minnesota, 197
Miracles, Myers, 193
Miss Florida pageant, 77
Miss Indian River, 77
Missile Test Project, 23
Mississippi, 198
Biloxi Bay, 198
Moldenhauer, Thomas J., 231
Moldenhauer, Tom, 108, 121, 134
Moore, William A., 106, 227
Mr. Canova, 54
Muldrew, Dick, 92, 122
Muldrew, Richard B., 231
Mullet Creek, 11
Mullins, Dr. Mark, 209
Mullins, Joe, 176
Murray Elaine, Stone, 39, 240
Myers, Tom, 136

N

NAS Melbourne, 15
NASA Boulevard, 7, 22, 109, 214
NASA's, 163, 195, 201, 240,
National Academy Foundation, 190
National Bank of Melbourne, 25, 135, 213, 234
National Industry Recovery Act, 34
Naval Air Stations, 14, 16
Naval Expansion Act, 14, 62
Naval Expansion Act of 1938, 62
Navigation Company, 50
Navy Knox, 15
Negro census, 79
Neimeyer, Charles, 231
New Falmouth, Jamaica, 141
New Haven Avenue, 60, 78, 85, 155, 213
New Smyrna, 58
New York's LaGuardia Airport, 177
Newcomb, William W., 231
Niel, R.E.L., 227
Niel, Robert E.I., 56
Nixon, Richard, 66
Noel, S.D., 50
Nohrr, Donald, 232
Nohrr, Maxine, 157, 160, 232

Noll, Steven, 66
North Africa, 234
North American Rockwell Corporation, 31
North side of Turkey Creek, 9
Northrop-Grumman, 42, 205

O

Ocala, 65
Office of the High Representative (OHR), 242
Oklawaha River, 66
Oleanders Hotel, 79
Operation Unity, Inc. (OUI), 125
Ordinance 66-1, 175
Orlando, 1-242
Orlando Chamber of Commerce, 57, 202
Orlando Evening Star, 68, 75, 77, 81-85, 94-98, 100, 102, 103, 105-107, 109, 110, 115-119, 130, 131, 134
Orlando International Airport, 1, 40, 41, 57, 128, 175, 179, 204, 240, 242
Orlando Regional Chamber, 199, 201
Orlando Sentinel, 5, 29, 35, 41, 48, 53, 55, 57, 79, 83-88, 91-96, 98-112, 115, 117, 130-132, 134, 135, 140-142, 147, 150, 151, 157, 161, 165, 166, 201, 202, 234
Stewart, Linda, 156
Osceola Country, 10, 86, 149, 183
Outlaw, Beville, 108, 130, 131, 232
"outside harbor", 82
O'Connell, Dan, 167
O'Kelley, Harold, 119, 128

P

Palm Bay, 5-235
Palm Bay (Tillman), 226
Palm Bay Chamber of Commerce, 5, 88, 182, 227, 229-231, 233
Palm Bay Community Hospital (PBCH), 34
Palm Beach, 49, 53, 58, 60, 103
Palm Shores, 118, 121, 226

Palmer, Pasty, 141
Park, Wickham, 108, 109, 183
Parrish, J.J., 59, 60
Passman, Harry M., 31, 32
Patrick AFB, 18, 69
Patrick Air Force Base, 69, 74, 81, 83, 87, 101, 107, 109, 134
Patterson, Eugene W., 143
Pave Mover Radar Program, 36
Peel, David, 52
Peltonen, Nancy, 211
Pence, Herschel, 231
Pensacola News Journal, 51
Peoples, Brent, 170, 208, 215, 223, 232
Perkins, Frank, 39, 128, 240
Perrine, Jim, 231
Peters, George, 23
Pickett, Bylynn, 198
Pineda Causeway, 101, 102, 104, 197
Pino, Larry, 201
Piper, 31, 212
Platt, Cecil, 116
Platt, Sidney, 78, 81, 98
Poehailos, Tom, 202, 232
Pokrywa, Todd, 208, 232
Pompano Beach, 147
Pooley, Bert, 93, 108
Port Canaveral, 14, 61-63
Port Malabar, 29, 30, 89, 94, 126
Potter, Dave, 214
Potter, Davison E., 102, 231
Potter, William C., i, iv, 40, 232, 242, 179,
Powell, Bill, 122
Price, Charles E., 231
Price, Wayne, 191
Proctor, Travis, 167, 200, 201, 205, 223, 232
Proulx, Art, 106, 108
Proulx, Arthur, 231
Pruitt, James, 65
Public Utilities Commission, 74

Q

Quick, Garrett, 231

R
Radiation, 20-22, 25, 29, 39, 40, 89, 117, 119, 121, 126, 128, 240
Raytheon Technologies, 33
RCA's Systems Analysis section, 23
Reagan, Ronald, 6, 160, 161, 235
Reed, Cheryl, 183
Reid, Jackie, 94, 96, 140, 175
Reid, Victoria, 191
Remington Arms Company, 23
Revell, Walter, 141
Rice, Clare I., 32
Ridenhour, Jim, 232
Riverview Park, 79
Robbins Skyways, 70
Robbins, Vic, 70
Robbins, Victor, 231
Robert, 11, 23, 25, 27, 56, 57, 166, 227
Robison, Jeff, 232
Rockledge, 56, 209
Rockwell Collins operations, 154, 213
Rodes, John B., 49
Rossetter, Carrie, 80
Rotary and Kiwanis clubs, 57
Rouede, Maurice T., 232
Ryals, Jack, 232

S
Sanders, Ken, 107, 231
Sanford Burnham Prebys Medical Discovery Institute in Lake Nona, 202, 242
Sarnoff, Dr. Robert, 25
Satellite Beach, 36, 101, 118, 120-122, 152, 193, 226
Satellite Communications Division, 22
St. Johns River, 10, 29, 51, 62, 76, 101
Sawyer, F.M., 227
Schaefer, Gayla, 234
Schausel, Chris, 136
Schillo, Kathi, 198
Schubert, Paul, 227
Scott, Jack, 167
Scott, Rick, 209

Sea Island Association, 72, 73
Sea Island Beaches, 76
Sebastian Inlet, 59, 64, 65, 73, 74, 80, 87, 89, 90, 94, 100, 102, 109, 112
Sebastian Inlet bridge, 94
Sebastian Inlet State Park, 100
Sebastian Inlet Tax District, 65
Sebastian River, 75
Shares, J. J., 57
Shares, John O., 54-56
Shaw, George, 20, 21, 25, 29, 39, 40, 117
Shepard, Betty, 131
Shinn, Sally, 199
Skurla, George, 35, 41
Sidewalk Art Festival, 94
Silberhorn, Ed, 232
Singleton, C.P., 48, 55
Skelton, Betty, 72
Smith, Adger, 83, 131, 132, 165, 231, 232
Smith, Charlie, 11
Smith, Patrick, 156
Sosin, Milt, 76
South Brevard Beaches Chamber of Commerce, 5, 87, 89, 90, 99, 227, 231
south Brevard County, iii, 2, 8-11, 13, 17, 20, 23, 29, 30, 34, 35, 38, 39, 41, 61, 69, 70, 73, 78, 80, 91, 93, 96, 99, 100, 102, 111, 115, 117-121, 125, 128, 166, 183, 194, 217, 226, 229, 233, 240
South Brevard Water Authority, 183
South Korea, 203
Southern Association of Colleges and Schools (SACS), 26
Southern United States, 13
Southworth, Walt, 122, 125
Soviets launched Sputnik, 18, 69
space age university, 97
Space Bowl Game, 100
Space Coast World Trade Council, 169
Space Shuttle fleet, 155

Space University, Lift-Off of Florida Institute of Technology, 240
Spencer, Natasha, 232
Spessard Holland Park, 94
Sputnik, 18, 69
St Johns Heritage Parkway, 149
St. Augustine, 51
St. Cloud, 48
St. Johns Water Management District, 140
St. Petersburg Chamber of Commerce, 27
Standard Metropolitan Statistical Area (SMSA), 120
Stanford University, 23
State Railroad Commission, 59
State Road A1A, 102
State Road Department Dredge, 60
Stewart, Charles H., 48
Storms, Elting, 116, 122
Strawbridge (Doc) William G., 146, 162
Strawbridge Avenue, 6, 7, 135, 139, 147
Stuart, Jacob, 199, 201, 202
Stuhlmiller, Bob, 232
Sugarman, Jennifer, 211
Sullivan, William, 232
Suntree Country Club, 34, 42
Surplus Property Act, 17

T

T. Price, Wayne, 197, 201, 208
Tallahassee, 4, 56, 58, 73, 117, 118, 122, 141, 148, 198, 210, 213, 215, 240
Tampa Bay Times, 53, 96, 187
Tampa Tribune, 49, 50, 53
TDC, 208
TechXpo, 203, 204
Tegeder, David, 66
Texas Christian University, 27, 96
The Chamber of Commerce of South Brevard, 6, 152, 157, 172, 182, 228, 230, 232, 233
The Cross State Road, 48
The entire East Coast, 85, 89
The Great Escape, 234
The Florida Historical Society Press, 240
The Greater Melbourne Chamber of Commerce, 60, 75-81, 84, 86, 87, 98, 115, 214
The Harris story, 40, 240
The Logical Location for a Large City, 53
The New York Times, 30
The South Florida Developer, 56
The Space Coast Tech Council, 204
Tillman, John, 9
Tin Can Tourists, 78, 81
Titusville Chamber, 54
Titusville-Cocoa, 16
Tokyo, 233, 234
Tomlinson, George, 109
Traft, William Howard, 44
Trailer Haven, 78, 81, 176
Truman, 18, 69
Tullis, Richard, 22
Turpin, Hazel, 227

U

U.S. Bureau of Public Roads, 87
U.S. Chamber of Commerce, 45, 46, 57, 146, 152, 153, 172, 173, 181, 203
U.S. Coast Guard, 59
U.S. space program, 18, 23, 31, 69
Union Cypress Company, 10, 51
United States Chamber of Commerce, 6, 7, 44, 46, 172
University of Georgia, 152
University of Michigan Law School, 242
University of Michigan's Institute of Science and Technology, 21
University of Virginia, 23
University Press of Florida, 66
Upper St. Johns-Indian River Canal, 56

V

V-2 rocket, 18, 20, 69
Viera Business Alliance, 7, 209
Valkaria, 15, 17, 75, 226

Vero Beach Press Journal, 57, 61, 197
Viera, 7, 34, 38, 42, 84, 155, 181, 185, 188, 198, 206, 209, 215, 226
Viera/Suntree Business Council, 209
Virginia, 20, 23, 134, 200
Vocelle, L.B., 89
Vogt, John, 144
Vorkeller, Albert, 51, 52, 231

W
Walter A, 80
War Department, 64
Warner, Roy C., 231
Waverly Place, 25
Weatherman, Lynda, 187
Webb, W.D., 231
Webster, Alfred, 110
Webster, Alfred D., 227, 228
Wedler, Fred, 227
Weil, Joseph, 26
Wenner, Lee, 92, 93
Weona, Cleveland, 39, 40, 128, 240
Werley, Bernice, 227
Werley, Van G., 80, 231
west coast, 49
West Melbourne Chamber of Commerce, 5, 86, 87, 115-117, 227, 231, 234
West Palm Beach, 60, 103
White House Conference, 150
Whitley, Jim, 232
Wickham (known as "Papa Joe"), 183
Wickham Road, 34, 148, 149, 183, 185, 197, 212
Wickham, Joe, 103, 108, 110, 120, 183
Wickham, Joseph H., 231
Wilcox, Alfred, 11
William D. Ellis, 40
William "Doc" Strawbridge, 147
William, Potter, 40, 240
Williams, Reidy, 166
Wilson, John, 108, 166
Winton, Dr. J. B., 231

Wolf Creek swamps, 10
Wolff, Irving, 25
Woody Burke Road, 22
World War II, iii, 13, 14, 16, 17, 20, 25, 31, 47, 65, 69
Worley, Dwight R., 177
Wright Brothers, 9
Wright, Captain Peter, 9
Wysor, Cathleen, 38, 64, 128, 179

Y
Y.M.C.A., 125
Youngberg, 5

www.ingramcontent.com/pod-product-compliance
Lightning Source LLC
LaVergne TN
LVHW061629070526
838199LV00071B/6626